THE SPECIAL EDUCATION PROGRAM ADMINISTRATOR'S HANDBOOK

DAVID F. BATEMAN

Shippensburg University

KIMBERLY L. BRIGHT

Shippensburg University

DOROTHY J. O'SHEA

Slippery Rock University of Pennsylvania

LAWRENCE J. O'SHEA

Intermediate Unit 1, Coal Center, Pennsylvania

BOB ALGOZZINE

University of North Carolina at Charlotte

PEARSON

Boston   New York   San Francisco
Mexico City   Montreal   Toronto   London   Madrid   Munich   Paris
Hong Kong   Singapore   Tokyo   Cape Town   Sydney

Executive Editor: *Virginia Lanigan*
Editorial Assistant: *Scott Blaszak*
Marketing Manager: *Kris Ellis-Levy*
Production Editor: *Gregory Erb*
Editorial Production Service: *Walsh & Associates, Inc.*
Composition Buyer: *Linda Cox*
Manufacturing Buyer: *Megan Cochran*
Electronic Composition: *Peggy Cabot*
Cover Administrator: *Elena Sidorova*

Library of Congress Cataloging-in-Publication Data

The special education program administrator's handbook / David F. Bateman . . . [et al.].—
   1st ed.
      p. cm.
   Includes bibliographic references and index.
   ISBN 0-205-37673-8
      1. Special education—United States—Administration—Handbooks, manuals, etc. 2. Students with disabilities—Education—United States—Handbooks, manuals, etc. 3. School administrators—United States—Handbooks, manuals, etc. I. Bateman, David (David F.)

LC3981.S624 2007
371.904—dc22

2006041651

Printed in the United States of America

10 9 8 7 6 5 4 3 2 1   RRD-VA   10 09 08 07 06

To special education administrators who labor mightily each day to improve the lives of students with disabilities and the professionals and parents who teach, work, and live with them.

CONTENTS

Preface xiii

Contributors xvii

CHAPTER ONE

Understanding the Law   1

OVERVIEW   1

SPECIAL EDUCATION LAW   1

Education for All Handicapped Children Act (PL 94-142)   1

The Rehabilitation Act of 1973   14

The Americans with Disabilities Act of 1990   14

Family Education Rights and Privacy Act   15

PUTTING PRINCIPLES INTO PRACTICE   16

Tips   17

Pitfalls to Avoid   17

RESOURCES   18

IDEA 2004 Law and Regulations   18

REFERENCES   19

CHAPTER TWO

504 Accommodation Plans   21

OVERVIEW   21

SECTION 504 REGULATIONS AND DEFINITIONS   21

Regulations   21

Definitions   22

EDUCATIONAL ASPECTS   22

Determining Need for Section 504   23

Free Appropriate Public Education   24

Least Restrictive Environment   24

Appropriate Evaluation and Placement   25

Evaluation and Reevaluation   26

Placement   26

Procedural Safeguards   27

504 Accommodation Plans and Responsibilities   27

Section 504 versus IDEA   28

PUTTING PRINCIPLES INTO PRACTICE   29
Tips   29
Pitfalls to Avoid   29
RESOURCES   30
REFERENCES   30
APPENDIX: SAMPLE NOTICES AND AGREEMENTS   31

CHAPTER THREE

Preparing for Due Process Hearings and Mediation   39

OVERVIEW   39
REGULATIONS   40
PUTTING PRINCIPLES INTO PRACTICE   42
Tips for Avoiding Due Process Hearings   42
Tips for Handling Inevitable Pitfalls   44
Tips for Protecting the IEP Team Process   45
When All Else Fails   46
How to Guarantee a Due Process Hearing   47
RESOURCES   48
Websites and Technical Assistance   48
REFERENCES   49

CHAPTER FOUR

Dealing with Discipline   51

OVERVIEW   51
REGULATIONS   51
Change of Placement for Disciplinary Reasons   51
Authority of School Personnel   52
Authority of Hearing Officer   53
Determination of Setting   53
Manifest Determination Review   53
Behavior Determined Not a Manifestation of Disability   54
Parent Appeal   54
Placement during Appeals   54
Protections for Children Not Yet Eligible for Services   55
Expedited Due Process Hearings   56
Referral to and Action by Other Authorities   56
PUTTING PRINCIPLES INTO PRACTICE   56

Tips   57
Pitfalls to Avoid   57
RESOURCES   58

CHAPTER FIVE

Dealing Effectively with Child Find   59

OVERVIEW   59
CHILD FIND REQUIREMENTS   59
Regulations   59
Changes in Child Find Activities through the IDEA 2004   61
PUTTING PRINCIPLES INTO PRACTICE   62
Reasons for Maintaining Awareness Strategies over Time   62
Tips   63
Pitfalls to Avoid   64
RESOURCES   64
Websites   64
Technical Assistance   65

CHAPTER SIX

The Referral and Evaluation Process   67

OVERVIEW   67
THE REFERRAL PROCESS   68
Regulations   68
Putting Principles into Practice   70
THE EVALUATION PROCESS   75
General Requirements: Regulations   75
Putting Principles into Practice   83
RESOURCES   85
Websites   85
Technical Assistance   85

CHAPTER SEVEN

Monitoring Students in Special Education and Related Services   87

OVERVIEW   87
REGULATIONS   88
Changes in Monitoring Activities through the IDEA 2004   91
PUTTING PRINCIPLES INTO PRACTICE   92

Tips   92
Pitfalls to Avoid   95

RESOURCES   95
Websites   95
Technical Assistance   96

CHAPTER EIGHT

Understanding Placement Issues   97

OVERVIEW   97

REGULATIONS: INDIVIDUALIZED EDUCATION PROGRAMS   98
IEP Content   99
IEP Team Attendance   101
Provisions Related to Students Transferring into the LEA   101
Amending the IEP   102
Multiyear IEP Demonstration   103

EXISTING REGULATIONS   103

PUTTING PRINCIPLES INTO PRACTICE   111
Tips   111
Pitfalls to Avoid   112

RESOURCES   113
Websites   113
Technical Assistance   114

CHAPTER NINE

**Dealing Effectively with Transition Services in the
Individualized Education Program (IEP)   115**

OVERVIEW   115

REGULATIONS   116

PUTTING PRINCIPLES INTO PRACTICE   117
Planning Stages   118
Tips   119
Pitfalls to Avoid   120
Frequently Asked Questions about Transition Services   121

RESOURCES   123
Example of a Transition Plan   123
Organizations   125

REFERENCES   127

CHAPTER TEN

Working Effectively with Parent Groups   129

    OVERVIEW   129

    PUTTING PRINCIPLES INTO PRACTICE   129

        Organizing New Groups   129

        Working with Existing Groups   130

    RESOURCES   131

CHAPTER ELEVEN

Effectively Supporting Within District and School Transitions   137

    OVERVIEW   137

    WHAT WE KNOW ABOUT WITHIN DISTRICT AND SCHOOL TRANSITIONS   137

        How Transferring Affects Students   139

    PUTTING PRINCIPLES INTO PRACTICE   142

        Critical Elements   143

        Transition Tips   144

        A Dozen Facts to Know about Transitions   145

    REFERENCES   147

CHAPTER TWELVE

Managing Federal Funds   151

    OVERVIEW   151

    REGULATIONS   151

    TIPS AND PITFALLS TO AVOID   160

    RESOURCES   163

CHAPTER THIRTEEN

Managing Special Education Budgets   165

    OVERVIEW   165

    BUDGETING CYCLE   165

    BUDGET PREPARATION ACTIVITIES   166

    ACCOUNTING CODES: FUNCTIONS AND OBJECTS   167

        Generally Accepted Accounting Principles (GAAP)   167

    CALCULATING AND BUDGETING FOR THE TOTAL COST OF OPERATION   172

TIPS AND PITFALLS TO AVOID   176

RESOURCES   179

REFERENCES   180

CHAPTER FOURTEEN

Independent Educational Evaluation (IEE)   181

OVERVIEW   181

REGULATIONS   181

PUTTING PRINCIPLES INTO PRACTICE   183

Appropriateness of Evaluation   183

Scope of Evaluation   184

Utility of Evaluation for IEP Development   184

Final Tips   185

Pitfalls to Avoid   186

REFERENCES   186

CHAPTER FIFTEEN

Contracting with Outside Service Providers   187

OVERVIEW   187

REGULATIONS   187

ROLES OF SERVICE PROVIDERS   188

Audiology Services   188

Counseling Services   188

Early Identification and Assessment   189

Medical Services   189

Occupational Therapy Services   189

Orientation and Mobility Therapy Services   190

Parent Counseling and Training   190

Physical Therapy   190

Psychological Services   191

Recreation Services   191

Rehabilitation Counseling Services   191

School Health Services   192

Social Work Services in Schools   192

Speech-Language Pathology Services   192

Transportation Services   193

PUTTING PRINCIPLES INTO PRACTICE   193

Tips   193

Avoiding Inadequate Contracted Services   194

Pitfalls to Avoid   195

RESOURCES   195

Websites   195

Other Agencies   196

Government Agencies   197

Government-Supported Organizations   199

CHAPTER SIXTEEN

Navigating the Mental Health System   201

OVERVIEW   201

REGULATIONS   203

STUDENTS' MENTAL HEALTH ISSUES   204

GUIDELINES AND TIPS ON NAVIGATING INTERAGENCY COORDINATION   209

PUTTING PRINCIPLES INTO PRACTICE   211

Tips   212

Guidelines for Avoiding Inadequate Mental Health Services   213

RESOURCES   214

Websites   214

Other Agencies   214

REFERENCES   215

CHAPTER SEVENTEEN

Running Efficient and Effective Staff Meetings   217

OVERVIEW   217

SUGGESTIONS FOR EFFECTIVE MEETINGS   217

PUTTING PRINCIPLES INTO PRACTICE   218

Tips   219

Pitfalls to Avoid   220

REFERENCES   220

CHAPTER EIGHTEEN

Building Relationships with Special Education Staff   223

OVERVIEW   223

REGULATIONS   223

PUTTING PRINCIPLES INTO PRACTICE   224

Building Interpersonal Skills   224

Managing Special Education   227

REFERENCES   231

CHAPTER NINETEEN

Evaluating Special Education Staff   233

OVERVIEW   233

REGULATIONS   233

PUTTING PRINCIPLES INTO PRACTICE   233

Observing and Evaluating Teachers   234

Developing or Adapting an Evaluation Framework   237

REFERENCES   240

SUGGESTED READINGS   241

CHAPTER TWENTY

Working with Other Administrators   243

OVERVIEW   243

REGULATIONS   243

PUTTING PRINCIPLES INTO PRACTICE   243

The Superintendent   243

The School Board   244

The Building Principal and Assistant Principal   245

General Tips for the Administration Team   247

REFERENCES   250

Index   251

PREFACE

The Special Education Program Administrator's Handbook is a practical guide for special education administrators charged with operating special education programs for the first time or for veteran administrators who seek practical information on how to provide support and services to students with disabilities and their families. Many special education administrators are armed to meet the challenges with a broad formal education and years of experience. Most are prepared to tackle any problem related to teaching and learning, personnel selection and evaluation, basic financial management, community relations, or general legal matters. With the support of the superintendent, many are confident they are ready to deal with most anything that will come along.

Soon after the first bell rings, however, many special education administrators will face one area of responsibility in which they feel less confident. They will suddenly be thrust into situations in which they must become the final arbiter on matters related to strange-sounding terms such as "IEPs," "504 decisions," requests for "mediation or due process hearings," and "IDEA compliance." They are required to be an expert on all levels and types of special education services available within and outside of the district, each and every disability, and all aspects of special education programming from early intervention through transition to adult life.

Not only that, but they find these responsibilities are very time consuming. Regrettably, there are few places to turn for help in making these new decisions, because unlike a principal who can turn to the other building principals for advice, there is only one special education administrator in many districts. Everyone assumes the special education administrator is the person with the greatest expertise in these matters. Unfortunately, most new special education administrators come to their positions ill-prepared to deal with these problems.

BACKGROUND

Tremendous changes have occurred over the past decade in the provision of services to students with disabilities. Federal mandates continue to define requirements for free, appropriate public education in the least restrictive environment. The present climate of school restructuring is placing new leadership demands on all administrators, especially those in special education. In addition, the move to educate students with disabilities in more inclusive settings necessitates shared responsibility and schoolwide collaboration among supervisors, principals, general and special education teachers, and related service personnel. To be effective, today's leaders must be knowledgeable about programs for students with disabilities and must provide appropriate support to teachers.

Recognizing that few special education administrators feel adequately prepared for these new roles, *The Special Education Program Administrator's Handbook* will enable practicing administrators to support and supervise teachers of students with disabilities.

The idea for this book was born after a group of administrators, college professors, teachers, students, and hearing officers were discussing the dilemma—a shortage of well-prepared and effective special education administrators. Our combined experiences in research and practice guided our planning of the handbook so that it was easy to read and interpret—not a theoretical framework, but rather a handbook with specific answers.

INTENDED AUDIENCE

This book is intended for novice and veteran special education administrators, assistant principals, and building administrators. It provides information about the effective implementation of special education, especially how it involves administrators.

In addition, *The Special Education Program Administrator's Handbook* will benefit certification programs and professional development workshops conducted for teachers. It will also serve as a reference tool for other administrators and principals.

ACKNOWLEDGMENTS

Collectively we want to thank Virginia Lanigan and the professional staff at Allyn and Bacon. Virginia's continuing support for the book and her insightful comments helped to start the project and bring it to completion, and the assistance we received in all aspects of producing the book was outstanding. We would also like to thank the following reviewers for their time and input: Bonnie S. Billingsley, Virginia Tech University; Jean Crockett, Virginia Tech University; Inge Jacobs, Capital Region BOCES; and James Yates, University of Texas at Austin.

PERSONAL ACKNOWLEDGMENTS

Good leaders make good schools. Thank you to all the leaders out there who are working to make good schools for all students. You do not have an easy job, but it is one of the most important.

David F. Bateman

I feel fortunate to contribute to a book that will help countless special education administrators provide strong special education programs and services to children and youth with disabilities, their parents, and teachers. To those on the front line, I acknowledge your diligence, respect your commitment, and honor your position. A special acknowledgment to Michel Miller for offering the idea as she transitioned from special education teacher to special education supervisor.

Kimberly L. Bright

I dedicate this book to the leaders of special education programs and services. Leaders embody trust and commitment to students, families, and professionals. Leaders are willing to take risks and facilitate change, as the world becomes a more trusting and committed learning setting for all diverse people.

Dorothy J. O'Shea

Leaders in the field of special education, including teachers, administrators, and parents, are those individuals who each day work to do the right thing for the right reasons in order to make the lives of students with disabilities and their nondisabled peers more enriching. To these courageous leaders I dedicate this book.

Lawrence J. O'Shea

I have never written a book without the constant and continuous support of my family. While they may not see it and often bring it in very clever ways, they are an inspiration for me always and I am grateful for it. I am also thankful for those who remind me every day that leadership is important, that learning requires vigilance and attention, and that teaching is a great way to spend your life.

Bob Algozzine

CONTRIBUTORS

Richael Barger Anderson works at Slippery Rock University in the Special Education Department. She is a former classroom teacher.

Michael Dunsmore is the Director of Special Education and Student Services in the Mount Union Area School District, Mount Union, Pennsylvania.

Deborah Forest is a law student at Widener University. She is a former classroom special education teacher.

Michael Jazzar is an Assistant Professor in the Department of Educational Leadership at the University of North Carolina at Charlotte.

Ann McColl is an Associate Professor in the Department of Educational Leadership at the University of North Carolina at Charlotte. She was formerly an attorney in private practice and Legal Counsel and Director of Policy for the North Carolina School Boards Association.

Joseph Merhaut works at Slippery Rock University in the Special Education Department. He is a former building administrator in the public schools.

Mary Beth Roth is a principal in Concord, North Carolina.

Gina Scala is a professor at East Stroudsburg University. She is a formal classroom special education teacher and administrator.

Brooke Shambach is a special education teacher in the Bermudian Springs School District, Biglerville, Pennsylvania.

CHAPTER ONE

UNDERSTANDING THE LAW

with DEBORAH FOREST

OVERVIEW

Effective implementation of special education in any district relies on a solid understanding of the rules and regulations governing special education. In this chapter we enumerate key laws as promulgated by the federal government that influence special education. As is clarified in other chapters, there are often numerous unwritten rules existing as a part of any organization, especially districtwide implementation of special education polices and procedures. It is important to note that the specific regulations in your state may be slightly different from those promulgated by the federal government. The regulations provided by the federal government serve as the minimum required for implementation.

Additionally, litigation affects the implementation of the regulations. We summarize some of the more important cases in this chapter, but there is probably a specific case affecting the implementation of special education in your district. Special education program administrators are strongly encouraged to join a chapter of CASE (Council of Administrators of Special Education), attend statewide or regional special education law conferences, and join electronic (and other) mailing lists devoted to special education administration and law (a list of helpful websites is included at the end of this chapter).

SPECIAL EDUCATION LAW

The most important laws governing the education of students with disabilities are the Education for All Handicapped Children Act (PL 94-142), the Individuals with Disabilities Education Act (IDEA 2004), Section 504 of the Rehabilitation Act of 1973, the Americans with Disabilities Act (ADA), and the Family Education Rights and Privacy Act (FERPA). In addition to the laws passed by Congress are the codifying regulations that provide the specific "rules" for how special education should be implemented in order to get federal reimbursement. Each will be addressed in turn. Understanding each will assist in providing appropriate services in your school.

Education for All Handicapped Children Act (PL 94-142)

This is the law that provides the basis for the implementation of special education as it is known and practiced today. Some have written that, in fact, we have a profession that is defined by this law (Yell, 2004). This is only partially correct. Special education clearly existed before 1975 when this law was enacted; however, the manner in which it is practiced and the experiences of teachers and students are clearly very different because of this law.

Public Law 94-142 established that all children with disabilities were to receive a free appropriate public education. Additionally, they were to receive this education as a result of a nondiscriminatory evaluation that was completed with parental permission and assistance, resulting in each child's receiving an individualized education program (IEP) (Turnbull, Turnbull, Stowe, & Wilcox, 2000). There are several other important characteristics of this law: States (and in turn localities) were to receive financial assistance to meet the demands of providing services, and the law was to be revisited every five years to see if any changes were warranted.

In 1990, Congress reauthorized the Education of All Handicapped Children Act of 1975 in the form of Public Law 101-476, the Individuals with Disabilities Education Act (IDEA). This change in the title of the law was a result of the changes that occur every five years. With each change, there is some "tinkering" with the rules and regulations, meaning there most likely will be changes in forms, policies, and procedures. The latest change, or reauthorization, occurred in November 2004 (PL 108-446; IDEA 2004). Special education program administrators complain that once they master the old rules and regulations, it is time to learn new ones.

The current title of the law is the Individuals with Disabilities Education Improvement Act or IDEA 2004. The first significant point of the 1990 Amendments was the rewording of the title. In 1975, the law used the term "handicapped children." The new terminology, "individuals with disabilities," reflects the philosophy that the individual should be recognized first and the condition second. Additionally, the new title emphasized the preference for the term "disability" over the label "handicap," which is viewed as demeaning.

In providing appropriate special education, administrators must be vigilant regarding key components of the law:

1. All children with disabilities are entitled to receive a free and appropriate education.
2. Students with disabilities are to be educated in the least restrictive environment.
3. Parents are expected to participate in all decision making.
4. Related services must be provided, if needed.
5. Identification, placement, and evaluation procedures must be unbiased.
6. Due process procedures need to be followed.
7. Transition plans are to be developed for when the student leaves school.

Regulations.   When a law is written, it contains parts in which key sections (§§) of the legislation are described, defined, and delimited. We present information to describe the purposes, to define key terms (such as *a child with a disability, a free appropriate public education, least restrictive environment, parent involvement,* and *related services*), and to delimit basic practices such as identification, evaluation, and placement, due process, and transition, which are represented in the most current Individuals with Disabilities Education Act.

§300.1 Purposes.   The fundamental purpose of contemporary special education law is to ensure that *all* children with disabilities have available to them a free appropriate public education that emphasizes special education and related services designed to meet their unique needs and prepare them for employment and independent living.

The original title of IDEA 2004 was the Education for All Handicapped Children Act (PL 94-142). Congress used that title to emphasize how important it was for all children to be included. Schools had historically barred children with disabilities because of the perception that they were not able to benefit from education or that they were not "ready" for school. Congress wanted to emphasize that no child with a disability was to be excluded from receiving special education services (Stainback & Stainback, 1992).

§300.7 Child with a Disability.   The term *child with a disability* means a child who is evaluated as having mental retardation, a hearing impairment including deafness, a speech or language impairment, a visual impairment including blindness, a serious emotional disturbance (hereafter referred to as emotional disturbance), an orthopedic impairment, autism, traumatic brain injury, another health impairment, a specific learning disability, deaf-blindness, or multiple disabilities, and who, by reason thereof, needs special education and related services.

The IDEA 2004 definitions are not as broad or as inclusive as the definitions put forward by Section 504 of the Rehabilitation Act of 1973. For example, an individual who is alcohol dependent could have a disability under Section 504. Eligible individuals under Section 504 have an impairment, have a record of an impairment, or are regarded as having an impairment (see definition on page 14). The definitions under IDEA 2004 are categorical in nature, whereas definitions under Section 504 are functional in nature, meeting one of the three life-defining criteria.

§§300.300–300.313 Free Appropriate Public Education.   The term *free appropriate public education* (or FAPE) means special education and related services that

(1) Are provided at public expense, under public supervision and direction, and without charge.
(2) Meet the standards of the State Education Agency.
(3) Include preschool, elementary school, or secondary school education in the State.
(4) Are provided in conformity with an individualized education program (IEP) that meets the requirements of §§300.340–300.350.

§§300.550–300.556 Least Restrictive Environment.   The IDEA 2004 directs that all children with disabilities receive a free appropriate public education that emphasizes special education and related services designed to meet their unique needs. To the maximum extent appropriate, children with disabilities, including those in public or private institutions or other care facilities, are expected to be educated with children without disabilities.

This is known as the *least restrictive environment* provision of the law and means that states are expected to provide a continuum of alternative placements to meet the unique needs of each child with a disability.

At one time, the term *mainstreaming* was used to describe circumstances in which special education teachers integrated students with disabilities into general education classrooms or activities as a means of providing education as much like normal as possible. Often used synonymously with inclusion, mainstreaming as a term does not exist in any of the legislation. *Inclusion* is the preferred word, because it clarifies the intent of the law and the regulations. In mainstreaming, the students with disabilities prove themselves before participating with students who do not have disabilities (Laski, 1991). Different from this, inclusion's presumption is that the student will be in the general education classroom with supports, until it has been shown that the child cannot benefit from education in the general classroom (Kauffman & Hallahan, 1995). It is not the intent of this chapter to discuss full inclusion, rather to clarify the law. The law states:

> Schools must maintain a continuum of alternative placements such as special classes, resource rooms, and itinerant instruction to meet the needs of students with disabilities. (cf. Rothstein, 2000)

The services and location of those services are listed on the individualized education program. Some students can be appropriately placed solely in the regular classroom with little additional assistance from special education teachers; however, some students require residential settings, totally separated from students without disabilities (Gorn, 2000).

Often forgotten is that the law stipulates services are to follow students—that is, services are to be tailored to the unique needs of the individual in the most appropriate setting. It is not acceptable for students to be assigned solely those services designated for a particular disability or those programs that are available or convenient. Just because a student is identified as having severe mental retardation does not mean the student has to be placed in a self-contained classroom when a partial-day program or a resource room might be more suited for that child. The school district needs to have available a continuum of services including everything between the regular classroom and hospital-type settings (Gorn, 2000).

§§300.500–300.517 Parental Involvement and Procedural Safeguards.   Historically, parents often have been shut out of the decision-making process because it was assumed that they were the cause of the child's disability (e.g., Bruno Bettelheim and autism [Bettelheim, 1950, 1967]). Professionals viewed parents as ignorant of their children's educational needs, believing that only they knew what was best for the children (Turnbull & Turnbull, 1997). Actually, parents and guardians have essential information about their children with disabilities (Mahoney & Wheeden, 1997). Legislators realized this and outlined provisions in PL 94-142 ensuring parental participation in the special education process (Rothstein, 2000). Procedures were enumerated for notification, access to records (see the discussion of FERPA below), consultation, and participation in advisory panels.

Shared decision making protects the rights of students by ensuring there is someone involved in the process who has a long-term interest in the child (Turnbull & Turnbull, 1997). Additionally, it could be argued that what affects the student with a disability also affects the parents (O'Shea, O'Shea, Algozzine, & Hammitte, 2001); therefore, most educators regard parents as important stakeholders.

IDEA 2004 states that parents need to be aware of, and consent to, every step of the process (O'Shea et al., 2001). This includes the initial evaluation, the eligibility meeting, the development of the IEP, annual reviews, and the triennial evaluation process. Parents also need access to all the records kept on their children and the assurances about confidentiality (Yell, 1998).

The early childhood amendments to IDEA 2004 have added requirements for parent involvement: Districts must establish a public awareness campaign, a comprehensive child-find program, and a central director of information. School systems also have an obligation to work with families when the child is identified as needing special education services. Early childhood personnel should start working with families as soon as possible after the child is born, providing the child with as much assistance as possible before he or she enters school for the first time.

Schools also must develop an Individualized Family Services Plan (IFSP). Similar to the development of the IEP, the IFSP includes a heavy family component because there is a realization that families play a vital role in the development and nurturing of their child (O'Shea et al., 2001). One component is working with the family to help them meet the needs of the family member. This can be accomplished either through training of family members to carry out specific duties or in collaborating with them to determine the best methods for working with the family member who has a disability (O'Shea et al., 2001). The IFSP is more than just an IEP with a family twist, though; it is a multidisciplinary document designed to enhance children's development and minimize delays by enhancing the family's capacity to meet family members' needs (Gorn, 2000).

Another important component of the early childhood amendments is the realization that one service provider does not have to be the sole discipline working to address circumstances for the child with a disability and family members (O'Shea et al., 2001). Ideally, multiple agencies must work together to provide combinations of approaches and interventions.

§300.24 Related Services.   In addition to the educational services students with disabilities receive, there are other services the child might require to benefit from special education. These are called related services. Related services include many components:

> Transportation, and such . . . other supportive services (including speech pathology and audiology), psychological services, physical and occupational therapy, recreation, including therapeutic recreation and social work services, and medical and counseling services, including rehabilitation counseling (except that such medical services shall be for diagnostic and evaluation purposes only), as may be required to assist a child with a disability to benefit from special education, and includes the early identification and assessment of disabling conditions in children.

Several conditions must be met before the child receives related services. First, to be entitled to related services, a child must be eligible for special education services. Unfortunately, there are students who might benefit from these related services, but because they are not eligible for special education, they cannot receive related services. In the absence of this eligibility, these students do not qualify for related services. Second, only those services necessary to aid a child with a disability to benefit from special education must be provided, regardless of how easily a school nurse or lay person could furnish them. For example, if a particular medication or treatment may appropriately be administered to a child other than during the school day, a school is not required to provide nursing services to administer it. Third, the regulations state that medical services must be provided only if they can be performed by a nurse or other qualified person, not if a physician is required (Rothstein, 2000; Yell, 1998).

Just as classroom placement is individually determined for the child with a disability, the need for related services should be determined in the same manner and listed on the IEP. Finally, this requires school districts to provide delineated IEP-related services, regardless of whether they are currently available.

§§300.530–300.536 Evaluation Procedures. Historically, there have been problems in the testing and placement of children with disabilities, including things such as not testing in their primary language, not measuring adaptive behavior, or the reliance on a single test for classification and placement. These practices resulted in court cases stipulating correct procedures for the assessment and classification of children with disabilities (Rothstein, 2000).

The courts have issued guidelines stating (and the federal regulations have further codified):

1. All children are to be tested in their primary language.
2. IQ tests alone cannot be used for the placement of children into special education programs.
3. Unvalidated tests cannot be used.
4. Parents must be notified before any testing may begin (there are procedures for bypass if parents do not consent to testing).
5. Group tests are not to be used for determining eligibility.
6. Adaptive behavior must be taken into account when considering eligibility.

There are two other important points:

7. Districts need to seek out and evaluate each child with a suspected disability in their jurisdiction.
8. Districts need to implement procedures to screen preschool-age children for disabilities.

Procedures for notifying parents of testing can include announcements in the newspaper, as well as notices in grocery stores, gas stations, physicians' offices, and churches (for more information, see the chapters on child find and the referral process). These notices would have dates and locations for screening to determine eligibility for services before entering school at age 5 or 6. Regardless of the age of the child, school districts must identify the specific nature of a child's disability and determine the type and extent of special education and related services required.

Additionally, the evaluation of the child must be an individualized assessment of all areas related to the suspected disability. *Individualized* means that if the child has a suspected reading disability, the focus relates to the problems in reading. If the suspected problem relates to behavior, the focus is on the behavior problem and how it manifests itself in school. A team must make the eligibility decision, with at least one member of the team experienced in the suspected disability category. The job of the team is to determine whether a child is eligible for special education and related services. Districts must also notify parents of their right to an independent evaluation at public expense if they disagree with the results or procedures of the school district's evaluation. If the team finds the student eligible, an individualized education program needs to be developed based on the results of the assessments.

The eligibility process is repeated every three years. Historically, children were placed inappropriately in special education and remained there for the duration of their schooling. Therefore, the law mandates at least a three-year, or triennial, evaluation to determine that a child still qualifies for special education services.

After the individualized evaluation with a finding of eligibility, the team develops an individualized education program (IEP). The IEP is a legal document developed by a team of individuals describing the special education and related services designed to meet the needs of a child who has a disability. The team details the IEP provisions in writing. It contains a statement of the child's present level of educational performance, and goals and objectives based on this functioning. Specifically, it describes the following in detail:

1. Who will provide the services.
2. Where the services will be provided.
3. The dates and anticipated duration of services to be provided.
4. The related services necessary to reach those goals and objectives.
5. The extent to which they are to be provided.

The IEP also defines objective criteria and evaluation procedures. It defines schedules for determining, on at least a regular basis (at least as regularly as nondisabled students get feedback), progress toward IEP goals.

The IEP is more than a document outlining goals and objectives. It serves as a written commitment by the local education agency to provide the services (Bateman & Linden, 1998). This is an important point for special education program administrators. When the IEP is signed by a representative of the district, it states to the student with a disability and his or her parents that the program will be in place for their child, including the requisite finances. Additionally, the district is stating to the parents that the program as delineated in this IEP will provide a free appropriate public education for this child. These are several important points for special education program administrators to understand. For example, do not write IEPs that state the child is to receive education one-on-one 100 percent of the time unless this is clearly what the child needs or that the child will receive computer instruction 100 percent of the time. However, if this is what the child needs, ensure the financial wherewithal to guarantee it is implemented appropriately (see the chapter on budgets for more information).

The IEP team decides where the child is to receive his or her education. It is important that this be a team decision, one not based solely on available space in the district special education classrooms. The IEP describes the special education placement to be provided (this should not be decided until the IEP meeting) and the amount and location of the participation with students who do not have disabilities (Bateman & Linden, 1998). If a student is not going to participate with students without disabilities, documentation is necessary stating why this will not occur, and when such placement might occur.

§§300.500–300.517 Due Process.   One main component of the law for children with disabilities is the opportunity for parental decision making on all the different levels affecting the child's eligibility for special education services. If parents or guardians disapprove of the methods used for determining eligibility and educational programming for children with disabilities or disapprove of the resulting decisions, due process procedures allow interested parties to challenge the school system (see the chapter on preparation for due process for a greater discussion of this). Due process protection comes out of the Fifth and Fourteenth Amendments of the United States Constitution in that "... no person shall be deprived of life, liberty, or property without due process of law."

Appropriate notification is one essential element of procedural due process. The law is very specific about requirements relating to notice. The law requires written notice before the schools can (i) propose to initiate or change or (ii) refuse to initiate or change the identification, evaluation, or educational placement of the child or the provision of an appropriate education. The schools also must convey the details of the proposed action and the reasons for the action (O'Shea, Bateman, O'Shea, & Algozzine, 2004).

Parents may request a due process hearing if they are not happy with any or all aspects of the procedures or the education of their child with a disability. The purpose of the due process hearing is to resolve differences of opinion between parents and school officials regarding the education, placement, or services for the child with a disability. If the parents request a hearing, a hearing officer independent of the local education agency conducts the hearing. The hearing is at a time and place suitable to the parents.

By describing the cases in terms of wins or losses, a due process hearing tends to be an antagonistic process (O'Shea et al., 2004). It usually ends with both parties unhappy about the results or feeling they received less than they wanted. It is a legal procedure, and like any other legal procedure, there are problems. Due process hearings require an enormous amount of energy, time, and money (O'Shea et al., 2004). However, due process procedures are an invaluable means of ensuring an appropriate education and the participation of parents in the education of their children.

Instead of due process hearings, more individuals and school systems are using another form of resolution called mediation (O'Shea et al., 2004). Mediation involves the use of less formal, less adversarial, more negotiated-settlement meetings for resolving disputes. Usually in mediation, a neutral party hears the issues and helps to find an acceptable solution. There has been a significant increase in the number of cases using mediation (O'Shea et al., 2004).

§300.29 Transition.   Originally, under PL 94-142 there was no mention of transition services. The law provided access to school for students with disabilities; it did not consider issues of postschool life for these individuals.

In 1984, transition from school to work for students with disabilities became a major priority for the Office of Special Education and Rehabilitative Services (OSERS) (Bateman, 1994). Many individuals around the nation who had never thought of transition as a part of the function of special education now had at least heard about the need for transition services. These initiatives stressed that students with disabilities could potentially move into integrated employment in the community rather than simply into a sheltered workshop or work activity center (Bateman, Bright, & Boldin, 2003).

Three main factors brought about the changes in transition services for students with disabilities: (a) the lessons of history, (b) the realizations that students with disabilities were leaving a free appropriate public education and entering a system where there are no mandates, and (c) the students educated in special education were not achieving desired outcomes (Bateman et al., 2003).

The definition of transition services is a coordinated set of activities for a student, designed within an outcome-oriented process, that promotes movement from school to postschool activities, including postsecondary education, vocational training, integrated employment (including supported employment), continuing and adult education, adult services, independent living, and/or community.

What Is an Appropriate Education?   Historically, students with disabilities were placed in a disability specific classroom regardless of whether that placement would provide them an "appropriate" education (Sailor, 1991). The term *appropriate,* however, has caused confusion both before and after the implementation of the Act. What one parent, supervisor, principal, or teacher finds appropriate, another might deem completely inappropriate. This term has caused a great deal of confusion relating to the education of students with disabilities. The Supreme Court tried to help define the definition on appropriateness in the *Board of Education of Hendrick Hudson School District v. Rowley* (458 U.S. 176 [1982]).

In the Rowley case, Amy Rowley was a child with a hearing impairment who was fully mainstreamed in regular education except for one hour of instruction by a hearing therapist. She also received speech therapy and had the use of an FM amplification system. Her classroom performance was better than average when measured against her peers, and she was advancing regularly from grade to grade. It was also clear that if Amy had the benefit of a sign language interpreter at all times, she would have performed even better. It is important to keep in mind that the achievement of passing marks and advancing from grade to grade was viewed by the Court as "one important factor in determining educational benefit." Amy was not only passing from grade to grade, she was in the upper half of her class. However, the Court went on to say in *Rowley,* "we do not hold today that every handicapped child who is advancing from grade to grade in regular public schools is automatically receiving a free appropriate public education." Further, the Court stated, "we do not attempt today to establish any one test for determining the adequacy of educational benefits conferred upon all children covered by the Act."

The Court adopted the following general principles for determining when a program is appropriate:

1. Compliance with procedural requirements of the Act is required in every case.
2. The program must be personalized, individually designed and reasonably calculated to enable the child to receive educational benefit.
3. The school district is not required to maximize the potential of every student with a disability.

State and local education agencies receive federal funding for special education by providing an appropriate education for all students with disabilities in their jurisdiction. This is demonstrated through the development to the IEP. As elaborated by the Supreme Court, the definition of appropriate education is a process definition. A process definition is such that if the district follows a certain process in the development and implementation of the IEP, then the student should be receiving an acceptable result. This is why it is imperative that special education program administrators have a full and complete understanding of the IEP process. Additionally, they need to become active participants to ensure that not only the district follows appropriate procedures, but also that the student receives an appropriate education.

The recent reauthorization of the IDEA 2004 made subtle changes to the requirements relating to IEPs:

1. Changes regarding present levels of educational performance.
   - IEPs must include:
     - Present levels of academic achievement and functional performance; and
     - A statement of measurable annual goals, including both academic and functional goals
   - IEPs must include a description of benchmarks or short-term objectives only for children who take alternate assessments aligned to alternate achievement standards.
   [614(d)(1)(A)(i)(I)]

2. Changes regarding assessments in the IEP.
   - A statement of any individual appropriate accommodations that it is necessary to measure:
     - Academic achievement and functional performance on statewide and districtwide assessments.
   - If the IEP team determines that the child will take an alternate assessment, a statement must be provided that indicates why the IEP team selected a particular alternate assessment and why it is appropriate for the child.
   [614(d)(1)(A)(i)(VI)(aa), (bb)(BB)]

3. Changes to annual goals.
   - IEPs are required to include:
     - A statement of measurable annual goals, including academic and functional goals.
   [614(d)(1)(A)(i)(II)]

4. Changes to measuring progress and reporting.
   - IEPs are required to include:
     - A description of how the child's progress toward meeting the annual goals will be measured; and
     - A description of when periodic progress reports will be provided to the parents.
   - Reporting may include:
     - Quarterly reports; or
     - Other periodic reports concurrent with issuance of report cards.
   [614(d)(1)(A)(i)(III)]

5. Changes to statement of services.
   This change adds to the statement of the special education and related services and supplementary aids and services, for the child or on behalf of the child—that they be based on peer-reviewed research, to the extent practicable.
   [614(d)(1)(A)(i)(IV)]

6. Changes to transition requirements.
   Beginning not later than the first IEP to be in effect when the child turns 16 [note: eliminates age 14 requirements] and then updated annually thereafter, the IEP must include:

- Appropriate measurable postsecondary goals based upon age-appropriate transition assessments related to training, education, employment and independent living skills, where appropriate.
- Transition services needed to assist the child in reaching those goals, including courses of study.
- Beginning not later than one year before the child reaches the age of majority under state law, a statement that the child has been informed of the child's rights under this title, if any, that will transfer to him or her on reaching the age of majority.
  [614(d)(1)(A)(i)(VIII)]

7. Requirements for children with disabilities transferring within a state and between states.
  - Within-state transfers:
    - In the case of a child with a disability who transfers school districts within the same academic year, who enrolls in a new school, and who had an IEP that was in effect in the same state, the new local educational agency (LEA) must provide such child with a free appropriate public education (FAPE), including services consistent with the previous district's IEP, in consultation with parents, until it adopts the previously held IEP or develops and implements a new IEP that is consistent with federal and state law.
  [614(d)(2)(C)(i)(I)]

  - Between-state transfers:
    - In the case of a child with a disability who transfers school districts within the same academic year, who enrolls in a new school, and who had an IEP that was in effect in another state, the new LEA must provide such child with FAPE, including services consistent with the previous IEP, in consultation with parents, until the new LEA conducts an evaluation pursuant to Section 614(a)(1), if determined to be necessary by such agency, and develops a new IEP that is consistent with federal and state law.
  [614(d)(2)(C)(i)(II)]

  - Transmittal of records: To facilitate the transition for a child described above, the new school shall take reasonable steps to promptly obtain and transfer the child's records, including the IEP and supporting documents and any other records relating to the provision of special education or related services to the child, from the previous school; and the previous school must take reasonable steps to promptly respond to such request.
  [614(d)(2)(C)(ii)]

Questions the special education program administrator needs to keep in mind in the determination of an appropriate education and the correct process include:

1. Was the child evaluated in a nondiscriminatory fashion?
2. Is everybody certified for his or her role in the development and implementation of the IEP?
3. Is the IEP individualized?
4. Are the necessary related services listed?

5. Are all the components listed for service on the IEP being implemented?
6. Is there clear documentation on the level of functioning of the child with a disability in comparison to the goals and objectives on the IEP?
7. Is the child receiving educational benefit from the program?
8. Are all the objectives of the IEP behaviorally written?
9. Have the parents or guardians been involved in every step of the development of the IEP?
10. Have the parents or guardians been made aware of their due process rights?
11. Is the student integrated with non-disabled students to the maximum extent possible?
12. If there is no provision for integration, is there a plan for the future integration of the student with students who are non-disabled? (Bateman & Bateman, 2001)

One of the most important components of the process definition is it places the burden on professionals who develop and implement the IEP to show it was based on correct information (testing and observations). Districts also need to show it was properly developed and implemented, and that proper monitoring occurred during its implementation (Rothstein, 2000).

The recent reauthorization of the law added very specific language relating to the No Child Left Behind Act and discipline. In the No Child Left Behind Act and the new IDEA 2004, states must establish goals for the performance of children with disabilities that:

- Promote annual yearly progress.
- Address graduation rates and dropout rates, as well as such other factors as the state may determine.
- Are consistent, to the extent appropriate, with any other goals and standards for children established by the state.

In addition, the state must establish performance indicators it will use to assess progress toward achieving the goals described in Section 612(a)(15)(A) of IDEA, including measurable annual objectives for progress by children with disabilities under Section 1111(b)(2)(C)(v)(II)(c) of the ESEA (612(a)(15)(A) and (B) of IDEA). Additionally, states will annually report to the secretary and to the public on its progress, and the progress of children with disabilities, toward meeting these goals. Also, if the state has adopted alternate academic achievement standards permitted under the regulations, the state shall measure the achievement of children with disabilities against those standards.

Discipline is covered extensively in another chapter. However, it is important to point out the specific changes.

1. School personnel may consider any unique circumstances on a case-by-case basis when deciding to order a change in placement for a child with a disability who violates a student conduct code.

2. A new standard exists regarding manifestation determinations. Within ten school days of any decision to change the placement of a child with a disability because of a violation of a code of student conduct, the local educational agency (LEA), parent, and relevant members of the individualized education program (IEP) team (as determined by the parent and LEA) shall review all relevant information in the student's file, includ-

ing the child's IEP, any teacher observations and any relevant information provided by the parents to determine if conduct was:

- Caused by, or was in direct and substantial relationship to, the child's disability; or
- A direct result of the LEA's failure to implement the IEP.

3. The determination that a behavior was a manifestation of the disability. If the LEA, parent, and relevant members of the IEP team . . . determine that the conduct was a manifestation of the child's disability, the IEP team shall:

- Conduct a functional behavioral assessment and implement a behavioral intervention plan for the child; or
- If a behavioral intervention plan has been developed, review the existing plan and modify it as necessary to address the behavior.
- If the behavior is a manifestation of the child's disability, the child is returned to the placement from which he or she was removed, unless the parent and LEA agree otherwise.

4. New rules for special circumstances. A school is permitted to remove a child with a disability to an alternative educational setting for not more than forty-five school days without regard to whether the behavior is determined to be a manifestation of the child's disability, in cases where a child:

- Carries or possesses a weapon to or at school, on school premises, or to or at a school function under jurisdiction of a state educational agency (SEA) or LEA;
- Knowingly possesses or uses illegal drugs, or sells or solicits the sale of a controlled substance, while at school, on school premises, or at a school function under the jurisdiction of an SEA or LEA; or
- Has inflicted serious bodily injury upon another person while at school, on school premises, or at a school function under the jurisdiction of an SEA or LEA. [615(k)(1)(G)]

5. Adds a new definition of Serious Bodily Injury: Defined in USC 1365(g) to mean a bodily injury that involves a substantial risk of death; extreme physical pain; protracted and obvious disfigurement; or protracted loss or impairment of the function of a bodily member, organ, or faculty. [615(k)(7)(D)]

6. Changes the authority of hearing officers. In making the determination under Section 615(k)(3)(B)(i), the hearing officer may order a change in placement of a child with a disability . . . in such situations, the hearing officer may return a child with a disability to the placement from which the child was removed or order a change in placement of a child with a disability to an appropriate interim alternative educational setting for not more than forty-five school days if the hearing officer determines that maintaining the current placement of such child is substantially likely to result in injury to the child or to others. [615(k)(3)(B)(ii)]

7. Changes the placement during appeals. When an appeal under Section 615(k)(3) has been requested by either the parent or the LEA, the child shall remain in the interim alternative educational setting pending the decision of the hearing officer, or until the

expiration of the time period provided for in Section 615(k)(1)(C), whichever occurs first, unless the parent and the SEA or LEA agree otherwise. [615(k)(4)(A)]

8. New timeline for expedited hearing. The SEA or LEA shall arrange for an expedited hearing, which shall occur within twenty school days of the date the hearing is requested, and shall result in a determination within ten school days after the hearing. [615(k)(4)(B)]

The Rehabilitation Act of 1973

Commonly referred to as the "Rehab Act," or "Section 504," this law authorized federal funds to be paid to institutions after they comply with regulations concerning the education of students with disabilities (and withholding of funds for noncompliance). The main component of Section 504 of the Rehab Act states:

> "No otherwise qualified individual with handicaps shall solely by reason of her or his handicap, be excluded from the participation in, be denied the benefits of, or be subjected to discrimination under any program or activity receiving Federal financial assistance" (29 U.S.C. Sec. 706).

This act protects from discrimination any person, including students who meet one of three criteria. Any person who

> (i) has a physical or mental impairment which substantially limits one or more of such person's major life activities, (ii) has a record of such an impairment, or (iii) is regarded as having such an impairment (29 U.S.C. Sec. 706)

is considered as having a disability under this law. For the purposes of Section 504, major life activities include caring for one's self, performing manual tasks, walking, seeing, hearing, speaking, breathing, learning, and working. The law protects individuals who are discriminated against both intentionally and unintentionally. Under Section 504, individuals who have a disability might need assistance to qualify for the related services necessary for them to benefit from education. In addition, Section 504 has provisions for nondiscriminatory employment.

The definition used for Section 504 for individuals with a disability and the descriptors of major life events are the same as the definitions used in the Americans with Disabilities Act (ADA). For a greater discussion of Section 504, the reader is referred to that chapter.

The Americans with Disabilities Act of 1990

Though the Rehab Act was passed in 1973, individuals with disabilities continued, as a group, to occupy an inferior status in our society and were severely disadvantaged socially, vocationally, economically, and educationally. Congress strengthened the law through its subsequent amendments and with the passage of the Americans with Disabilities Act (ADA) in 1990 (PL 101-336). The language of ADA is analogous to the language of the Rehab Act in this respect:

Subject to the provision of this title, no qualified individual with a disability, shall by reason of such disability, be excluded from participation in or be denied the benefits of services, programs, or activities of a public entity, or be subjected to discrimination by such entity. (The Americans with Disabilities Act of 1990, Section 12132)

The Rehabilitation Act of 1973 and The Americans with Disabilities Act of 1990 are important additions to lives of children with disabilities because they allow statutory venues for remediation of complaints (Bateman, 1996). This provides individuals with disabilities, their families, and employees an avenue through which they can file complaints against public schools. If these complaints are valid, schools can have their federal funds terminated. An example is a student with diabetes who does not require special assistance for his education and, therefore, is not classified as needing special education. However, he still meets the definition of having a disability under the three-part definition of Section 504 of the Rehab Act. Under Section 504, it would be illegal to discriminate against this child regarding activities, events, or classes. Section 504 of the Rehab Act and ADA are broader and more inclusive than the Individuals with Disabilities Education Act are.

The ADA strives for "equality of opportunity, full participation, independent living, and economic self-sufficiency" (42 U.S.C. 12101, et seq., Sec. 2[a][8]) for persons with disabilities. The main purpose of the ADA is to provide civil rights to the 43 million Americans with disabilities who have been unable to access their communities and necessary services. Critics argue the ADA prevents businesses from expanding and wrecks small business (Turnbull, Bateman, & Turnbull, 1991). However, its main interest is to promote equal access and freedom for people with disabilities. As long as the requirements of accessibility and nondiscrimination based on disability are articulated, ADA should not be a time-consuming burden (Turnbull et al., 1991).

Family Education Rights and Privacy Act

Known also as the Buckley Amendment, the Family Educational Rights and Privacy Act of 1974 (FERPA) defines who may and may not see student records. There are several major points that are important to consider as a principal relating to FERPA.

1. FERPA guarantees the parents or guardians of a student the right to inspect and review their child's records.
2. FERPA establishes policies through which parents can challenge the accuracy of student records.
3. FERPA also establishes a mechanism through which parents can appeal concerning alleged failures to comply with the law.
4. FERPA prohibits the release of information about a student without the parent(s) or guardian(s) consent, except to those who have a legitimate right to know.
5. Districts need to establish a written policy about who will have access to student records.

Special education program administrators need to realize that all of the information obtained as a part of the assessment process to determine whether a student has a disability is to be placed in the student's file. The only exceptions to this may be the actual test protocols used by the individual administering the psychological and educational assessments. Additionally, the file should include evaluation reports, IEPs, and summaries of attainments toward the IEP goals and objectives.

The important component about FERPA is that all of a student's records are located in the files, parents have access to them, they can challenge them, and the files contain confidential information. Knowing this, one should be very judicious about who has access. In addition, it is necessary to safeguard the files and ensure that the appropriate information remains in the files.

PUTTING PRINCIPLES INTO PRACTICE

Parents of children with disabilities experience a range of emotions including guilt, anger, frustration, and helplessness as they struggle to raise this child while also working to increase the odds that their child will become an independent, self-sufficient member of society. The laws governing the education of students with disabilities are complex, and parents will look to the special education program administrator as the final arbiter within their district.

When you are called about a student with a disability within your district, you will probably feel empathy and an immediate desire to help. The first impulse may be to place a telephone call to the specific school official and, by your actions, resolve the problems experienced by these parents and child. Giving in to this impulse may give short-term relief to parents and child, but will usually do little to resolve the real problems. You must realize that problems with students with disabilities can generate emotional responses, and it is important to get both sides of the issue. Contact the teachers/local administrators about the issue and if necessary bring everyone together to resolve the matter.

Understanding the law as outlined above and keeping abreast of the frequent changes will help with preventing problems but will also let you know what to do when problems do occur. You will also know where to look to find more detailed answers to point you and the parents in the proper direction to ensure that the child will receive appropriate special education services.

It is hoped that the special education program administrator will only be involved in the lives of students with disabilities for a limited amount of time and that the parents will work closely with teachers to resolve any problems. This is important because the goal should be the education of the student, and it is the teacher who should have more day-to-day impact on that level than the special education program administrator. The special education program administrator must be aware that he or she will only be involved with the student for a short period of time. Yet the impact of the disability will continue. The parents might struggle to secure and maintain an appropriate level of special education services, often for many years. The parents must learn to deal effectively with the school system and should be able to talk with the school staff whenever they have legal questions.

It is important that the special education program administrator develop a clear understanding about the nature of the disability, the laws, and how to measure educational benefit when a child is in a special education program. To do this, special education program administrators need to develop an understanding of the law so they can identify the specific legal and factual issues. Special education legal matters almost always relate to one of two areas of the law: procedural or factual. Procedural matters involve whether there are violations of timelines, the nature of the disability, the process for evaluation, eligibility for services, and failure to implement an IEP. Factual issues relate to the progress made over the past two years, whether the IEP was implemented, whether the child is due compensatory education services or tuition reimbursement for private school, and whether the child is educationally benefiting or regressing under the public school's special education program.

In all cases it is important to develop an understanding of the facts so that you can identify and target the specific factual issues.

Tips

- Stay current. This is important for both legal and educational issues. For example, it is important to keep in mind and follow the changes in education as a result of No Child Left Behind. There are also methodological changes in the education of students with disabilities.
- Be open to suggestions from parents for creative methods of solving problems and working with their children.
- Meet with parents regularly. Promptly return their phone calls and emails.
- Attend conferences related to education law, especially if they have a special education strand.
- Join different professional organizations. Do not just join organizations for special education program administrators (which is important), but also join parent groups to learn what interests them, and professional special education organizations to understand the latest methodologies and issues.
- Meet with staff regularly to keep aware of their needs (see the chapter on staff meetings). Important, do not hold meetings just to see staff. Go out into the schools. Visit their classrooms. See the behavior problems, understand the physical layout of the staff's responsibilities, and as more students with disabilities are educated in the general education classroom, talk with those teachers about the services and expectations they have.
- Hold pertinent in-services. Make sure the information is useful, research tested, is needed by the staff, and can be used by them.
- Keep the timelines in mind. Provide the resources for the staff to complete the necessary evaluations, develop the reports, and schedule the meetings. If secretarial or staff support is needed, make sure they have what they need and are able to keep their focus on the educational needs of the students in the classroom.

Pitfalls to Avoid

- Staying in the office. Get out among the teachers and the staff and help them. If you do not know how to help them yourself, get them the help they need.
- Not keeping the superintendent informed of potential litigation. Let him or her know when problems are imminent and provide regular updates.
- Saying to the parents, "We don't do that in our district." The child's needs drive the services, not the other way around.

- Giving in to parents' demands. If you as a team really feel this child needs these services, work to make sure the child gets what is necessary (this may involve mediation or due process). This should not be taken lightly—it is important for the child to get what he or she deserves.
- Not meeting with parents on a regular basis.
- Not returning parents' phone calls or emails.
- Not changing how you implement the rules and regulations when there might be a better way. Do not change just for change sake, but also do not hold on to the old methods just because that is the way it has always been done.

RESOURCES

IDEA 2004 Law and Regulations

The Individuals with Disabilities Education Act Amendments of 2004 (PL 108-446), were signed by the president on December 3, 2004. The law and its associated regulations are available in several different formats, including enhanced versions that take full advantage of the linking capabilities of the web.

Sources for more information:

American Speech and Hearing Association (ASHA)
www.asha.org

Association for Career and Technical Education (ACTE)
www.acteonline.org

Council for Children with Behavior Disorders (CCBD)
www.ccbd.net

Council for Exceptional Children (CEC)
www.cec.sped.org

The Federation for Children with Special Needs (FCSN)
www.fcsn.org

IDEA Partnership
www.ideapartnership.org

National Association for Bilingual Education (NABE)
www.nabe.org

National Association of Elementary School Principals (NAESP)
www.naesp.org

National Association of School Psychologists (NASP)
www.nasponline.org

National Association of Secondary School Principals (NASSP)
www.nassp.org

National Education Association (NEA)
www.nea.org

National Resource Center for Paraprofessionals (NRCP)
www.nrcpara.org

Parent Advocacy Coalition for Educational Rights (PACER)
www.pacer.org

REFERENCES

Bateman, B. D., & Linden, M. A. (1998). *Better IEPs: How to develop legally correct and educationally useful programs* (3rd ed.). Longmont, CO: Sopris West.

Bateman, D. F. (1994). Transitional programming: Definitions, models, and practices. In A. Rotatori & J. O. Schwenn (Eds.), *Advances in special education* (Vol. 8, pp. 109–136). New York: JAI Press.

Bateman, D. F. (1996). Legal issues of special education. In M. B. Goor (Ed.), *Case studies in special education administration* (pp. 40–60). New York: Harcourt Brace Jovanovich.

Bateman, D. F., & Bateman, C. F. (2001). *A principal's guide to special education.* Reston, VA: Council for Exceptional Children.

Bateman, D. F., Bright, K. L., & Boldin, A. (2003). Parents as educators in and out of the classroom. In D. Wandry & A. Pleet (Eds.), *A practitioner's guide to facilitating the role of families in the transition process.* Reston, VA: Council for Exceptional Children.

Bettelheim, B. (1950). *Love is not enough.* New York: Macmillan.

Bettelheim, B. (1967). *The empty fortress.* New York: Free Press.

Board of Education of Hendrick Hudson School District v. Rowley, 458 U.S. 176 (1982).

Gorn, S. (2000). *The answer book on special education law* (3rd ed.). Horsham, PA: LRP Publications.

Kauffman, J. M., & Hallahan, D. P. (1995). *The illusion of full inclusion.* Austin, TX: Pro-Ed.

Individuals with Disabilities Education Act (IDEA). (2004). 20 U.S.C. Sec. 1401-1482.

Laski, F. J. (1991). Achieving integration during the second revolution. In L. H. Meyer, C. A. Peck, & L. Brown (Eds.), *Critical issues in the lives of persons with severe disabilities* (pp. 409–421). Baltimore, MD: Paul H. Brookes.

Mahoney, G., & Wheeden, C. A. (1997). Parent-child interaction—the foundation for family-centered early intervention practice: A response to Baird and Peterson. *Topics for Early Childhood and Special Education, 17,* 165–184.

O'Shea, D., Bateman, D. F., O'Shea, L.O., & Algozzine, R. (2004). *The special education due process handbook.* Longmont, CO: Sopris West.

O'Shea, D. J., O'Shea, L., Algozzine, B., & Hammitte, D. J. (Eds.). (2001). *Families and teachers: Collaborative orientations, responsive practices.* Boston: Allyn and Bacon.

Rothstein, L. (2000). *Special education law.* New York: Addison Wesley.

Sailor, W. (1991). Special education in the restructured school. *Remedial and Special Education, 12*(6), 8–22.

Stainback, S., & Stainback, W. (1992). Schools as inclusive communities. In W. Stainback & S. Stainback (Eds.), *Controversial issues confronting special education: Divergent perspectives* (pp. 29–43). Boston: Allyn and Bacon.

Turnbull, A. P., & Turnbull, H. R. (1997). *Families, professionals, and exceptionality: A special partnership* (3rd ed.). Upper Saddle River, NJ: Prentice-Hall.

Turnbull, H. R., Bateman, D. F., & Turnbull, A. P. (1993). Family empowerment. In P. Wehman (Ed.), *The Americans with Disabilities Act* (pp. 157–174). Baltimore, MD: Paul H. Brookes.

Turnbull, H. R., Turnbull, A. P., Stowe, M., & Wilcox, B. L. (2000). *Free appropriate public education: The law and children with disabilities.* Denver, CO: Love Publishing.

Yell, M. L. (2004). *The law and special education.* Upper Saddle River, NJ: Prentice-Hall.

CHAPTER TWO

504 ACCOMMODATION PLANS

BROOKE SHAMBACH

OVERVIEW

Many who are involved with students with disabilities know of the Individuals with Disabilities Act (IDEA); however, an amendment to the Rehabilitation Act of 1973 greatly affects the education of students with disabilities in the public school setting. Section 504 of the Rehabilitation Act (Section 504) makes programs and activities accessible and functional to all individuals with disabilities.

This chapter will define and discuss the implications of Section 504 on public school districts including implementation, evaluation, placement, and procedural safeguards. Due to the nature of the law and the wide variety of environments that it entails, this chapter will focus on the impact of the law on schools receiving federal financial assistance. This law provides many opportunities for children who need accommodations to be successful.

SECTION 504 REGULATIONS AND DEFINITIONS

Regulations

General

No qualified individual with a disability . . . shall solely by reason of her or his disability, be excluded from participation in, be denied the benefits of, or otherwise be subjected to discrimination under any program or activity which receives or benefits from Federal financial assistance. 29 U.S.C. §794(a).

Definitions

A person is considered to be an individual with a disability under Section 504 when he or she has a physical or mental impairment which substantially limits one or more of such person's major life activities, has a record of such an impairment, or is regarded as having such an impairment. 29 U.S.C. §706(8)(B).

Discrimination Prohibited

For purposes of this part, aids, benefits, and services, to be equally effective, are not required to produce the identical result of level of achievement for handicapped and nonhandicapped persons, but must afford handicapped persons equal opportunity to obtain the same result, to gain the same benefit, or to reach the same level of achievement, in the most integrated setting appropriate to the person's needs.

Definitions

The Rehabilitation Act of 1973, a civil rights act, protects the rights of people with disabilities. It states that any recipient of federal financial assistance cannot discriminate based on disability. The original act focused mostly on employment. Section 504 was expanded in 1993 to include all who receive federal financial assistance, including schools. Compliance with Section 504, however, does not grant the programs additional state or federal funding. This statute's purpose is to prevent discrimination, both intentional and unintentional, against individuals with disabilities, those who are believed to have a disability, or family members of a person with a disability.

An individual who is covered under Section 504 may have visible disabilities and/or disabilities that may be unknown. Section 504 defines an "individual with a disability" as a person who:

(a) has a physical or mental impairment which substantially limits one or more major life activities,

(b) has a record of such an impairment, or

(c) is regarded as having such an impairment.

The key element of the definition and in determining eligibility is if the individual's disability affects his or her ability to perform a major life activity, whether permanent or temporary. Disabilities, mental or physical, that are not always readily evident or obvious to others, known as hidden disabilities, are also covered by Section 504.

These disabilities include such things as learning disabilities, ADHD, and allergies where you would not be able to determine that an individual had a disability without some evaluation method. Under Section 504, it is the program's responsibility to seek out all individuals with disabilities to ensure that they are receiving services (U.S. Department of Education Office for Civil Rights, 1995).

EDUCATIONAL ASPECTS

The Office of Civil Rights (OCR) in programs and activities receiving funds from the U.S. Department of Education (ED) enforces Section 504. Each federal agency has its own set of Section 504 regulations applying to its programs. Part 104 of the Code of Federal Regulations states the guidelines for implementing Section 504 in educational settings.

Subpart D—Preschool, Elementary, and Secondary Education (34 C.F.R.)

§104.31 Application of this subpart
Subpart D applies to preschool, elementary, secondary, and adult education programs and activities that receive or benefit from the Federal financial assistance and to recipients that operate, or that receive or benefit from Federal financial assistance for the operation of, such programs or activities.

§104.32 Location and notification
A recipient that operates a public elementary or secondary education program shall annually:

(a) Undertake to identify and locate every qualified handicapped person residing in the recipient's jurisdiction who is not receiving a public education; and

(b) Take appropriate steps to notify handicapped persons and their parents or guardians of the recipient's duty under this subpart.

§104.33 Free appropriate public education

(a) General. A recipient that operates a public elementary or secondary education program shall provide a free appropriate public education to each qualified handicapped person who is in the recipient's jurisdiction, regardless of the nature or severity of the person's handicap.

(b) Appropriate education.

(1) For the purpose of this subpart, the provision of an appropriate education is the provision of regular or special education and related aids and services that (i) are designed to meet individual educational needs of handicapped persons as adequately as the needs of nonhandicapped persons are met (ii) are based upon adherence to procedures that satisfy the requirements of §104.34, §104.35, and §104.36.

§104.34 Educational setting
(a) Academic setting. A recipient to which this subpart applies shall educate, or shall provide for the education of, each qualified handicapped person in its jurisdiction with persons who are not handicapped to the maximum extent appropriate to the needs of the handicapped person.

Determining Need for Section 504

It is the responsibility of preschool, elementary, and secondary programs receiving federal financial assistance to identify all students in their jurisdiction who may be qualified persons with disabilities. Under Section 504 a person who has a disability, in the educational setting, is:

- of an age that individuals without disabilities are provided the services.
- of an age that the services are mandatory under state law.
- a person who, under the Individuals with Disabilities Act (IDEA), is required to receive a free appropriate public education (FAPE).

The responsibility of the educational program, under the Section 504 regulation, is to seek out and serve qualified individuals. The recipients of federal financial assistance must:

- identify and locate all children with disabilities annually.
- provide a "free appropriate public education" to students with disabilities.
- provide education in the "least restrictive environment." This means that students with disabilities will be educated to the maximum extent possible with nondisabled peers.
- construct evaluation and placement guidelines to ensure appropriate identification of the student.
- provide parents and/or guardians with procedural safeguards allowing them to participate in the evaluation and placement of their children.
- give all students with disabilities an equal opportunity to participate in all activities and services.

The greatest challenge of the educational program is the responsibility to identify the students with hidden disabilities. These students represent the part of the student population who are typically not properly diagnosed. Due to this, they appear to be "problem" students who are often described by others as lazy or having discipline issues. However, it is important to know that because of hidden disabilities these students cannot demonstrate their true potential and academic ability. Due to disabilities, they are not able to benefit the same as students without disabilities. An appropriate education is one that meets the needs of all students, disabled or not disabled, and provides them with the same opportunities.

Free Appropriate Public Education

One responsibility of the school district is to provide a "free appropriate public education" (FAPE) to all students with a disability as defined by Section 504. FAPE is defined in IDEA as specially designed instruction (adaptations and modifications), and related services provided at no extra cost, to meet the student's individual and unique needs provided regardless of the severity of the disability. These related services include, but are not limited to, identification, assessments, and transportation. These services and specially designed instruction should enable the student with a disability to have the same opportunities as students without disabilities (Rothstein, 2000).

FAPE plays a major role in Section 504. It relates directly to the regulations, which state that each person in the program must have "equal opportunity to obtain the same result, to gain the same benefit, or to reach the same level of achievement, in the most integrated setting." To comply with Section 504, the student needs to be provided FAPE in the least restrictive environment.

Least Restrictive Environment

The educational component of Section 504 tells how and where the services are to be provided. The concept that relates to this is the least restrictive environment (LRE), which comes from IDEA regulations. The LRE is to provide an education for students with disabilities along with those who are not disabled, to the maximum extent appropriate, without sacrificing the quality of instruction for those involved (see, e.g., the Circuit Court decisions in *Sacra-*

mento School District v. Rachel H., Oberti v. Board of Education of Clementon School District, and *Daniel R. R. v. State Board of Education).* This does not mean that all students with disabilities are to be placed in the regular education classrooms. The LRE is different for each individual. The appropriate placement depends on the individual and his or her disability.

There are multiple reasons that support educating students with disabilities with those who are nondisabled. A principle behind LRE is the benefit of socialization. Students with disabilities would have role models and others that portray appropriate behaviors. Another reason is that the student with the disability would not be singled out and stigmatized by a separate education. Even though instruction in the regular education environment can greatly benefit a student with disabilities, it is not the cure-all. For example, just because one student with a specific learning disability functions and achieves in the regular classroom with supports and services does not mean that all students with learning disabilities can. The education provided must be individualized pertaining to the student being placed and appropriate to meet his or needs (Rothstein, 2000).

Appropriate Evaluation and Placement

§104.35 Evaluation and placement

(a) **Preplacement evaluation.** A recipient that operates a public elementary or secondary education program shall conduct an evaluation in accordance with the requirements of paragraph (b) of this section of any person who, because of handicap, needs or is believed to need special education or related services before taking any action with respect to the initial placement of the person in a regular or special education program and any subsequent significant change in placement.

(b) **Evaluation procedures.**

(1) Tests and other evaluation materials have been validated for the specific purpose for which they are used and are administered by trained personnel in conformance with the instruction provided by their producer;

(2) Tests and other evaluation materials include those tailored to assess specific areas of educational need and not merely those which are designed to provide a single general intelligence quotient; and

(3) Tests are selected and administered so as best to ensure that, when a test is administered to a student with impaired sensory, manual, or speaking skills, the test results accurately reflect the student's aptitude or achievement level or whatever other factor the test purports to measure, rather than reflecting the student's impaired sensory, manual, or speaking skills (except where those skills are the factors that the test purports to measure).

(c) **Placement procedures.** In interpreting evaluation data and in making placement decisions, a recipient shall—

(1) draw upon information from a variety of sources,

(2) establish procedures to ensure that information obtained from all such sources is documented and carefully considered,

(3) ensure that the placement decision is made by a group of persons, including persons knowledgeable about the child, the meaning of the evaluation data, and the placement options, and

(4) ensure that the placement decision is made in conformity with §104.34.

Evaluation and Reevaluation

The first initial step of Section 504 is "child find." Each school program is responsible to identify and locate all students with disabilities. This is done to ensure that all students are given the opportunity to reach their fullest potential. Every year the district must attempt to find every qualified student in that district, whether receiving a public education or not.

The evaluation process begins with a team of individuals who are knowledgeable about the student. The main focus of this team is to ensure that the student's best interests are represented and that he or she is not incorrectly labeled or misclassified. Parents must receive a notice informing parents of the identification, evaluation, and placement of their children. It does not have to be written consent; however, many districts obtain it as documentation. There is no requirement for parental consent under Section 504.

An evaluation must be conducted before any placement changes or decisions are made. The evaluation procedures that pertain to Section 504 parallel those under IDEA. The evaluation procedures must make certain that:

- Tests and other evaluation materials have been validated.
- Evaluations are administered by trained personnel.
- Evaluations are tailored to assess specific areas of educational need.
- Tests are selected and administered that accurately reflect the factors the test purports to measure.

At the conclusion of the evaluations and observations, data is collected and all the information is used to make a collaborative decision.

There are no timelines for evaluations; however, they must be conducted in a reasonable amount of time. After evaluations have been conducted and completed, the school must document the information that has been considered. This will ensure that authorities have taken all the steps necessary for a proper identification.

Reevaluations are periodically required to determine continued need for services. This can be conducted at parent's request, schools request, or at set interval of time. This reevaluation is very similar to the IDEA regulations.

Placement

After a student is identified as needing services, a placement decision must be made based on the definition of least restrictive environment. Again, Section 504 relates to IDEA when is comes to placement decision procedures. The school district decides the makeup of the team. Under Section 504, parents do not need to be included; however, it is a good idea to involve them in the entire process. Services that the student is receiving must be documented in the student's file. This documentation should include modifications in academic requirements and expectations that are necessary to meet the needs of a particular student. The plan should list the accommodations needed so that the student can participate in the general education program.

If a student has a change of placement due to suspension or expulsion, the placement team must reconvene. Under Section 504, if a student is suspended for more than ten days, the team must decide if a significant change of placement is occurring and if the behavior is a result of the student's disability. If the action is found not to be connected to the student's disability, the student's discipline would be based on the school's regular procedures. If it is a result of the disability, the student cannot be expelled or suspended for more than ten days.

§104.36 Procedural safeguards

A recipient that operates a public elementary or secondary education program shall establish and implement, with respect to actions regarding the identification, evaluation, or educational placement of persons who, because of handicap, need or are believed to need special instruction or related services, a system of procedural safeguards that includes a notice, an opportunity for the parents or guardian of the person to examine relevant records, an impartial hearing with opportunity for participation by the person's parents or guardian and representation by counsel, and a review procedure. Compliance with the procedural safeguards of §300.504 of the Individuals with Disabilities Education Act is one means of meeting this requirement.

Procedural Safeguards

There are no set procedural safeguards concerning Section 504 regulations. The schools may adopt their own, or they can use the ones set forth by IDEA. The procedural safeguards must include notice, opportunity for parents and/or guardians to examine data, impartial hearing giving parents and/or guardians the right to be represented by counsel, and review procedures. Impartial hearings for Section 504 violations vary from state to state. If a state does not have hearings to rule on issues, then the school district must provide another method by which the parents can voice their concerns. Many states allow an IDEA hearing officer to rule on Section 504 issues.

Complaints of violations may be filed with the school district's compliance officer or be filed with the Office for Civil Rights (OCR). These complaints must be filed within 180 days of the regulation violation. An investigation will occur. If an individual is filing a complaint, he or she may go through a process call Early Complaint Resolution (ECR). OCR will then issue a decision that will be either no violation or identifying violations and steps to take to correct them. Failure to employ remedial actions may cause federal education funds to be terminated.

504 Accommodation Plans and Responsibilities

Throughout the entire identification, evaluation, and placement process, it is very important that the school and parents of the student with a disability work together to create an accommodation plan. This plan will provide the student with accommodations and modifications to be successful in the school setting. There are no legal requirements for what the accommodation plans need to contain—they should set forth what the student needs to be able to benefit from his or her educational program. Key elements of a 504 accommodation plan include:

- Identification of student. Name, Birthdate, . . .
- Team members. Identify individuals on team and their relationship with the student.
- Sources of evaluation information. Section 504 requires a variety of sources, and each should be listed on the plan.
- The physical or mental impairment. Name the impairment for which services, accommodations, and modifications are necessary.
- The major life activity that is affected.
- Degree of impact. The severity of the impairment and that it impairs a major life activity.
- Required accommodations, modifications, aids, and services that are necessary for the student to receive an educational opportunity proportionate to his or her peers.
- Parent signature and date stating that he or she received notification of the plan and the procedural rights.

Sample accommodations include:

- Homework notebook
- Modified/adapted physical education
- Providing study guides and guided notes
- Communication notebook
- Modified tests and quizzes
- Preferential seating
- Medication plans

After an accommodation plan is created, all staff who work with the student should be informed about the document. Then it can be implemented to ensure the student an appropriate free appropriate education in the least restrictive setting. The individuals who develop the plan have other responsibilities in the process as well.

Section 504 versus IDEA

Section 504 and IDEA are statutes that affect the education of children with disabilities. Section 504 is a civil rights statute, which prohibits discrimination against individuals with disabilities, provides equal access, and compares the education of students with and without disabilities. IDEA is a statute that funds special education programs and provides more services to children with disabilities. The purpose of IDEA is to provide a free appropriate public education (FAPE) and the unique educational needs of a student. While both of these statutes focus on the education of children with disabilities, they also contain significant differences.

Section 504 contains a broader definition than IDEA. All students who are covered under IDEA are also covered under Section 504. Not all students covered by Section 504 are eligible for services under IDEA.

One major difference that affects the educational settings is that of funding. IDEA provides schools additional funding, while Section 504 does not. Being noncompliant with Section 504 can cause an educational setting to lose federal financial assistance.

Evaluation requirements, placement decisions, procedural safeguards, and testing are similar between the two statutes. An evaluation needs to take place under either statute. Each school district must establish standards and procedures for testing. Placement decisions in both statutes are based on the least restrictive environment. Schools may adopt a separate set of procedural safeguards for Section 504 or may utilize the ones set forth in IDEA. The Office for Civil Rights (OCR) enforces Section 504 and the Office of Special Education and Rehabilitative Services (OSERS) implements IDEA.

PUTTING PRINCIPLES INTO PRACTICE

Tips

The special education administrator is often assigned the responsibility of ensuring compliance with the requirements of Section 504. There are specific responsibilities that should be delineated:

School Responsibilities
- Provide a free appropriate public education (FAPE).
- Provide written assurance of nondiscrimination.
- Provide grievance procedures to resolve complaints.
- Annually identify and notify all qualified students with disabilities and parents.

District Responsibilities
- Provide accessible services or facilities.
- Conduct evaluations on policies, programs, and practices to make sure discrimination is not occurring.

504 Coordinator
- Assist the school in meeting 504 requirements and provide resources.
- Create and support teams to accommodate student needs.

Parents and Students
- Be involved in meetings.
- Participate in identification of accommodations.
- Identify aids, supports, and services that are working.
- Be knowledgeable of rights to postsecondary programs.
- Understand the disability and needs to be successful.

Pitfalls to Avoid

Throughout the identification, evaluation/reevaluation, and placement process, a large number of factors need to be taken into consideration in order for the Section 504 plan to be effective in the classroom environment. The following are common problems that can be avoided with proper planning and training of staff in regards to Section 504 plans:

- Making any assumptions about the staff's knowledge about Section 504.
- Not making sure the support staff knows that when a student has any type of problem he or she is considered for eligibility.
- Ignoring parents' request for evaluations.
- Ignoring information from parents related to hospitalizations.
- Not documenting discipline problems when they occur.
- Not initiating appropriate child find procedures at all levels, including all new student admissions.
- Not following through with the goals and accommodations listed on the Section 504 accommodation plan.
- Not individualizing the Section 504 accommodation plan.

RESOURCES

Learning Disabilities Online
www.ldonline.org

Office of Special Education and Rehabilitative Service
www.ed.gov/offices/OSERS/OSEP

U.S. Department of Justice
Civil Rights Division
Disability Rights Section
P.O. Box 66738
Washington, DC 20035-6738
1-800-514-0301 (voice)
1-800-514-0383 (TTY)

REFERENCES

Daniel R. R. v. State Board of Education, 874 F.2d 1036 (5th Cir. 1989).
Oberti v. Board of Education, 995 F.2d 1204 (3rd Cir. 1993).
Rehabilitation Act of 1973. 29 U.S.C. Chapter 16.
Rosenfeld, J. (2000). *Section 504 and IDEA: Basic similarities and differences.* Florida: EDLAW.
Rothstein, L. (2000). *Special education law.* New York: Addison Wesley.
Sacramento Unified School District v. Rachel H. 14 F.3d 1398 (9th Cir. 1994).
U.S. Department of Education Office for Civil Rights. (1995). *The civil rights of students with hidden disabilities under Section 504 of the Rehabilitation Act of 1973.* Washington, DC: U.S. Government Printing Office, 1995-0-396-916.

APPENDIX

SAMPLE NOTICES AND AGREEMENTS

ANNUAL NOTICE TO PARENTS

In compliance with state and federal law, the ABC School District will provide to each protected handicapped student, without discrimination or cost to the student or family, those related aids, services, or accommodations that are needed to provide equal opportunity to participate in and obtain the benefits of the school program and extracurricular activities to the maximum extent appropriate to the student's abilities. In order to qualify as a protected handicapped student, the child must be of school age with a physical or mental disability that substantially limits or prohibits participation in or access to an aspect of the school program.

These services and protections for "protected handicapped students" are distinct from those applicable to all eligible or exceptional students enrolled (or seeking enrollment) in special education programs.

For further information on the evaluation procedures and provision of services to protected handicapped students, contact Ms. Jones, Supervisor of Special Education, ABC School District, Street, Anytown, KS 12345, phone (123) 456-7890.

Sincerely,

Dr. Smith, Ed.D.
Superintendent

NOTICE OF DISTRICT-INITIATED EVALUATION AS A PROTECTED HANDICAPPED STUDENT

Date:

Dear _____:

The ABC School District believes that _____ should be identified/should no longer be identified/requires a change in or modification of the service agreement.

The basis for the belief that the student is or is no longer a protected handicapped student is:

The proposed change or modification in the service agreement is:

The procedures and types of tests that will be used in the evaluation are:

Additional information considered in the development of the service agreement:

If you have any additional information or medical records that will assist in this evaluation, please forward them to me or call me at (123) 456-7890 to discuss this information.

Parents have the right to review all relevant school records of the student, meet with appropriate school officials to discuss any and all issues relevant to the evaluation and accommodations of their child, and give or withhold their written consent to these evaluations.

Directions: Please check one of the options, sign, and return the form.

❒ I give my permission to proceed with the evaluation and/or modification of the service agreement.

❒ I do not give my permission to proceed with the evaluation and/or modification of the service agreement.

My reason for disapproval is:

❒ I request an informal conference to discuss the evaluation and/or modification of the service agreement.

_____   _____

Parent(s) Signature   Date

PROCEDURAL SAFEGUARDS

Dear Parent:

As part of the protections available to you if we cannot agree as to what related aids, services, or accommodations should or should no longer be provided to your child, the procedural safeguard system may be used to resolve the dispute. Following are some details of the avenues available to use.

Parental Request for Assistance

Parents may file a written request for assistance with the Department of Education if the school district is not providing the related aids, services, and accommodations specified in the service agreement and/or the school district has failed to comply with the regulations of the State Board.

The Department of Education will investigate and respond to requests for assistance and, unless exceptional circumstances exist, will, within 60 calendar days of receipt of the request, send written response to the request to the parents and school district.

Written requests should be addressed to: Department of Education
Bureau of Special Education
Anytown, KS 12345   PHONE: 717/783-6913

Informal Conference

Parents may file a written request with the school district for an informal conference with respect to the identification or evaluation of a student, or the student's need for related aid, service, or accommodation. Within 10 school days of receipt of the request, the school district shall convene an informal conference. At the conference, every effort shall be made to reach an amicable agreement.

Formal Due Process Hearing

Parents may file a written request with the school district for an impartial due process hearing. The hearing shall be held before an impartial hearing officer.

Following are some details about the due process hearing:

The hearing shall be held in the local school district at a place reasonably convenient to the parents. At the request of the parents, the hearing may be held in the evening.

The hearing shall be an oral, personal hearing and shall be open to the public unless the parents request a closed hearing.

(continued)

PROCEDURAL SAFEGUARDS (continued)

If the hearing is open, the decision issued in the case, and only the decision, shall be available to the public.

If the hearing is closed, the decision shall be treated as a record of the student and may not be available to the public.

The decision of the hearing officer shall include findings of fact, a discussion, and conclusions of law. The decision shall be based solely upon the substantial evidence presented at the hearing. The hearing officer shall have the authority to order that additional evidence be presented.

A written transcript of the hearing shall, upon request, be made and provided to parents at no cost.

Parents may be represented by any person, including legal counsel.

A parent or a parent's representative shall be given reasonable access to all educational records, including any tests or reports upon which the proposed action is based.

Any party may prohibit the introduction of any evidence at the hearing that has not been disclosed to that party at least five days before the hearing.

A parent or a parent's representative has the right to compel the attendance of and question witnesses of the school entity or agency who may have evidence upon which the proposed action might be based.

Any party has the right to present evidence and testimony, including expert medical, psychological, or educational testimony.

The Secretary of Education will contract with the Right to Education Office for the services of impartial hearing officers, who preside over initial hearings on behalf of local districts on behalf of the Department of Education and may compensate hearing officers for their services. The compensation shall not cause hearing officers to become employees of the Department. The hearing officer may not be an employee or agent of a school entity in which the parents or student resides, or of any agency that is responsible for the education or care of the student.

The following timeline applies to due process hearings:

1. A hearing shall be held within 30 calendar days after a parent's initial request for a hearing.
2. The hearing officer's decision shall be issued within 45 calendar days after the parent's request for a hearing.

Judicial Appeals

If the hearing pertains to Chapter 14 and 15 rights, the decision of the impartial hearing officer may be appealed to a panel of three appellate hearing officers. The panel's decision may be appealed further to a court of competent jurisdiction. If the hearing pertains to Chapter 15 rights, the decision of the impartial hearing officer may be appealed to a court of competent jurisdiction. Under some circumstances, parents may raise those claims directly under Section 504 without going through the due process hearing.

If, within 60 calendar days of the completion of the administrative due process proceedings under this chapter, an appeal or original jurisdiction action is filed in State or Federal Court, the administrative order shall be stayed pending the completion of the judicial proceedings, unless the parents and school district agree otherwise.

ABC SCHOOL DISTRICT
Anytown, KS 12345

SERVICE AGREEMENT

Student Name: _____   Date Services Begin: _____

Date Services End: _____ Initial Agreement: _____ Modified Agreement: _____

I am writing as a follow-up on our recent evaluation concerning your child and to summarize our recommendations and agreements for aids, services, or accommodations. The aids, services or accommodations are as follows:

The following procedures need to be followed in the event of a medical emergency:

The attached letter outlines your rights to resolve any disputes that you may have concerning the recommended aids, services, or accommodations. If you have any questions concerning your rights or the aids, services, or accommodations recommended, please feel free to contact me.

_____   _____
School District Administrator   Date

DIRECTIONS: Please check one of the options and sign this form.

❏ I agree and give permission to proceed as recommended.

❏ I do not agree and do not give permission to proceed as recommended.

❏ I would like to schedule an informal conference to discuss my concerns.

My reason for disapproval is:

_____   _____
Parent(s) Signature   Date

ABC SCHOOL DISTRICT
York Springs, Pennsylvania 17372-0501

SERVICE AGREEMENT

Student Name: _____ Shane L. _____ Date Services Begin: _12/15/05_

Parent's Name: _____ Mr. and Mrs. L. _____

Date Services End: 6/8/06   Initial Agreement: 12/15/01   Modified Agreement: 1/28/05

Modified Agreement: 3/2/05   Agreement ends the last day of the 2005–2006 School Year

School Year: 2005–2006   Student's Birthdate: 5/10/90   Phone No.: 000-123-4567

Student Social Security No. _____   Access No. 1234567890

I am writing as a follow-up on our recent evaluation concerning your child and to summarize our recommendations and agreements for aids, services, or accommodations. The aids, services or accommodations are as follows:

1) Physical Therapy—1 session per week—approximately 30 minutes per session—goal sheet attached

2) Occupational Therapy—1 session per week—approximately 30 minutes a session—goal sheet attached

3) Shane will be able to take breaks during writing assignments, and those will be adapted as needed—Shane will have access to the computer in the classroom to type assignments as needed.

4) Physical Education—modifications to regular physical education as needed. Shane will not participate in contact sports in phys. ed. class or at recess.

5) Additional Adaptive Physical Education class added.

6) Shane will be given preferential seating in the classroom close to the teacher.

7) The bathroom handrails, in the handicapped stall, will be utilized in order for Shane to maintain stability in the bathroom. Shane will be offered assistance as needed, when he vocalizes this to the classroom teacher.

8) Shane will be given additional time to arrive at and depart from classes, and this will be modified by the classroom teacher as the needs change throughout the year.

9) Adult supervision will be provided:

    a) getting off the bus in the morning—escort to the classroom
    b) escort at dismissal time ahead of other students to the bus
    c) during emergency drills
    d) at recess

(continued)

ABC SCHOOL DISTRICT (continued)

   e) movement in the hallway between classes

   f) Lunch—upon student request the aide will get student lunch

   g) adult supervision in hallways to special classes

10) The above plan will be explained to Shane by a building principal. His cooperation will be sought to implement the following plan to provide a safe and secure environment.

11) A classroom aide will be assigned on a trial basis to supervise lunch, lunch recess, afternoon recess, writing assignments, and dismissal procedures.

The following procedures need to be followed in the event of a medical emergency:

Contact parent at home: 123-4567
Emergency #: Jill Smith, 345-6789, Dad at work: 333-4567

The attached letter outlines your rights to resolve any disputes that you may have concerning the recommended aids, services, or accommodations. If you have any questions concerning your rights or the aids, services, or accommodations recommended, please feel free to contact me.

_____   _____

School District Administrator   Date

DIRECTIONS: Please check one of the options and sign this form.

   ❑ I agree and give permission to proceed as recommended.

   ❑ I do not agree and do not give permission to proceed as recommended.

   ❑ I would like to schedule an informal conference to discuss my concerns.

My reason for disapproval is: _____

CHAPTER THREE

PREPARING FOR DUE PROCESS HEARINGS AND MEDIATION

ANN McCOLL

OVERVIEW

In the world of wishes for successful special education administrators, teachers and parents work together to identify the needs of children with disabilities, and teachers execute these plans with support from parents and feedback on how well the process is working. If disagreements occur, there is a simple process for going to someone outside of the system who can resolve the dispute. This person may have qualifications like a judge, but the process is far less formal than a courtroom trial, and the dispute is quickly resolved, at least within 45 days. With the dispute resolved, the parents and educators quickly get back to the task of educating the child in accordance with how the dispute was resolved. Because the process is straightforward, simple to use, and of minimal cost, both teachers and parents feel comfortable using it in order to protect the interests of the child.

In the world of realities for most administrators, the process is not often so simple. Consider a few examples from practice:

- An administrative law judge presides over the dispute; the hearings often are conducted in courtrooms, and, more often than not, both sides are represented by attorneys.
- Special education disputes follow the same procedural rules as other types of cases heard by these administrative law judges; this means that special education cases follow the same procedures as protracted civil litigation in deposing witnesses in advance of the hearing or discovering evidence through written interrogatories or requests for documents.
- Especially when the dispute involves an expensive educational service or placement, expert witnesses are likely to be used, increasing the cost and length of the trials.
- Instead of being resolved within the requisite 45-day period, the vast majority of cases exceed the time frame. In fact, 85 percent of due process cases closed during fiscal year 2001–2002 exceeded this time frame (N.C. Department of Public Instruction, 2002).

In North Carolina, and elsewhere, the process of "settling" special education disputes sometimes means long trials and, often, great expense related to attorney fees, administrative hearings costs, and reimbursements to the parents for the cost of their attorney if they prevail in the hearing (Rawson, 2000). Litigation rates in special education are at historically high levels (cf. O'Shea, Bateman, Algozzine, & O'Shea, 2004; Mann, 1998; McColl, 1998; Yell, 2005; Yell, Katsiyannis, Bradley, & Rozalski, 2000; Ysseldyke, Algozzine, & Thurlow, 2000; Zirkel, 1997). Special education disputes have contributed significantly to this phenomenon and continue to grow at alarming rates (Rawson, 2000; Rothstein, 2000; Yell, 2005). In this chapter, we provide fundamental information related to key parts of dispute resolution procedures: mediation and due process hearings.

The Supreme Court has also recently weighed in on the extensive costs and time of litigation. In her recent decision in *Schaffer v. Weast,* Justice Sandra Day O'Connor wrote of the extensive costs and time commitments of litigation. This case also clarified that the burden of showing an IEP as inappropriate is the responsibility of the party requesting the hearing, typically the parents.

REGULATIONS

Section 615. Procedural Safeguards

Mediation

In General—Any State educational agency or local educational agency that receives assistance under this part shall ensure that procedures are established and implemented to allow parties to disputes involving any matter, including matters arising prior to the filing of a complaint, to resolve such disputes through a mediation process.

Requirements—Such procedures shall meet the following requirements:

The procedures shall ensure that the mediation process—

(i) is voluntary on the part of the parties;

(ii) is not used to deny or delay a parent's right to a due process hearing or to deny any other rights; and

(iii) is conducted by a qualified and impartial mediator who is trained in effective mediation techniques.

Impartial Due Process Hearing

In General—

(A) Hearing—Whenever a complaint has been received, the parents or the local educational agency involved in such complaint shall have an opportunity for an impartial due process hearing, which shall be conducted by the State educational agency or by the local educational agency, as determined by State law or by the State educational agency.

(B) Resolution Session

(i) Preliminary Meeting—Prior to the opportunity for an impartial due process hearing, the local educational agency shall convene a meeting with the parents and the relevant member or members of the IEP Team who have specific knowledge of the facts identified in the complaint—within 15 days of receiving notice of the parents' complaint. The meeting shall include a representative of the agency who has decision-making authority on behalf of such agency; which may not include an attorney of the local educational agency unless the parent is accompanied by an attorney; and, where the parents of the child discuss their complaint and the facts that form the basis of the complaint and the local educational agency is provided the opportunity to resolve the complaint, unless the parents and the local educational agency agree in writing to waive such meeting, or agree to use the mediation process.

(ii) Hearing—If the local educational agency has not resolved the complaint to the satisfaction of the parents within 30 days of the receipt of the complaint, the due process hearing may occur, and all of the applicable timelines for a due process hearing under this part shall commence.

Written Settlement Agreement—In the case that a resolution is reached to resolve the complaint at a meeting, the parties shall execute a legally binding agreement that is signed by both the parent and a representative of the agency who has the authority to bind such agency; and enforceable in any State court of competent jurisdiction or in a district court of the United States.

Review Period—If the parties execute an agreement, a party may void such agreement within 3 business days of the agreement's execution.

Disclosure of Evaluations and Recommendations

In General—Not less than 5 business days prior to a hearing, each party shall disclose to all other parties all evaluations completed by that date, and recommendations based on the offering party's evaluations, that the party intends to use at the hearing.

Simply put, parents have a right to request assistance and an impartial hearing when a conflict surfaces related to their child's education. Mediation and/or a due process hearing can be the beginning in a series of legal challenges that can lead to appellate court decisions. Mediation, before or after filing a due process hearing request, is the procedure of choice for attempting to resolve most disagreements. Federal law requires that opportunities be available for mediation that provides an opportunity for the parties to try to work out their differences with the help of a trained facilitator. School districts are still obligated to meet all legal requirements for serving the child, but within these parameters, mediation can be successful for working out issues. Mediation is especially productive when the main barrier is communication. If there is a complex legal dispute or great expense is involved in the requested services or placement for the child, mediation may not help.

Deciding when to request mediation is a balancing of concerns. Sometimes parents do not believe that they are being taken seriously until after they file a due process hearing request. If so, they may want to file a request and then seek mediation opportunities. The disadvantage is that filing a due process hearing request before mediation creates a more adversarial tone that may affect the success of mediation. For parents who are seeking changes in legal interpretations of the law or have been advised by their lawyer that mediation is not the best way to get a change, then more formal due process proceedings are more likely to be part of the dispute.

The resolution session is an opportunity after filing a complaint for another meeting between the parent and relevant members of the IEP team and a LEA representative with decision-making authority. It is an option that can be used instead of mediation. It may be helpful in circumstances where filing the complaint (1) has made the problems and potential resolution more clear; or (2) causes the school district to pay more attention. It obviously is not much help if everyone is in a deadlock or has reached the point of not being able to communicate or if the issues have been worked over in this environment without success.

PUTTING PRINCIPLES INTO PRACTICE

Clearly, there are many times when due process hearings should be avoided. These are situations where it is not so much a legal dispute as it is a breakdown in communication and cooperation between the parents and educators. There is a loss of trust. Parents may believe that the educators do not have the interests of their child at heart or that the educators are not willing to listen to them about what they know about their child and his or her needs. Educators may believe that the parents are being unreasonable in their demands or that they are being difficult to work with. In these situations, all a due process hearing can do is to resolve the particular dispute at that time. It cannot mend the relationship, and, in fact, it will probably make it worse. These are the types of cases where as soon as the parties are out of the due process hearing, they will once again find themselves in disagreement, perhaps even over how the orders from the hearing are to be implemented.

Tips for Avoiding Due Process Hearings

There are strategies that school districts can use effectively to avoid due process hearings at all stages of their relationship with parents. They generally revolve around knowledge of legal responsibilities and appropriate actions related to them.

1. *Be knowledgeable about the purpose and requirements of disabilities laws.*

Educators must be knowledgeable of the legal rights of children with disabilities and their parents. Not knowing them can cause the school district to unintentionally violate rights, such as failing to provide proper notice to parents (Davidson & Algozzine, 2002). It also can give the impression that the school district doesn't really care about its students with disabilities. Parents who have become educated about their rights and their children's rights are especially likely to be critical of educators who appear to know less than they do about the law.

There is a distinction between a superficial understanding of the law and the kind of understanding that leads to meaningful implementation. Educators have to make sure necessary forms are completed with appropriate signatures. But when parents believe that all the educators care about is getting the forms completed, they will leave a meeting frustrated that the educators only seem interested in compliance, not in making their child successful. By comparison, meaningful implementation means that the team of educators understands and has fully adopted as a part of its educational philosophy the key elements of the law including zero reject, child find, free appropriate public education, and least restrictive environment.

While a regular education teacher may not need to know everything the special education director knows, each educator must have a reasonable understanding of the law based upon his or her responsibilities. This is not an easy task and requires a commitment at the school and school district level to ongoing professional development.

2. *Believe in the principles of disabilities laws.*

Laws can establish requirements but they cannot force individuals to believe in the requirements. Until educators believe in the capabilities of children with disabilities and the ability to educate them in the least restrictive environment, the law will never be fully implemented as intended. Sometimes teachers complain that the principal doesn't support the disability services or there is tension between the special education department and regular education. Research repeatedly finds that provisions in IDEA have not been implemented as intended because the educators did not really believe in the principles established by the law (cf. O'Shea et al., 2004; Yell, 2005; Ysseldyke et al., 2000; Zirkel, 1997).

Parents can quickly tell the difference between a teacher or administrator who just seems to be going through the motions and one that is truly committed. If parents believe that school personnel are truly doing all they can, they are much more willing to be patient and work with them. A lack of belief may be the single element most likely to drive parents to due process because they do not see any other way to get the school to commit. This can be particularly obvious in matters involving families speaking native languages other than English—for example, there is a difference between going through the motions of having a translator or really making sure parents understand what is being said. There is no value to having met a "responsibility" by having a translator present when parents have not understood the educational or legal jargon controlling the meeting.

3. *Know how to serve children with disabilities.*

Educational practices continue to evolve in working with children with different types of disabilities. Understanding how to serve children may affect the kinds of goals and objectives identified for the child and will certainly have an impact on how the IEP is implemented. Parents who have become educated about their child's disability and have learned about effective educational practices will be especially disheartened by trying to work with educators who do not seem to be current in their professional field.

If parents present ideas, educators should investigate them. Sometimes parents have been exposed to other ways of serving children from working with other school districts in the same state or another state, or they may have attended workshops. Not only might educators learn some new ways of working with the child, but also it will do wonders for the relationship with the parents for them to see that their ideas are taken seriously.

4. *Adopt a team approach.*

The law requires a team approach. But it is possible to meet the letter of the law without meeting the spirit of the law. For example, the legal requirements for the IEP meeting are met if all the appropriate persons are in attendance (34 C.F.R. 300.344). But the spirit of the law is broken when most of the attendees are mute while one person drives the process.

The law reflects a belief that people from multiple disciplines and with different experiences with the child can best develop a plan for serving the child. No one person should carry the weight of developing the IEP. And yet, this still occurs in schools. This is evident when one person walks through a draft IEP with little or no input from anyone else in the meeting. By comparison, a team that has embraced this concept has lively discussions in the meeting. When reflecting on the meeting, participants will say, "we decided," "we thought about," or "we were concerned."

If the solo voice is one that the parent trusts, then it may not matter too much to him or her whether there is a true team concept. The problem occurs when the parent does not like or respect a solo voice. At that point, it is much more likely to feel to the parent that it is just the parent versus this one educator and that there is little choice but to pursue more litigious strategies. By comparison, if there is a full team behind a decision, it is likely to be more credible to the parent, even if there are individuals on the team that the parent doesn't like.

5. *Communicate effectively with parents.*

Good communication skills are essential. Communication is how educators can convey all the things that they do well: They can demonstrate what they know about the parent's and child's legal rights, their beliefs in the principles of the law, their knowledge of how to effectively educate the child, and their commitment to working with the parent as a team.

Good communication also is the best tool educators have when things go wrong. Given the complexity of disabilities law and the practical issues many schools face in providing services, the likelihood is pretty high that, at some point, the child's records will be out of compliance or educators will not have met all the legal requirements in serving the child. While fixing these issues is important, the most effective way to avoid due process over unintended deficiencies may be for educators to be able to sincerely say to the parents that they are sorry.

Without good communication skills, educators may appear arrogant, disinterested, uncaring, and insensitive. Not surprisingly, parents faced with educators that they perceive in this light will be extremely frustrated and disappointed and either give up and withdraw from the process or fight back. They way they fight back may depend on their own communication skills and style. It becomes like the dynamics in domestic conflicts where the parties get stuck in an unhealthy relationship. And while this will make the entire IEP team process unpleasant for all participants, the bigger concern is that what has taken center stage is the relationship between the educators and the parents, not the education of the child.

Ideally, all educators should receive training in cooperative behaviors, conflict resolution, and effective listening. When this is not possible, at least some of the educators who serve on the IEP team should have the training so that they can take the lead in communication when necessary and use their facilitation skills to improve relationships.

Tips for Handling Inevitable Pitfalls

"Trouble" begins when educators or parents realize that they are having difficulty working together and resolving issues related to the child's education. When problems, pitfalls, and provisos take over, all of the strategies mentioned above are critical. In addition, consider the following strategies.

1. *Focus on establishing a clear complaint.*

The importance of a complete and direct complaint is very important, since it is the basis for a resolution session (if held), and parents are precluded from raising issues in the due process hearing that are not listed in the complaint. If the complaint is deemed frivolous, parents also can be liable for the school district's attorney fees. Clearly an ounce of direction is worth a pound of correction when formulating the complaint.

2. *Implement additional communication strategies.*

Educators should have additional communication strategies ready to implement when trouble begins. For example, school districts can adopt the following practices:

- A member of the IEP team notifies personnel in the school district exceptional children's office about the problems so that they can intervene if appropriate. For example, they might assign the case to someone to review the file and participate in the IEP meeting or even to contact the parent to discuss the parent's concerns.
- Find someone whom the parent trusts to be the link between the school and the parent. While educational decisions can only be made in the IEP meetings, a contact person can talk with the parent between meetings to help plan the IEP meeting in a way to meet the parent's needs and concerns.
- Determine if there are communication skill problems with any of the educators who are participating in the IEP meeting or working with the child. If there are, the school should provide training and/or set clearer expectations with the person or give the role to another educator who is similarly qualified to participate.

3. *Seek legal advice if necessary to make sure the school district is meeting legal requirements.*

The law is complex, and sometimes even educators who are reasonably knowledgeable about the law may be uncertain about particular requirements. In situations where educators are not as knowledgeable as they should be, it is even more important to have the school district's lawyer review the case and make sure that legal requirements are being met and that whatever positions the educators are taking are legally defensible.

Tips for Protecting the IEP Team Process

Federal law places great emphasis on educational decisions being made by the IEP team. Before turning to other processes to resolve disputes, two other strategies may help make the IEP team be successful in working out differences. Either educators or parents could recommend these strategies.

1. *Suggest using an impartial facilitator to conduct the IEP meeting.*

If the problems are primarily communication problems, either the parent or the educators could suggest using an impartial facilitator to conduct the IEP meeting. The facilitator does not offer his or her views, but helps the parents and educators work together. This is especially helpful, if like in a bad marriage, the parents and educators simply cannot listen or respond effectively to each other. Perhaps the parents are too quick to jump to conclusions, or perhaps the educators are not listening closely enough to realize that the parent is offering some flexibility. A facilitator can work to make sure everyone gets a fair opportunity to be heard and to help the parties come to agreement.

2. *Suggest an impartial on-site review.*

If the root of the problem is more of a factual dispute about how well the child is doing or the appropriateness of the IEP or placement, either the parent or educators could suggest an impartial on-site review. An on-site reviewer would observe the child and review the education/medical records. The function is similar to an Independent Education Evaluation (IEE) in that it is intended to bring an objective outside opinion. Unlike the IEE, an impartial on-site review is not a part of federal law and so it is purely voluntary. It also can have a broader scope, since the review might offer an opinion on an array of topics related to the content of the IEP and its delivery.

When All Else Fails

When strategies within the IEP team process have failed, it is time to look to other forms of interventions. Schools have the right to seek due process in certain circumstances, including for the purpose of obtaining permission to evaluate a child when the parent has refused or for seeking temporary removal of the child from its regular placement due to behavior and safety concerns. In the vast majority of circumstances, it is the parent who seeks due process. This section primarily addresses the parent as the initiator.

1. *Offer mediation.*

Rather than wait for a request for mediation, the school district can offer to enter into mediation with the parent once it realizes that other strategies have not succeeded.

2. *Make a reasonable offer.*

If the parent has filed a request for a due process hearing, then the parent had to provide an explanation of concerns and offer a resolution. At any time more than ten days before the due process hearing begins, the school district has the opportunity to respond to the parent by making an offer. With rare exception, if the parent rejects the school district's offer but fares no better through the due process hearing, the parent cannot be awarded reimbursement of attorney fees from the school district. Thus, even if the school district is found at fault in the due process hearing and the decision is in favor of the parent, the parent will not be able to be awarded the attorney fees if the order is not better than the school district's offer. Given how high attorney fees can climb in lengthy litigation, this creates a powerful incentive for the school district to make a good offer and for parents to carefully consider whether they are likely to do any better in a hearing. It is the best chance left for avoiding a due process hearing.

How to Guarantee a Due Process Hearing

Nobody wants disputes with parents. Nobody wants to go to court to resolve them. The best defense in the land of special education litigation is a good offense. Put simply this means there are many "hot buttons" to avoid in dealing with legal matters related to providing special education services. Here is a "Top Ten List of Ways to Move Closer to (Rather than Away from) a Due Process Hearing":

1. *"We don't do it that way here."* Besides the fact that "it" might be legally required, this message is contrary to working as a resourceful team. It sends the message to parents that we are not willing to listen to your ideas. This message could land you straight in a due process hearing.

2. *"That costs too much money."* This statement sends a red flag to parents that the school may not have its priorities in order. While federal standards and most state standards do not require a Cadillac version of education, there are definite limitations on how much the issue of funding can be considered.

3. *"I can take care of that."* There are two problems with this statement. The first is the "I." All educational decisions are to be made by the team and not determined in advance by any individual. The second is the suggestion that this is purely negotiation and satisfying parental requests. The school district's obligation is always first to meet its legal requirements to the child.

4. *"We don't have to give you another IEP meeting since you failed to show up."* Educators can get so wrapped up in what they are legally required to do that they fail to use common sense. They may not legally be required to hold another meeting in some circumstances or respond to some other parent request, but educators should carefully consider whether rejecting the parent request is worth the cost to the relationship.

5. *"It doesn't matter what services your child received at the other school."* This is partly another version of the "we don't do it that way here." It also raises problems in that there may be valuable information from the other school about how the child responded to a particular placement or service. If the parent wants the same provisions at this school, the educators should at least check it out before saying no.

6. *"We don't have to provide an Independent Education Evaluation in this situation."* This is another version of the "we legally can't be required so we won't do it" mentality. While there are times that schools can contest a parent's request for an IEE, if it would help bring some clarity, make the parent feel more involved, then spending the extra funds now may save a lot more later if a due process hearing is avoided.

7. *"We only provide that service for children with this other disability."* Children are to be served, not the disability. Limiting the availability of services to only certain disability classifications is contrary to the law.

8. *Educators repeatedly document in the regular education records that the child is "lazy" and "doesn't pay attention" but there is no evaluation.* What educators write in regular education records matters when it comes to special education. These are the easy cases for parents where the educators have documented the basis for knowledge of a disability without then taking steps to identify and evaluate the child. The school district

should have some sort of tickler system to make sure comments like this are not made repeatedly without some follow-through.

9. *The IEP team marks on the form that the "child's behavior interferes with the child's learning or the learning of others," but there are no behavior objectives or plan, and the child is frequently suspended.* What educators say through the special education records also matter. A lack of follow-through, like this example, is an easy way to end up in due process.

10. *"It's not our fault the child didn't get the education—the parents wouldn't agree."* The school district retains the legal responsibility for educating the child, no matter what. That's why school districts can also pursue due process hearings when necessary to obtain appropriate decisions for the child. When a child has been inadequately served, courts don't think much of a school district's excuse that they relented to the parent's choice in order to get along. The courts will say that the educators are supposed to be the experts and ultimately must make decisions in accordance with legal requirements, not what will make the parent happy. This is when acting to avoid a due process hearing is not the right thing to do.

RESOURCES

Resources available online and in individual *community and state* information services can be very helpful in avoiding a litigation train wreck in contemporary special education. The following listing of resources may be helpful in dealing with mediation and due process procedures when settling disputes related to providing special education services.

Websites and Technical Assistance

The World Wide Web provides ready access to a variety of resources related to mediation and due process hearings. Here is a sample.

Oregon Department of Education
www.ode.state.or.us
A section of the Oregon Department of Education's Office of Special Education website provides a variety of information on resolving disagreements involving students with disabilities and their educational needs. Similar resources are available on the websites of other education agencies:

- California Department of Education
- Confederation of Oregon School Administrators
- Connecticut State Department of Education
- Pennsylvania Department of Education

Wrightslaw
www.wrightslaw.com
Wrightslaw provides administrators, teachers, parents, advocates, and attorneys with accurate, up-to-date information about special education law and improving services

for children with disabilities. Several parts of the website address mediation and due process hearings and provide a variety of resources related to better understanding these processes in relation to special education.

REFERENCES

Davidson, D. N., & Algozzine, B. (2002). Administrators' knowledge of expected special education practices. *Educational Leadership and Administration, 14,* 135–147.

Mann, J. (1998). Response to the Center's article on special education disputes in North Carolina. *North Carolina Insight, 17*(4)/*18*(1), 65–68.

McColl, A. (1998). Red rape and raw nerves: Special education disputes in North Carolina. *North Carolina Insight, 17*(4)/*18*(1), 45–62.

North Carolina Department of Public Instruction, Exceptional Children Division. (2002). *Annual Report for Special Education Due Process Hearings and Formal Written Complaints, July 1, 2001–June 30, 2002.* Raleigh: Author.

O'Shea, D. J., Bateman, D., Algozzine, B., & O'Shea, L. J. (2004). *The special education due process handbook.* Longmont, CO: Sopris West.

Rawson, M. J. (2000). *A manual of special education law for educators and parents.* Naples, FL: Morgen Publishing.

Rothstein, L. (2000). *Special education law.* New York: Addison Wesley.

Schaffer v. Weast, 126 S.Ct. 528 (2005).

Yell, M. (2005). *The law and special education.* Upper Saddle River, NJ: Prentice-Hall.

Yell, M. L., Katsiyannis, A., Bradley, R., & Rozalski, M. E. (2000). Ensuring compliance with the discipline provisions of IDEA. *Journal of Special Education Leadership 13,* 3–18.

Ysseldyke, J. E., Algozzine, B., & Thurlow, M. L. (2000). *Critical issues in special and remedial education* (3rd ed.). Boston: Houghton Mifflin.

Zirkel, P. A. (1997). The "explosion" in education litigation. *West's Education Law Reporter, 114,* 341–351.

CHAPTER FOUR

DEALING WITH DISCIPLINE

MICHAEL JAZZAR

OVERVIEW

Disciplining students with disabilities has proven to be a continuously controversial and complex issue. Although the Individuals with Disabilities Education Act (IDEA) and Section 504 of the Rehabilitation Act of 1973 established laws that are quite detailed in many areas, until recently specific federal guidelines regarding the disciplining of students with disabilities did not exist. Following much heated testimony, Congress added a section to the IDEA Amendments of 1997 that specifically addressed discipline issues. In doing so, Congress sought to strike a balance between school officials' duty to ensure that schools are safe and conducive to learning and their continuing obligation to ensure that students with disabilities receive a free appropriate public education.

The chapter presents the information needed to understand the background of the disciplinary components of IDEA, the general requirements, some tips for putting the principles into practice, and a listing of resources. The procedures outlined in this chapter are designed to facilitate school leaders in dealing with the requirements evident in discipline procedures of the IDEA.

REGULATIONS

Change of Placement for Disciplinary Reasons

For purposes of removal of a child with a disability from the current educational placement, a change of placement occurs if the removal is for more than ten consecutive school days or the child is subjected to a series of removals that constitute a pattern because they cumulate to more than ten school days in a school year, and because of factors such as the length of each removal, the total amount of time the child is removed, and the proximity of the removals to one another.

Authority of School Personnel

A change of placement may be ordered to the extent that removal would be applied to children without disabilities, the removal of a child with a disability from the child's current placement for not more than ten consecutive school days for any violation of school rules, and additional removals of not more than ten consecutive school days in that same school year for separate incidents of misconduct (as long as those removals do not constitute a change of placement); after a child with a disability has been removed from his or her current placement for more than ten school days in the same school year, during any subsequent days of removal the public agency must provide services; and to an appropriate interim alternative educational setting for the same amount of time that a child without a disability would be subject to discipline, but for not more than forty-five days, if the child carries a weapon to school or to a school function under the jurisdiction of a state or a local educational agency; or the child knowingly possesses or uses illegal drugs or sells or solicits the sale of a controlled substance while at school or a school function under the jurisdiction of a state or local educational agency.

Either before or not later than ten business days after either first removing the child for more than ten school days in a school year or commencing a removal that constitutes a change of placement under §300.519, including the action described in paragraph (a)(2) of this section—

(i) If the LEA did not conduct a functional behavioral assessment and implement a behavioral intervention plan for the child before the behavior that resulted in the removal described in paragraph (a) of this section, the agency shall convene an IEP meeting to develop an assessment plan.

(ii) If the child already has a behavioral intervention plan, the IEP team shall meet to review the plan and its implementation, and modify the plan and its implementation as necessary, to address the behavior.

(2) As soon as practicable after developing the plan described in paragraph (b)(1)(i) of this section, and completing the assessments required by the plan, the LEA shall convene an IEP meeting to develop appropriate behavioral interventions to address that behavior and shall implement those interventions.

(c)

(1) If subsequently, a child with a disability who has a behavioral intervention plan and who has been removed from the child's current educational placement for more than ten school days in a school year is subjected to a removal that does not constitute a change of placement under §300.519, the IEP team members shall review the behavioral intervention plan and its implementation to determine if modifications are necessary.

(2) If one or more of the team members believe that modifications are needed, the team shall meet to modify the plan and its implementation, to the extent the team determines necessary.

(d) For purposes of this section, the following definitions apply:

(1) *Controlled substance* means a drug or other substance identified under schedules I, II, III, IV, or V in section 202(c) of the Controlled Substances Act (21 U.S.C. 812(c)).

(2) *Illegal drug—*

> (i) Means a controlled substance; but

> (ii) Does not include a substance that is legally possessed or used under the supervision of a licensed health-care professional or that is legally possessed or used under any other authority under that Act or under any other provision of Federal law.

(3) *Weapon* has the meaning given the term "dangerous weapon" under paragraph (2) of the first subsection (g) of section 930 of title 18, United States Code.

(Authority: 20 U.S.C. 1415(k)(1), (10))

Authority of Hearing Officer

A hearing officer may order a change in the placement of a child with a disability to an appropriate interim alternative educational setting for not more than 45 days if the hearing officer, in an expedited due process hearing—

(a) Determines that the public agency has demonstrated by substantial evidence (i.e., beyond a preponderance of the evidence) that maintaining the current placement of the child is substantially likely to result in injury to the child or to others; (b) Considers the appropriateness of the child's current placement; (c) Considers whether the public agency has made reasonable efforts to minimize the risk of harm in the child's current placement, including the use of supplementary aids and services; and (d) Determines that the interim alternative educational setting that is proposed by school personnel, who have consulted with the child's special education teacher, meets the expected requirements.

Determination of Setting

The interim alternative educational setting must be determined by the IEP team and must be selected so as to enable the child to continue to progress in the general curriculum, although in another setting, and to continue to receive those services and modifications, including those described in the child's current IEP, that will enable the child to meet the goals set out in that IEP, and include services and modifications to address the behavior determining eligibility for services and to prevent the behavior from recurring.

Manifestation Determination Review

If an action is contemplated regarding behavior involving a removal that constitutes a change of placement for a child with a disability who has engaged in other behavior that violated any rule or code of conduct of the LEA that applies to all children—

(1) Not later than the date on which the decision to take that action is made, the parents must be notified of that decision and provided the procedural safeguards notice; and,

(2) Immediately, if possible, but in no case later than ten school days after the date on which the decision to take that action is made, a review must be conducted of the relationship between the child's disability and the behavior subject to the disciplinary action. The review must be conducted by the IEP team and other qualified personnel in a meeting and determine

that the behavior of the child was not a manifestation of the child's disability only if the IEP team and other qualified personnel consider, in terms of the behavior subject to disciplinary action, all relevant information, including (i) evaluation and diagnostic results, including the results or other relevant information supplied by the parents of the child; (ii) observations of the child; and (iii) the child's IEP and placement; and then determine that (i) in relationship to the behavior subject to disciplinary action, the child's IEP and placement were appropriate and the special education services, supplementary aids and services, and behavior intervention strategies were provided consistent with the child's IEP and placement; (ii) the child's disability did not impair the ability of the child to understand the impact and consequences of the behavior subject to disciplinary action; and (iii) the child's disability did not impair the ability of the child to control the behavior subject to disciplinary action.

Behavior Determined Not a Manifestation of Disability

If the result of the review is a determination that the behavior of the child with a disability was not a manifestation of the child's disability, the relevant disciplinary procedures applicable to children without disabilities may be applied to the child in the same manner in which they would be applied to children without disabilities. If the public agency initiates disciplinary procedures applicable to all children, the agency shall ensure that the special education and disciplinary records of the child with a disability are transmitted for consideration by the person or persons making the final determination regarding the disciplinary action. If a parent requests a hearing to challenge a determination made through a review that the behavior of the child was not a manifestation of the child's disability, the hearing is to occur on an expedited basis.

Parent Appeal

In general, if the child's parent disagrees with a determination that the child's behavior was not a manifestation of the child's disability or with any decision regarding placement, the parent may request a hearing. The State or local educational agency shall arrange for an expedited hearing in any case if a hearing is requested by a parent. In reviewing a decision with respect to the manifestation determination, the hearing officer shall determine whether the public agency has demonstrated that the child's behavior was not a manifestation of the child's disability consistent with the requirements set forth in the law. In reviewing a decision to place the child in an interim alternative educational setting, the hearing officer shall apply appropriate standards as well.

Placement during Appeals

If a parent requests a hearing or an appeal regarding a disciplinary action to challenge the interim alternative educational setting or the manifestation determination, the child must remain in the interim alternative educational setting pending the decision of the hearing officer or until the expiration of the appropriate time period, whichever occurs first, unless the parent and the State agency or local educational agency agree otherwise. If a child is placed in an interim alternative educational setting and school personnel propose to change the child's placement after expiration of the interim alternative placement, during the pendency of any proceeding to challenge the proposed change in placement, the child must remain in the current placement (the child's placement prior to the interim alternative educational setting). If school personnel maintain that it is dangerous for the child to be in the current placement (placement prior to removal to the interim alternative education setting) during the pendency of the due process proceedings, the LEA may request an expedited due process hearing. In determining whether the child may be placed in the alternative educational setting or in another appropriate placement ordered by the hearing officer, the hearing officer shall apply appropriate standards. Such a placement ordered may not be longer than 45 days and the procedure may be repeated, as necessary.

Protections for Children Not Yet Eligible for Services

A child who has not been determined to be eligible for special education and related services and who has engaged in behavior that violated any rule or code of conduct of the local educational agency may assert any of the protections provided if the LEA had knowledge that the child was a child with a disability before the behavior that precipitated the disciplinary action occurred. An LEA must be deemed to have knowledge that a child is a child with a disability if—

(1) The parent of the child has expressed concern in writing (or orally if the parent does not know how to write or has a disability that prevents a written statement) to personnel of the appropriate educational agency that the child is in need of special education and related services;

(2) The behavior or performance of the child demonstrates the need for these services;

(3) The parent of the child has requested an evaluation of the child; or

(4) The teacher of the child, or other personnel of the local educational agency, has expressed concern about the behavior or performance of the child to the director of special education of the agency or to other personnel in accordance with the agency's established child find or special education referral system. A public agency would not be deemed to have knowledge as a result of conducting an evaluation and determining that the child was not a child with a disability; or determining that an evaluation was not necessary; and providing notice to the child's parents of such determination.

If an LEA does not have knowledge that a child is a child with a disability prior to taking disciplinary measures against the child, the child may be subjected to the same disciplinary measures as measures applied to children without disabilities who engaged in comparable behaviors. If a request is made for an evaluation of a child during the time period in which the child is subjected to disciplinary measures, the evaluation must be conducted in an expedited manner. Until the evaluation is completed, the child remains in the educational placement determined by school authorities, which can include suspension or expulsion without educational services. If the child is determined to be a child with a disability, taking into consideration information from the evaluation conducted by the agency and information provided by the parents, the agency shall provide special education and related services.

Expedited Due Process Hearings

Expedited due process hearings must meet the requirements that a State may provide that the time periods identified for purposes of expedited due process hearings are not less than two business days, and be conducted by a due process hearing officer who satisfies the law's requirements. Each State shall establish a timeline for expedited due process hearings that results in a written decision being mailed to the parties within 45 days of the public agency's receipt of the request for the hearing, without exceptions or extensions. The timeline must be the same for hearings requested by parents or public agencies. A State may establish different procedural rules for expedited hearings than it has established for other due process hearings. The decisions on expedited due process hearings may be appealed.

Referral to and Action by Other Authorities

Nothing in this part prohibits an agency from reporting a crime committed by a child with a disability to appropriate authorities or to prevent law enforcement and judicial authorities from exercising their responsibilities with regard to the application of Federal and State law to crimes committed by a child with a disability. An agency reporting a crime committed by a child with a disability shall ensure that copies of the special education and disciplinary records of the child are transmitted for consideration by the appropriate authorities to whom it reports the crime. An agency reporting a crime under this section may transmit copies of the child's special education and disciplinary records only to the extent that the transmission is permitted by the Family Educational Rights and Privacy Act.

Disciplining students with disabilities is a complex issue. This is not to say that students with disabilities are immune from a school's disciplinary procedure. Schools may use procedures such as reprimands, detention, restriction of privileges, response cost, in-school suspensions (if the student's education is continued), and out-of-school suspensions (ten days or less) as long as the procedures are not abused or applied in a discriminatory manner. Disciplinary procedures that effectively change a student's placement are, however, not legal if not done in accordance with the procedural safeguards afforded students with disabilities. Such procedures include suspension (if over ten days) and expulsion. If students with disabilities bring weapons to school or they use, possess, or sell illegal drugs, school officials may unilaterally remove them to an interim alternative setting for forty-five school days. During this time the IEP team should meet to consider appropriate actions. In general, knowledge and adherence to the laws are imperative in disciplining students with disabilities with adequate documentation being critical.

PUTTING PRINCIPLES INTO PRACTICE

Discipline is among the most salient concerns of administrators, parents, teachers, and students in U.S. schools. Fueled by occasional incidents of extreme levels of school violence, maintaining safe and orderly schools is a continuing quest and challenge. The tips below focus on ways to improve the environment that is the classroom of today; they will help special education administrators think about ways and means for dealing with discipline based on individual students' needs.

Tips

In order to comply with federal discipline regulations of children with disabilities, school personnel shall . . .

- Ensure that children with disabilities be provided equal access to public education. Failure to provide appropriate special education may result in a court injunction as well a mandatory compensatory education.
- Document, collect, and safeguard formative data about the behavior of each student with disabilities.
- Use disciplinary procedures reasonably and for legitimate educational purposes, not compromising a student's free appropriate public education.
- Budget and utilize adequate funding for programs for students with disabilities, not using budgetary constraints as a basis to deny children with disabilities a public education.
- Organize and implement a staff development plan to prepare all teachers to work effectively with children who are disabled. These activities should be coherent, continuous, and well supported by the district.
- Realize that possible liability challenges occur when educators fail to perform certain related services properly.
- Respect and address parental rights in matters relating to evaluation and IEP development.
- Implement discipline sanctions in consideration of students' disabilities and seek legal guidance when disciplining students with disabilities for behavior that is associated with their known disabilities.
- Provide students with disabilities educational services even though a long-term suspension is legally sanctioned; school officials should be familiar with the latest IDEA amendments regarding discipline of such students and be certain that the amendments are incorporated into district policy.
- Prepare to pay assessed attorney fees if a parent prevails in a suit for violation of IDEA.
- Plan to provide the burden of proof as it rests with the school district in determining whether misbehavior by a student with disabilities is attributed to the disability.
- Ensure that architectural barriers do not prevent individuals with disabilities from receiving services or participating in programs or activities provided by the district.
- Provide educational services beyond the regular school year for students with disabilities, depending on the student's unique needs.

Pitfalls to Avoid

- Inconsistent discipline policies and procedures. Formulate and disseminate discipline policies and procedures with alignment to IDEA of 2004.
- Uninformed parents. Ensure that parents have access to and understanding of the school district policies.
- Unclear policies on student property and student privacy. Student handbooks should include statements regarding student property and the diminished right of student privacy in regard to lockers and school property.

- Unclear student conduct and behavior rules. Delineate inappropriate student behavior and conduct through school rules. Specify consequences for violating school rules.
- Disregard for due process. Extend due process rights at all times. If students are suspended for ten days or less, notify students of charges and give them an opportunity to respond. If suspended over ten days or expelled, notification, opportunity to respond, and more formalized hearing procedures are required.
- Not recognizing the dual disciplinary standard. Suspension leading to a change of placement for ten days is allowed. No long-term suspension or expulsion should be used unless the behavior is unrelated to the disability (and this can only be determined during a manifestation hearing). There is not to be a cessation of educational services. If a student brings a weapon or uses or sells drugs, he or she may be placed in another setting with educational services for forty-five days.
- Not including a behavior intervention plan in students' IEP accommodation plans. The plan should be based on a functional assessment, including positive procedures and consequences. Delineate consequences that may be used (e.g., in-school suspension, timeout) and a crisis intervention plan.
- Not documenting. Document, document, document! All behavior incidents should be described in writing. In situations involving problem behavior, document disciplinary actions taken in writing and notify parents.
- Not conducting continuous evaluations. Evaluate continuously the effectiveness of disciplinary procedures and interventions of students with disabilities.

RESOURCES

There are many sources focused on discipline of students with disabilities. The World Wide Web provides access to a variety of resources that contain useful material. Here are some that have been particularly useful.

Council of Exceptional Children
www.cec.sped.org/
Professional development, training, and events; professional standards, recognition, and awards; public policy, advocacy, legislative action center.

IDEA Practices
www.ideapractices.org/law/header.php
IDEA practices; laws; rules and regulations.

IDEA '97 Regulations—Navigation Page
www.ideapractices.org/law/regulations/regindex.php
Procedural safeguards.

Rules and Regulations Stated
www.pattan.net/regsforms/School-AgeFormsandFormats.aspx
Suspension reviewed; expulsion stated; legal reference presented.

CHAPTER FIVE

DEALING EFFECTIVELY WITH CHILD FIND

OVERVIEW

"Child Find" provisions under the IDEA require the local educational agency (LEA) to identify, locate, and evaluate all students with disabilities, including those attending private schools, regardless of the severity of their disabilities (20 U.S.C.1412[a][3]).

Special education program administrators will work with district or community personnel and parents to conduct awareness activities to inform parents and interested citizens of special education programs or services and the means by which to access these programs or services. The public must be informed of child identification activities and of the procedures followed to ensure confidentiality of information pertaining to eligible young children or students with disabilities.

In this chapter, we review information related to roles played by special education program administrators in locating, identifying, and screening children suspected of having a disability as prescribed by federal legislation, as well as reasons for maintaining awareness strategies over time. The Individuals with Disabilities Education Improvement Act (IDEA 2004) of 2004 (i.e., PL 108-446) added a change at §612(a)(10)(A)(ii) to existing Child Find procedures when defining services to parentally placed children with disabilities. We describe and explain the change in the reauthorized law. Further, the requirement for consultation at §612(a)(10)(A)(iii) has expanded to include the Child Find process. We cover this change in the reauthorized law.

CHILD FIND REQUIREMENTS

Regulations

34 CFR §300.125 Child Find

General requirement.

(1) The State must have in effect policies and procedures to ensure that—

I. All children with disabilities residing in the State, including children with disabilities attending private schools, regardless of the severity of their disability, and who are in need of special education and related services, are identified, located, and evaluated; and

II. A practical method is developed and implemented to determine which children are currently receiving needed special education and related services.

(2) The requirements of paragraph (a)(1) of this section apply to—

(i) Highly mobile children with disabilities (such as migrant and homeless children); and

(ii) Children who are suspected of being a child with a disability under §300.7 and in need of special education, even though they are advancing from grade to grade.

(b) Documents relating to Child Find. The State must have on file with the Secretary the policies and procedures described in paragraph (a) of this section, including—

(1) The name of the State agency (if other than the SEA) responsible for coordinating the planning and implementation of the policies and procedures under paragraph (a) of this section;

(2) The name of each agency that participates in the planning and implementation of the Child Find activities and a description of the nature and extent of its participation;

(3) A description of how the policies and procedures under paragraph (a) of this section will be monitored to ensure that the SEA obtains—

(i) The number of children with disabilities within each disability category that have been identified, located, and evaluated; and

(ii) Information adequate to evaluate the effectiveness of those policies and procedures; and

(4) A description of the method the State uses to determine which children are currently receiving special education and related services.

(c) Child Find for children from birth through age 2 when the SEA and lead agency for the Part C program are different.

(1) In states where the SEA and the State's lead agency for the Part C program are different and the Part C lead agency will be participating in the Child Find activities described in paragraph (a) of this section, a description of the nature and extent of the Part C lead agency's participation must be included under paragraph (b)(2) of this section.

(2) With the SEA's agreement, the Part C lead agency's participation may include the actual implementation of Child Find activities for infants and toddlers with disabilities.

(3) The use of an interagency agreement or other mechanism for providing for the Part C lead agency's participation does not alter or diminish the responsibility of the SEA to ensure compliance with the requirement of this section.

(d) Construction. Nothing in the Act requires that children be classified by their disability so long as each child who has a disability listed in §300.7 and who, by reason of that disability, needs special education and related services is regarded as a child with a disability under Part B of the Act.

(e) Confidentiality of Child Find data. The collection and use of data to meet the requirements of this section are subject to the confidentiality requirements of §§300.560–300.577.

(Authority: 20 U.S.C. 1412(a)(3)(A) and (B))

The state is responsible for ensuring that districts "find" students suspected of having a disability and conduct screening processes prior to the student's referral for special education. Importantly, special education program administrators will work in an efficient and effective manner in their districts to find and name young children eligible for early intervention services. Special education program administrators will work also to find and identify older students who may be experiencing academic and behavioral problems. Based on screening activities, district personnel must name students who may need special education services and programs once these students are served in kindergarten through grade 12 programs.

Once a student has been screened and is thought to be eligible for special education, districts then have an obligation to perform a full and complete evaluation on that child to determine whether that child is a "child with a disability" and to determine his or her educational needs.

Changes in Child Find Activities through the IDEA 2004

The state must ensure that all children with disabilities, including children who are homeless, wards of the state, and parentally placed private school children, are identified, located, and evaluated [§612(a)(3)]. A change through the IDEA 2004 relates to Child Find Activities. That is, the law states:

> Child Find activities shall be designed to ensure equitable participation and an accurate count, shall be similar to the activities for public school children and completed in a comparable time period. The cost of Child Find and individual evaluations does not count toward the proportionate share of federal money the district must spend on these children." [§612(a)(1)(A)(ii)].

Further, the IDEA 2004 has expanded the requirement for consultation. The reauthorized law states,

> Consultation is with private school officials and representatives of parents of parentally placed private school children. Topics for consultation include: the Child Find process; how these children can participate equitably; how parents, teachers and private school officials will be informed of the process; the determination of the proportionate share amount and how the amount was calculated; the consultation process . . . who, where and by whom special education and related services will be provided for these children . . . if the district disagrees with the views of private school officials on the provision of services, or the types of services . . . the district shall provide the private school official a written explanation of the reasons why the district chose not to provide the services directly or through a contract" [see §612(a)(10) (A)(iii)].

New Law Explained.   Many of the Child Find provisions were already in the regulations with the exception of the report that now must be made to the state education agency (SEA). That is, the state must receive from each district the numbers of children enrolled in private schools by their parents and in the same time frame as for children enrolled by their parents in public schools to ensure equitable participation and accuracy in reporting. Because the reauthorized law expanded the requirement for consultation, the district must initiate and maintain documentation of the consultation process with private school officials to the SEA, especially if there is disagreement between private school officials and representatives of parents of parentally placed private school children.

PUTTING PRINCIPLES INTO PRACTICE

In order to comply with federal Child Find regulations, school personnel conduct annual awareness activities to inform the public of special education programs and the means by which to access these services. For instance, school personnel can meet their obligations to provide annual public notification when they publish or announce district-related activities in newspapers or other media, or both, with circulation adequate to notify parents throughout the district of child identification activities and of the procedures followed to ensure confidentiality of information pertaining to students with disabilities or eligible young children. Most districts have specific collaboration activities for finding children suspected of having a disability. Special education program administrators may work with local physicians' offices, hospitals, or community agencies to provide flyers or brochures on special education services or programs and make these available to the public.

Reasons for Maintaining Awareness Strategies over Time

When districts work actively to maintain child awareness activities over time the following benefits occur.

- *Positive public relations increase.* The community gains an increase in the positive interactions district personnel create with parents when there is an active movement to provide support to area children and families.
- *Increased knowledge by the key players involved in screenings and identifications.* When districts create and maintain ongoing awareness campaigns, they support children, parents, teachers, nurses, administrative personnel, and any others concerned with students' welfare in school success.
- *Ongoing dissemination of data.* Effective child awareness activities over time help to supply information to and counsel with key players involved in Child Find activities in order to achieve the best possible school–home interactions.
- *Proper identification.* A smooth and efficient Child Find system underscores the proper identification of eligible students and avoids underidentification or overidentification practices. Eligible young children and students can be referred, through the proper authorities, to the appropriate agencies for supplemental diagnosis and assessment as

indicated by specific student needs. An effective system helps those in authority to keep adequate records on eligible children receiving programs and services in order to ensure the most effective continuing supports.

Tips

The following tips may help special education program administrators think about having on-going Child Find procedures that are easily accessible to the public. The tips consist of ideas to help identify and locate children at risk for or thought to be eligible for special education and related services, pursuant to federal requirements.

- Work with the local media to publicize notice of special education services, through a "Notice of Special Education Services." Written notices can appear in local newspapers each year and be made available to district residents during the school year to inform the public of special education programs and the means by which to access these services.
- Create and air radio and television notices of special education services on local stations during peak times of the school year. For example, air notices in spring prior to when parents register their kindergarten-age children for school services, or during fall when parents of preschoolers register their children for day care or preschool programs.
- Work with local interagency coordinating councils that deal with early intervention services, publicizing services available to young children in the district. Set up tables or booths to promote annual notices, such as through kiosks located at malls, department stores, or county fairs.
- Distribute a student handbook to district parents. The handbook can describe local, state, and federal student support services, Title 1 services, complaint procedures, special education services, or the district's specialized early intervention or afterschool programs that provide screening and support to children and families.
- Work with community agency personnel in local awareness activities to help parents consider whether their child may be a special needs student. For example, assign district personnel to attend community-sponsored health events, such as immunization and booster campaigns, blood-bank drives, or low-cost or free visual and hearing screenings.
- Establish and maintain specific prereferral services aimed at school-age children with problems in academics, ability, or behavior. Provide annual sensory and health screenings during periodic check points throughout the school year in elementary, middle, intermediate, junior high, and high school locations.
- Distribute a student support services handbook to district staff members, helping to increase the staff members' awareness of various District services, based on students' needs for guidance, health, instructional support, psychological services, special education, related services, student assistance programs, and/or federal programs.
- Establish and maintain ongoing professional development activities in the district to help faculty and staff locate students with problems. Offer training to district personnel in updated methods and procedures to identify students. Include parents, private school officials, and representatives of parents of parentally placed private school children to ensure meaningful participation by all young children and students with disabilities.

Pitfalls to Avoid

- Slacking on monitoring the annual public notification. Make ongoing changes to annual Child Find notices as federal and state laws evolve and are updated.
- Seeking out an inappropriate or limited media circulation. Target the largest media circulation in the area. The public may not receive adequate information if notices are published or announced in newspapers or other media, or both, with inadequate circulation to notify parents throughout the area served by the district.
- Limiting screening efforts. When the district is aware that an individual young child or student has problems (e.g., as evidenced by inadequate nutrition, poor health, low grades, disruptive behavior, inconsistent attendance, and so forth), initiate a screening as soon as possible. Invite the family for a conference to address immediately the student's suspected problems.
- Excluding Child Find activities and services to parentally placed children with disabilities. Remember that services may be provided on the premises of the private school, including a religious school, "to the extent allowed by law" [see §612(a)(1)(A)(i)(III)]. Special education program administrators will work and consult with private school officials pertaining to all located and identified, or need to be located and identified, children within the locale.

RESOURCES

There are many sources available online and in each individual community and state that will be helpful to advance Child Find activities. The following is a list of national resources that may be helpful when offering Child Find services.

Websites

The World Wide Web provides ready access to a variety of resources that contain useful material. Here are some that have been particularly useful to us.

CFR Titles—Part 1–99 and Part 101–299
www.access.gpo.gov/cgi-bin/cfrassemble.cgi?title=199834
Education Department General Administrative Regulations (Part 76); Family Education Rights and Privacy Act Regulations (Part 99) and Rehabilitation Act of 1973, Section 504—Regulations (Part 104). Important federal regulations related to confidentiality issues and discrimination practices for students and families.

CFR Titles—Part 300–Part 399
www.access.gpo.gov/nara/cfr/waisidx_99/34cfrv2_99.html
This website provides important information on Part 300 (Part B Regulations) and Part 303 (Part C Infant and Toddlers). The reader will be able to locate data on federal regulations related to infants, student, and youth with disabilities.

Federal Register Online

www.access.gpo.gov/su_docs/aces/aces140.html

Daily publication of Federal Register. Search back issues of Federal Register for relevant components relating to important national legislation.

IDEA Statute (PL 105-17)

www.access.gpo.gov/nara/index.html#pl

Statute (PL 105-17) for IDEA—June 4, 1997. Select 105th Congress (for 105-17) and must scroll to find PL 105-17, the federal law that guarantees students with disabilities their educational rights.

Technical Assistance

There are many forms of technical assistance available for Child Find requirements. Here are some associations and governmental organizations that provide widespread support.

National Association of Developmental Disabilities Councils

1234 Massachusetts Avenue, NW, Suite 103
Washington, DC 20005
(202) 347-1234
email: naddc@igc.apc.org
URL: http://www.igc.apc.orc/NADDC/

National Easter Seal Society

230 W. Monroe, Suite 1800
Chicago, IL 60606
1-800-221-6827 or (312) 726-6200
(312) 726-4258 (TTY)
URL: www.easterseals.com

National Parent Network on Disabilities (NPND)

1727 King Street, Suite 305
Alexandria, VA 22314
(703) 684-6763 (voice/TTY)
email: npnd@cs.com

Spina Bifida Association of America (SBAA)

4590 MacArthur Boulevard, NW, Suite 250
Washington, DC 20007-4226
1-800-621-3141 or (202) 944-3285
email: spinabifida@aol.com
URL: www.sbaa.org

United Cerebral Palsy Associations, Inc.
1660 L Street, NW, Suite 700
Washington, DC 20036-5602
1-800-872-5827
(202) 973-7197 (TDD)
email: ucnatl@ucpa.org

National Information Center on Deafness
Gallaudet University
800 Florida Avenue, NE
Washington, DC 20002-3695
(202) 651-5051
(202) 651-5054 (TTY)
email: judd103w@wonder.em.cdc.gov

CHAPTER SIX

THE REFERRAL AND EVALUATION PROCESS

with RICHAEL BARGER ANDERSON

OVERVIEW

To many special education program administrators, the referral process of special education can be wearisome. One, the paperwork can be intimidating, if not downright overwhelming. Two, the chain of command often becomes blurry. In other words, "Who is responsible for what action?" becomes a key question. Three, remaining in compliance with state and federal laws is a major concern to those involved, especially as state and federal laws evolve.

In this chapter, we examine referral issues in special education programs and services. We view terms such as *screening* and *prereferral strategies.* We illustrate examples of screening and referrals to facilitate special education program administrators' understanding of issues and concerns when considering students' eligibility for special education placements or services. We provide strategies in dealing with the special education referral process, as we hope to make the process as painless as possible for local educational agencies (LEAs), students, parents, and community agencies involved.

Further, the Individuals with Disabilities Education Improvement Act (IDEA 2004) of 2004 (i.e., PL 108-446) mandated important changes to procedures in evaluations and eligibility determinations that will affect the way special education program administrators work with multidisciplinary evaluation team members, including school or community personnel and parents, to evaluate and determine whether students are eligible and demonstrate a need for special education and related services [§614(a)(1)(A); §614(a)(2)(A); §614(b)(4)]. We explain existing regulations and new changes promulgated by the IDEA 2004 related to evaluations and eligibility requirements, and we focus on terms affected by the reauthorized law, such as *initial evaluations, reevaluations, conduct of evaluations, consent for evaluations,* and *eligibility mandates.*

The section on evaluation describes how LEAs evaluate, reevaluate, and/or make eligibility determinations for students with disabilities having a need for special education and related services or those thought to be students with disabilities and having a need for special education and related services. We provide relevant sections of the newly mandated IDEA 2004 for special education program administrators and explain the reauthorized law.

THE REFERRAL PROCESS

Regulations

34 CFR §300.320 Screening prior to initial evaluations

(a) Each public agency shall ensure that a full and individual evaluation is conducted for each child being considered for special education and related services under Part B of the Act—

(1) To determine if the child is a "child with a disability" under §300.7; and

(2) To determine the educational needs of the child.

(b) In implementing the requirements of paragraph (a) of this section, the public agency shall ensure that—

(1) The evaluation is conducted in accordance with the procedures described in §§300.53–300.535; and

(2) The results of the evaluation are used by the child's IEP team in meeting the requirements of §§300.34–300.350.

(Authority: 20 U.S.C. 1412(a), (b), and (c))

Not only do LEAs have an obligation to "find" children suspected of having a disability, as we discussed in Chapter 5 pursuant to Child Find obligations, LEAs also must implement a screening process prior to referral for special education. In order to remove a student from instruction with general education students for even part of the day, professionals must collect written evidence establishing the need for a change in placement and the type of instruction the student receives. Such removal begins with the screening process, resulting in the student's initial evaluation for special education consideration.

A *screening process* entails the input of administrators working with family members and school or community personnel to ascertain whether students demonstrating problems in ability, behavior, language, learning, and so forth, may be eligible and have a need for special education or related services. A student is eligible for special education if he or she is "a child with a disability . . . who by reason thereof, needs special education and related services" [34 CFR §300.7; 22].

Screenings.   In order to ascertain whether the student is eligible for and needs special education, school personnel work with families and community agencies to conduct screening activities. Screening activities in the referral process can help in instructional and behavioral decisions to determine appropriate support strategies in general education classes, based on individual students' needs and strengths. Activities can also provide important clues in how to serve students if and when they become eligible and require special education. Accordingly, the first screening activity in the referral process focuses on collecting important data about the nature and extent of the student's problems or concerns. Screening data include, but are not limited to the following:

- *Demographics and Relevant Family Information.* Parents or guardians and other family members can provide a plethora of relevant data regarding the student's early developmental milestones, such as age of crawling, walking, or talking. Home data may include information on the family dynamics, including the family members with whom the student lives, his or her living arrangements, number of siblings, and home roles or responsibilities. Parents or guardians may describe the student's social interactions with family members, neighbors, or community members. Their home data also may provide input into family members' perspectives of the problems exhibited by their children, which may differ greatly from descriptions provided by agency personnel.

- *Health and Sensory Information.* Additional home data that help in screening activities include information on the student's health needs and senses. For example, families may provide information on the child or family history of illnesses or diseases. Parents or guardians may describe relevant genetic predispositions common to parents, siblings, or other relatives. They may provide important information on the student's wellness checks and health care visits, or medications prescribed by physicians. These family data may also offer insights into health care workers' reporting on family-obtained speech and language, vision, hearing, motor, or other sensory testing results.
- *Cumulative School Files.* Screening activities may target data on the student's attendance records, school health records, lunch-program status, grades, achievement scores, permanent record cards, discipline incidents, and progress-reporting notations to parents, including remarks on report cards such as "approach to learning" (e.g., follows directions, uses time and materials productively, completes tasks) or "citizenship" (e.g., shares material and supplies, accepts responsibility for behavior, is responsible). These prior school records help in the referral process in order to ascertain trends in grade levels repeated, school achievement, past test results, anecdotal information, attendance patterns, and other important school variables (e.g., the student's participation in school or general education class activities, success of behavioral or instructional strategies already provided to students).
- *Current Classroom Progress.* Screening activities include the obtainment of progress descriptions in the present educational setting and written records of individual student progress in various general education curricula. Classroom progress data may focus on observation records by educators or other agency personnel. Anecdotal records, informal notations, or formal observations on students' behavior and academic functioning under varied conditions or settings can be useful. Many LEA personnel observe and screen students daily either by formal methods (e.g., checklists, rating scales, tests) or by informal methods (e.g., discussions with past teachers, unstructured comments based on informal meetings). Effective screening activities entail being able to discern students' patterns of normal and deviant behaviors or academic progress as students operate in their current placements.

Prereferral Strategies. Prereferral strategies consist of professional problem solving (i.e., consultation) and intervention based on screening data as the first steps of special education referral. Among relevant data required to refer a student for a change in educational placement is evidence that the student was provided with the full opportunity to remain in his or her least restrictive environment (LRE). All screening data collected to date supports the student's LRE.

The purposes of consultation meetings are twofold: (1) to generate general education class supports (i.e., prereferral strategies) to help the student remain in general education and

(2) to determine observation schedules needed to verify the student's progress toward the general education class prereferral strategies. To consider removing a student from the general education class for even part of the day, professionals must collect written evidence establishing the need for a change in placement and the type of instruction the student receives. Those important data relate to whether students who display differences from other students (e.g., differences in cognition, language, self-help, motor, behavior, social-emotional skills, or other areas) require assistance through specially designed instruction and/or related services. An important activity in prereferral documentation is promulgation of instructional or behavioral strategies employed in the general education class and an analysis of results of those strategies employed.

Examples of instructional strategies employed in the general education classroom include a focus on emphasizing key concepts by varying voice quality and use of cue words (e.g., teachers speaking key concepts with emphasis, writing key concepts on the blackboard, and/or repeating key concepts). Examples of behavioral strategies employed in the general education classroom include allowing students to use peer buddies for extra help on in-class assignments, reducing distracting noise or visual stimuli, or limiting the student's independent movement in the classroom environment. Providing students with predetermined signals (e.g., hand signals, verbal cues) can also assist students in their behavioral interactions.

Such prereferral strategies provide assistance to students and their teachers in the general education class, where the problems first arise. Teachers' implementation of such strategies can help students remain in the LRE. Today, with the provision of increased services in general education classes, professionals must collect data and the necessary paperwork on students' individual skills and abilities in the LRE, the setting closest to the general education class.

After the LEA faculty and staff have completed the data collection process and have determined the success of the prereferral strategies (i.e., once a student has been screened and is thought to be eligible for special education), LEAs then have an obligation to perform a full and complete evaluation on that child to determine whether that child is a "child with a disability" and to determine his or her educational needs (34 C.F.R. §300.320).

Putting Principles into Practice

Based on the previous discussions, what should special education program administrators be prepared to deal with as "most likely" screening and referral issues? Acquiring updated knowledge of the law; following the procedures established by the federal government, the state, and the LEA; and remaining fair and consistent are critical elements to successful screening and referral activities. Working with the LEA faculty and staff, community agencies, and family members within a team approach model all help to facilitate the referred student's needs first and foremost.

We offer practical suggestions below that will help special education program administrators think about ways and means to determine appropriate screening and referral strategies based on individual students' needs. The tips consist of ideas to simplify the referral process and make it effective for the local LEA. The tips have been broken down into three categories related to administrators' work with school faculty and staff, community and/or outside agencies, and families involved with the LEA in the referral process.

Tips.

Dealing Effectively with School Faculty and Staff Agencies Involved in the Referral Process

1. *Designate a screening and referral contact person from the school building.* LEA administrators should appoint a school building contact person for initial screening and referral activities. Guidance counselors or school psychologists are two choices. (Teachers often are not appropriate contacts. This is due to their demanding daily schedule and high percentage of time needed in the classroom. It is difficult for teachers to take phone calls, return phone calls, set meetings, and attend meetings throughout the day.) The contact will handle student referrals from teachers. This person is also responsible for communication between the families and the community agencies. The contact person should work to relay information from the families or agencies and attend all screening or referral meetings when possible. The contact may conduct many student observations to verify implementation and success of prereferral strategies implementation. The contact must keep accurate, detailed files on each student screened and referred.

2. *Create a filing system.* The contact person must keep accurate and organized records. Organization is essential! Useful information includes the parents' or guardians' names, parents' emails or phone numbers, and their work numbers. Other useful data are community agencies involved with the family and the agency caseworkers' names, work addresses, and emails or phone numbers. The file also requires the student's name and assigned student number, age, date of birth, prior school district(s) attended, health history (if significant), and any other important demographic information. If the student is housed in foster care, the contact may work with the special education administrator to devise a relevant information form from the sponsoring agency directly.

3. *Make teachers aware of the LEA contact.* Teachers need to be aware of all screening and referral activities for seeking help with an at-risk student needing special services. By creating awareness of the contact person, administrators alleviate unnecessary confusion. Also, they save the valuable time of all parties involved when administrators increase teachers' awareness of screening activities and referral steps.

4. *Establish a system for teachers to recommend students.* A routine system of referral is essential. Faculty or staff need to have confidence in screening activities and referral steps. The creation of a routine system develops trust between administrators and faculty or staff. Faculty or staff need to feel they are supported and all parties involved are working toward the same goal: helping the student. The following steps can help administrators establish and maintain the trust:

   a. *Completion of a referral form.* Administrators can work with their contact and faculty or staff to promote the creation of simple screening and referral form(s). Simple is the key word. Forms should not be long and tedious for LEA personnel to complete. On the other hand, forms need to be comprehensive with major problems indicated and referral reasons cited. The contact can develop these easily accessible forms. Administrators can help by offering a "drop box" or designated area specified for the return of completed forms.

    b. *Request for conference.* In certain cases, the need for a student referral may be immediate. For these special circumstances, it may be best to skip forms and screening activities and convene a meeting immediately with the referring teacher, other teachers, contact, and relevant administrators. The purpose is to devise an action plan. (Contacts may want to work with teachers on informing parents, or they may want to wait to contact parents until later.)

5. *Make an informational pamphlet.* It is always effective for administrators to put proper protocol in writing for any process. The special education referral process is no exception. Once the contact person has been established to act as a liaison between families, agencies, and teachers, and a buildingwide system of referral has been devised, all steps should be placed in writing. One of the easiest ways to disseminate screening and referral information is through a pamphlet. Remember, school administrators want faculty and staff to take the time read the information. Pamphlets are nonthreatening, easy to read, and conveniently stored for future use.

6. *Involve teachers in the process.* Developing a sense of ownership in creating a special education referral process can be an extremely effective technique. By involving teachers in the development and implementation of screening activities and referral steps is not only tapping a valuable resource, but it also creates a sense of cohesion between the administration and the faculty.

7. *Offer in-service training to* all *faculty and staff, not only to the teaching faculty.* In-service training is a crucial component to guarantee an educated faculty and staff. Knowledge is key! Presenters, consultants, and legal experts should be hired to conduct in-service trainings on changing screening and referral steps for the entire LEA faculty and staff. Not only can families or teachers make referrals, but also any school employee has the authority to initiate screenings or referrals. All employees need to know the importance and implications of screening for and referring a student to special education. School administrators create awareness of the initial evaluation process by contacting experts in the field to conduct training during special schoolwide meetings or during workshops held throughout the summer.

8. *Provide a suggestion box for improvement.* A suggestion box is a great way to get screening and referral input and feedback from the faculty and staff. Not only should the suggestion box be filled with new ideas, but it also encourages faculty and staff to share current successful practices. The suggestion box should be placed in an area with easy access for faculty and staff to use. Some possible location ideas include the school office, the faculty room, or the copier room.

9. *Conduct pupil personnel meetings (PPM) (or similarly titled meetings) regularly.* Pupil personnel meetings (PPM) should be conducted on a regular basis. These screening and referral meetings are attended by team members who consist of administrators, the contact, referring teacher or teacher(s), guidance counselors, the school psychologist, and any other pertinent LEA faculty or staff. The purpose of these meetings is to discuss and strategize the best approach for target students. Target students are those students who demonstrate classroom needs. An action plan to identify the student's

specific problems and to generate specific general education classroom strategies is established in the PPM. Further, an observation schedule to verify the success of prereferral strategies implemented within the general education class should be targeted during the PPM. All of these data help in initial evaluation processes of suspected students with disabilities that would warrant special education evaluations.

Dealing Effectively with Community and/or Outside Agencies Involved in the Referral Process

1. *Designate the school contact to work with community agency personnel involved in students' screenings and referrals.* Most community agencies prefer contact with one school designee. Administrators should appoint the contact. If there is more than one building in the LEA, it is best to have a contact designee for each building. Establishing a contact person for each building in the LEA provides stability for the agency, but also benefits the faculty, staff, and administration as well. Contacts will become familiar with a particular agency representative and establish a personal rapport. This relationship fosters trust between the school entity and the agency. This trust not only ensures a collaborative working relationship, but also ensures that the LEA is receiving valuable and reliable information on the student or services in question. Most often, the LEA contact is the same counselor or school psychologist assigned to assist the LEA faculty and staff. Again, teachers are not contacts due to their inflexible schedules and inability to take phone calls and attend meetings. Community agencies like to have consistency with LEAs. This saves time and energy for the caseworker assigned from the community agency.

2. *Identify available agencies in the area.* Identification of available agencies and resources in the area and what services they supply is valuable information to obtain. There are several avenues to pursue in order to gather and affirm this information. First, the LEA contact may fax, email, write, or telephone the county government. County commissioners often are knowledgeable of local agencies and may even provide the LEA with a directory. Second, local support programs, such as intermediate units, can provide a wealth of service data available through area agencies. Third, skimming through the phone book for categories may be beneficial. Once identification of agencies has been established, the LEA contact can develop an organization and file system, including what services are available and the agency liaison that has been established.

3. *Remain positive.* It is important to remember that no matter which step of the process administrators enter into, they must remain positive. Several roadblocks may be encountered along the way. Perhaps the agency contact retired or the agency is less than cooperative. The more positive and amiable LEA representatives are, the more progress will be made on the student's behalf.

Dealing Effectively with Family Agencies Involved in the Referral Process

1. *Encourage public awareness of the services available.* Families are usually not aware of the services available to them or their children through their LEA. Once a student has

entered the referral process for special education, many doors are opened in terms of services and changes occurring in state and federal laws and regulations. Administrators should work with their contacts to disseminate information about special education services and identification processes to families and taxpayers.

   a. *School website.* Almost every LEA has developed a website. This is a convenient way to post services available. It also should list phone numbers for family members to call for more information and provide answers to their common questions.
   b. *School calendar.* At the beginning of every school year, a school calendar is necessary. Mailing calendars to all LEA residents ensures a definite public display and disbursement of services in special education, along with the procedures for the screening and referral steps.
   c. *School newsletters.* A school newsletter is a popular way for LEAs to boast of current school achievements, awards, and upcoming events. It can also be a useful tool for reminding families of the special education screening activities and referral steps.

2. *Allow family members to have an active role in their children's education.* Parents or guardians want to be involved in their children's lives. They need to be presented with meaningful opportunities to participate in their children's education. Many times unconventional approaches are taken: Meetings may be required to be scheduled after school hours for working parents; phone conferences may be an option; home visits are another accommodation that may be made to allow parents or guardians a voice in the referral process. When administrators recognize that family members provide valuable information, they develop and maintain a nurturing and reciprocal relationship with significant individuals in students' lives.

3. *Communicate to family members with "family-friendly" language.* Educators have a tendency to talk a language of their own. Many times, to outsiders, it sounds like alphabet soup! Acronyms, such as IEP or MDE, have a specific meaning to educators. Outside the walls of the LEA and to the general public, these terms can be meaningless and confusing. Use of terminology that family members do not understand may intimidate them. From the initial point of correspondence, all family members need explanations of the screening and referral process in terms they can understand.

4. *Name the contacts for family members.* Inevitably parents or guardians will have questions about the special education referral process that they or the LEA initiated. These questions may surface any time. Administrators should inform family members of the specific LEA and agency contacts when questions arise. It is helpful to make family members feel comfortable to ask questions and reassure them that questions are normal.

5. *Invite the students to participate if appropriate.* Many times students play an active role in their own education. This builds a sense of ownership and pride. Administrators may invite students to participate in their own screening activities or referral steps, considering each student's maturity, as well as his or her age. Some students are active, meaningful participants in meetings, while other students may not be interested or willing to participate. Administrators should never force students to participate and should speak to parents or guardians to ascertain family opinions of student involvement.

6. *Embrace the "team" approach.* Families should be active, integral, and meaningful participants of the special education referral process. They should feel important at meetings and comfortable to contribute ideas, suggestions, and questions. They should feel free to ask other family members to join the meetings. Grandparents, aunts, or uncles may be interested in attending and participating in the referral process. Administrators can work actively to facilitate family comfort levels by encouraging open discussions, providing meaningful data on the student's progress, and demonstrating reciprocity and active listening to suggestions provided by family members. Such behaviors encourage effective and efficient screening activities and referral steps.

Pitfalls to Avoid.

- Getting behind on special education screenings and referrals. Monitor dates and timelines of all students' screening activities and referral steps to ensure appropriate initial evaluation decisions.
- Assuming community agency data are irrelevant. Agencies can supplement and enrich the classroom data provided by LEAs. The more knowledge and skills professionals can share and support, the more all professionals are assisted in their roles and responsibilities.
- Assuming family data are irrelevant. Recognize family contributions to the screening activities and referral steps. For many, this is the first time family members have been through referral activities. Administration, faculty and staff, and agency representatives participate in countless meetings. It is crucial not to assume parents or guardians understand the process. This is not just another meeting. This is their child. Family members can offer priceless contributions as members of the special education referral process if they receive the message that their data are valuable.

THE EVALUATION PROCESS

General Requirements: Regulations

(a) EVALUATIONS, PARENTAL CONSENT, AND REEVALUATIONS.—

(1) INITIAL EVALUATIONS.—

(A) IN GENERAL.—A State educational agency, other State agency, or local educational agency shall conduct a full and individual initial evaluation in accordance with this paragraph and subsection (b), before the initial provision of special education and related services to a child with a disability under this part.

(B) REQUEST FOR INITIAL EVALUATION.—Consistent with subparagraph (D), either a parent of a child, or a State educational agency, other State agency, or local educational agency may initiate a request for an initial evaluation to determine if the child is a child with a disability.

(C) PROCEDURES.—

(i) IN GENERAL.—Such initial evaluation shall consist of procedures—

(I) to determine whether a child is a child with a disability (as defined in section 602) within 60 days of receiving parental consent for the evaluation, or, if the State establishes a timeframe within which the evaluation must be conducted, within such timeframe; and (II) to determine the educational needs of such child.

(ii) EXCEPTION.—The relevant timeframe in clause (i)(I) shall not apply to a local educational agency if— (I) a child enrolls in a school served by the local educational agency after the relevant timeframe in clause (i)(I) has begun and prior to a determination by the child's previous local educational agency as to whether the child is a child with a disability (as defined in section 602), but only if the subsequent local educational agency is making sufficient progress to ensure a prompt completion of the evaluation, and the parent and subsequent local educational agency agree to a specific time when the evaluation will be completed; or (II) the parent of a child repeatedly fails or refuses to produce the child for the evaluation.

IDEA 2004 established a sixty-day timeline from receipt of parental consent for evaluation for eligibility to the determination of eligibility and the educational needs of the child, unless the state has already established a timeline for these activities. If the state has a deadline for completing the initial evaluation, the state deadline applies.

Exceptions to this timeframe address children moving between school districts and a parent's refusal to make the child available for evaluation. The sixty-day deadline is relaxed if the child enrolls in the LEA after the sixty days from consent has begun to run in the previous district and the previous district has not yet completed the evaluation. This exception to the sixty-day deadline applies only if the LEA into which the child has transferred is making sufficient progress to ensure prompt completion of the evaluation and the parent and district have agreed to a time when the initial evaluation will be completed.

(D) PARENTAL CONSENT.—

(i) IN GENERAL.—

H. R. 1350—57

(I) CONSENT FOR INITIAL EVALUATION.—The agency proposing to conduct an initial evaluation to determine if the child qualifies as a child with a disability as defined in section 602 shall obtain informed consent from the parent of such child before conducting the evaluation. Parental consent for evaluation shall not be construed as consent for placement for receipt of special education and related services.

(II) CONSENT FOR SERVICES.—An agency that is responsible for making a free appropriate public education available to a child with a disability under this part shall seek to obtain informed consent from the parent of such child before providing special education and related services to the child.

(ii) ABSENCE OF CONSENT.—

(I) FOR INITIAL EVALUATION.—If the parent of such child does not provide consent for an initial evaluation under clause (i)(I), or the parent fails to respond to a request to provide the consent, the local educational agency may pursue the initial evaluation of the child by utilizing the procedures described in section 615, except to the extent inconsistent with State law relating to such parental consent.

(II) FOR SERVICES.—If the parent of such child refuses to consent to services under clause (i)(II), the local educational agency shall not provide special education and related services to the child by utilizing the procedures described in section 615.

(III) EFFECT ON AGENCY OBLIGATIONS.—If the parent of such child refuses to consent to the receipt of special education and related services, or the parent fails to respond to a request to provide such consent—(aa) the local educational agency shall not be considered to be in violation of the requirement to make available a free appropriate public education to the child for the failure to provide such child with the special education and related services for which the local educational agency requests such consent; and (bb) the local educational agency shall not be required to convene an IEP meeting or develop an IEP under this section for the child for the special education and related services for which the local educational agency requests such consent.

(iii) CONSENT FOR WARDS OF THE STATE.— (I) IN GENERAL.—If the child is a ward of the State and is not residing with the child's parent, the agency shall make reasonable efforts to obtain the informed consent from the parent (as defined in section 602) of the child for an H.R. 1350-58 initial evaluation to determine whether the child is a child with a disability.

(II) EXCEPTION.—The agency shall not be required to obtain informed consent from the parent of a child for an initial evaluation to determine whether the child is a child with a disability if—(aa) despite reasonable efforts to do so, the agency cannot discover the whereabouts of the parent of the child; (bb) the rights of the parents of the child have been terminated in accordance with State law; or (cc) the rights of the parent to make educational decisions have been subrogated by a judge in accordance with State law and consent for an initial evaluation has been given by an individual appointed by the judge to represent the child.

(E) RULE OF CONSTRUCTION.—The screening of a student by a teacher or specialist to determine appropriate instructional strategies for curriculum implementation shall not be considered to be an evaluation for eligibility for special education and related services.

As in the existing regulations, a district must obtain consent from the parent before conducting an initial evaluation (and before conducting a reevaluation). However, if the parent fails to respond to a request for consent for an initial evaluation or refuses to consent, the district may pursue the initial evaluation by using the due process or mediation procedures. Although not clearly stated in IDEA 2004, the district may also pursue reevaluation by using the due process or mediation procedures to challenge a parent's refusal to consent to a reevaluation.

However, IDEA 2004 added additional procedures for obtaining parental consent for initial evaluation when the child is a ward of the state, including circumstances in which the agency is not required to obtain such consent. The law mandated that if a student is a ward of the state and not residing with a parent, the district shall make "reasonable efforts" to obtain consent for an initial evaluation from the parent of the child. However, the district is not obligated to obtain consent from the parent for an initial evaluation if the district cannot determine the whereabouts of the parent, the rights of the parent have been terminated under state law, or a judge has taken away from the parent the right to make educational decisions on behalf of the child and the court-appointed representative of the child has provided consent for the initial evaluation.

IDEA 2004 also mandated that a district cannot request dispute resolution to override a parent's refusal to consent for special education and related services. In these circumstances, the LEA is not responsible to provide FAPE, convene an IEP meeting, or develop an IEP. That is, parental consent for evaluation is not the same as consent for placement for receipt of special education services. The district must seek informed consent from the parent before providing special education and related services. If the parent refuses to consent to the initiation of services, the district shall not provide special education and related services to the student by utilizing the due process or mediation procedures. If the parent refuses to consent to the services, or does not respond to the request, the district is not in violation of the requirement to provide FAPE to a student with a disability for failure to provide the special education and related services for which consent was sought. The district does not have to convene an IEP team meeting or develop an IEP for this student for the special education and related services for which consent was sought.

(2) REEVALUATIONS.—

(A) IN GENERAL.—A local educational agency shall ensure that a reevaluation of each child with a disability is conducted in accordance with subsections (b) and (c)— (i) if the local educational agency determines that the educational or related services needs, including improved academic achievement and functional performance, of the child warrant a reevaluation; or (ii) if the child's parents or teacher requests a reevaluation.

(B) LIMITATION.—A reevaluation conducted under subparagraph (A) shall occur—(i) not more frequently than once a year, unless the parent and the local educational agency agree otherwise; and (ii) at least once every 3 years, unless the parent and the local educational agency agree that a reevaluation is unnecessary.

(b) EVALUATION PROCEDURES.—

(1) NOTICE.—The local educational agency shall provide notice to the parents of a child with a disability, in accordance with subsections (b)(3), (b)(4), and (c) of section 615, that describes any evaluation procedures such agency proposes to conduct.

IDEA 2004 mandated that the LEA shall conduct a reevaluation of a student if the LEA determines that the student's needs, including improved academic achievement and functional performance, warrant reevaluation, or if the student's parent or teacher(s) requests a reevaluation. However, IDEA 2004 modified the language related to the frequency of reevaluation, stating that it may not occur more than once a year unless agreed to by the parent and LEA, and that it must occur at least once every three years unless the parent and LEA agree it is unnecessary.

If the IEP team and other qualified individuals determine that no additional data are necessary to determine that the student continues to be a student with a disability and to determine his or her educational need, the IEP team shall notify the parent of the determination and the reasoning and the rights of the parents to request an assessment.

(2) CONDUCT OF EVALUATION.

In conducting the evaluation, the local educational agency shall—

(A) use a variety of assessment tools and strategies to gather relevant functional, developmental, and academic information, including information provided by the parent, that may assist in determining—(i) whether the child is a child with a disability; and H.R. 1350–59 (ii) the content of the child's individualized education program, including information related to enabling the child to be involved in and progress in the general education curriculum, or, for preschool children, to participate in appropriate activities;

(B) not use any single measure or assessment as the sole criterion for determining whether a child is a child with a disability or determining an appropriate educational program for the child; and

(C) use technically sound instruments that may assess the relative contribution of cognitive and behavioral factors, in addition to physical or developmental factors.

(3) ADDITIONAL REQUIREMENTS.—Each local educational agency shall ensure that—

(A) assessments and other evaluation materials used to assess a child under this section— (i) are selected and administered so as not to be discriminatory on a racial or cultural basis; (ii) are provided and administered in the language and form most likely to yield accurate information on what the child knows and can do academically, developmentally, and functionally, unless it is not feasible to so provide or administer; (iii) are used for purposes for which the assessments or measures are valid and reliable; (iv) are administered by trained and knowledgeable personnel; and (v) are administered in accordance with any instructions provided by the producer of such assessments;

(B) the child is assessed in all areas of suspected disability;

(C) assessment tools and strategies that provide relevant information that directly assists persons in determining the educational needs of the child are provided; and

(D) Assessments of children with disabilities who transfer from one school district to another school district in the same academic year are coordinated with such children's prior and subsequent schools, as necessary and as expeditiously as possible, to ensure prompt completion of full evaluations.

IDEA 2004 reconfirmed that the LEA must provide notice to the parent that describes any evaluation procedure that the LEA plans to conduct. When evaluating students for eligibility determinations for special education, the district must use a variety of assessment tools and strategies, not any single measure or assessment as the sole criterion. District personnel must use technically sound instruments that may assess the relative contribution of cognitive and behavioral factors, in addition to physical or developmental factors.

As in the previous regulations, the reauthorized law mandates that assessment and evaluation materials must be nondiscriminatory. However, IDEA 2004 changed the provision related to native language or other mode of communication to provide instead that evaluations are provided and administered in the language and form most likely to yield accurate information on what the child knows and can do academically, developmentally, and functionally, unless it is not feasible to so provide or administer. Assessment and evaluation materials must be used for purposes for which they are valid and reliable and administered according to the instructions provided by the materials producer.

Also, as in the previous federal law, the child must be assessed in all areas of suspected disability. The LEA must provide assessment tools and strategies that provide relevant data for determining the educational needs of the student. However, a new provision relates to a student transferring into a district during a school year. That is, the prior and subsequent schools shall coordinate to ensure that evaluations are completed promptly.

Using these sources and input from the parent, the IEP team and other qualified professionals then determine whether the student is a student with a disability (or continues to be a student with a disability). The team determines the present academic achievement and related developmental needs of the student, whether the student needs special education and related services (or continues to have such a need), and whether any additions or modifications to the special education and related services provided are necessary.

As part of an initial evaluation or reevaluation, the student's IEP team and other qualified professionals review existing data, such as evaluations and information provided by the parent, current classroom-based, local, and state assessments, and observations by teachers and other service providers. These data are relevant in determining whether the child is eligible and has a need for special education and related services.

(4) **DETERMINATION OF ELIGIBILITY AND EDUCATIONAL NEED.**—Upon completion of the administration of assessments and other evaluation measures—

(A) the determination of whether the child is a child with a disability as defined in section 602(3) and the educational needs of the child shall be made by a team of qualified professionals and the parent of the child in accordance with paragraph (5); and

(B) a copy of the evaluation report and the documentation of determination of eligibility shall be given to the parent.

After evaluation and assessment, the team of qualified professionals and the parent must make a determination as to whether the student is a student with a disability, pinpointing the educational needs of the student. A copy of the report of the evaluation and data related to the eligibility determination must be made available to the parent.

(5) **SPECIAL RULE FOR ELIGIBILITY DETERMINATION.**—In making a determination of eligibility under paragraph (4)(A), a child shall not be determined to be a child with a disability if the determinant factor for such determination is—H.R. 1350–60 (A) lack of appropriate instruction in reading, including in the essential components of reading instruction (as defined in section 1208(3) of the Elementary and Secondary Education Act of 1965); (B) lack of instruction in math; or (C) limited English proficiency.

IDEA 2004 mandated that a student shall not be determined to have a disability due to a lack of appropriate instruction in reading (including essential components of reading instruction), as defined by Section 1208(3) of the *Elementary and Secondary Act of 1965,* or math, or due to limited English proficiency [614(b)(5)].

(6) **SPECIFIC LEARNING DISABILITIES.**

(A) IN GENERAL.—Notwithstanding section 607(b), when determining whether a child has a specific learning disability as defined in section 602, a local educational agency shall not be required to take into consideration whether a child has a severe discrepancy between achievement and intellectual ability in oral expression, listening comprehension, written expression, basic reading skill, reading comprehension, mathematical calculation, or mathematical reasoning.

(B) ADDITIONAL AUTHORITY.—In determining whether a child has a specific learning disability, a local educational agency may use a process that determines if the child responds to scientific, research-based intervention as a part of the evaluation procedures described in paragraphs (2) and (3).

IDEA 2004 contained new language concerning the identification of students with learning disabilities. The new bill adds language related to determining whether a student has a specific learning disability, finding that the district is not required to consider whether a student has a severe discrepancy between achievement and intellectual ability in oral expression, listening comprehension, written expression, basic reading skill, reading comprehension, mathematical calculation, or mathematical reasoning. The regulations required a severe discrepancy between an individual's intelligence quotient (IQ) and achievement in order to identify a learning disability. For example, a student was considered to have a learning disability in reading when a severe discrepancy existed between the student's ability and reading achievement scores. However, IDEA 2004 allowed for the development of new approaches. That is, evaluation teams are no longer required to use the discrepancy model in making the determination, although there is nothing in the law that prevents its use. Rather, the new IDEA 2004 encouraged states and districts to use a process that determines whether the student responded to scientific, research-based interventions as part of the evaluation process for special education services. What entailed research-based intervention, however, remained left to interpretation by IEP teams and/or by the litigation system.

(c) ADDITIONAL REQUIREMENTS FOR EVALUATION AND REEVALUATIONS.—

(1) REVIEW OF EXISTING EVALUATION DATA.—As part of an initial evaluation (if appropriate) and as part of any reevaluation under this section, the IEP Team and other qualified professionals, as appropriate, shall—

(A) review existing evaluation data on the child, including—(i) evaluations and information provided by the parents of the child; (ii) current classroom-based, local, or State assessments, and classroom-based observations; and (iii) observations by teachers and related services providers; and

(B) on the basis of that review, and input from the child's parents, identify what additional data, if any, are needed to determine—(i) whether the child is a child with a disability as defined in section 602(3), and the educational needs of the child, or, in case of a reevaluation of a child, whether the child continues to have such a disability and such educational needs; (ii) the present levels of academic achievement and related developmental needs of the child; (iii) whether the child needs special education and related services, or in the case of a reevaluation of a child, whether the child continues to need special education and related services; and (iv) whether any additions or modifications to the special education and related services are needed to enable the child to meet the measurable annual goals set out in the individualized education program of the child and to participate, as appropriate, in the general education curriculum.

(H.R. 1350–61)

(2) SOURCE OF DATA.—The local educational agency shall administer such assessments and other evaluation measures as may be needed to produce the data identified by the IEP Team under paragraph (1)(B).

(3) PARENTAL CONSENT.—Each local educational agency shall obtain informed parental consent, in accordance with subsection (a)(1)(D), prior to conducting any reevaluation of a child with a disability, except that such informed parental consent need not be obtained if the local educational agency can demonstrate that it had taken reasonable measures to obtain such consent and the child's parent has failed to respond.

(4) REQUIREMENTS IF ADDITIONAL DATA ARE NOT NEEDED.—If the IEP Team and other qualified professionals, as appropriate, determine that no additional data are needed to determine whether the child continues to be a child with a disability and to determine the child's educational needs, the local educational agency—

(A) shall notify the child's parents of—(i) that determination and the reasons for the determination; and (ii) the right of such parents to request an assessment to determine whether the child continues to be a child with a disability and to determine the child's educational needs; and

(B) shall not be required to conduct such an assessment unless requested to by the child's parents.

The reevaluation requirement was modified by the 1997 IDEA Amendments to allow evaluation teams to forgo testing where new information is unnecessary to assist the IEP team in placement decisions. The IDEA 2004 continued to mandate that a team of qualified professionals and a parent should review existing evaluation data and provide a written conclusion regarding the need for additional data. The LEA should secure signature data from a psychologist, a regular education teacher, and parents as part of reevaluation decision making.

(5) EVALUATIONS BEFORE CHANGE IN ELIGIBILITY.—

(A) IN GENERAL.—Except as provided in subparagraph (B), a local educational agency shall evaluate a child with a disability in accordance with this section before determining that the child is no longer a child with a disability.

(B) EXCEPTION.—

(i) IN GENERAL.—The evaluation described in subparagraph (A) shall not be required before the termination of a child's eligibility under this part due to graduation from secondary school with a regular diploma, or due to exceeding the age eligibility for a free appropriate public education under State law.

(ii) SUMMARY OF PERFORMANCE.—For a child whose eligibility under this part terminates under circumstances described in clause (i), a local educational agency shall provide the child with a summary of the child's academic achievement and functional performance, which shall include recommendations on how to assist the child in meeting the child's postsecondary goals.

Before terminating a student's eligibility, the IDEA 2004 mandated that the LEA must conduct an evaluation of the student, unless the termination is due to graduation from high school with a regular diploma or due to the student's exceeding age eligibility. When the student's eligibility is terminated due to graduation or age, the LEA shall provide the student with a summary of his or her academic achievement and functional performance, which shall include recommendations on how to assist the student in meeting his or her postsecondary school goals.

Putting Principles into Practice

In order to comply with new evaluation and eligibility determination regulations mandated by the IDEA 2004, the following suggestions may help special education program administrators:

- Given the new sixty-day timelines unless the SEA has already established a timeline, special education program administrators should work with the SEA and district officials to identify what specific procedures and resources would be needed in order to implement this new timeline provision in an organized manner so as to not disrupt services to students and parents.
- Although an LEA cannot request dispute resolution to override a parent's refusal to consent for special education and related services and is therefore not responsible to provide FAPE, including meeting the IEP requirements, it would be helpful if special education program administrators collaborated with teachers and state officials on specific procedures for addressing students' needs to the extent possible. That is, using the general education curriculum as a guide, mailing a list of strategies and resources to all district parents (even those who refuse consent for placement, but whose children are eligible) may offer benefits to students despite the lack of special education and related service provisions.
- As to the frequency of reevaluations provision, special education program administrators must keep in contact with SEA and federal officials as provisions are clarified through final federal regulations, including documenting the parent and LEA agreement. Special education program administrators must support teachers, psychologists, counselors, community personnel, and other interested parties on their need for up-to-date, clarified provisions as all work toward dissemination efforts.
- The IDEA 2004's new provisions regarding providing students with summaries of academic achievement, functional performance, and recommendations to assist in meeting postsecondary goals, upon graduation or aging out of the programs, require clarification in final federal regulations. Special education program administrators remaining current on clarifications work toward disseminating to local officials, professionals, and parents important federal and SEA data as efficiently and effectively as possible through emails, television or radio communications, newsletters, and LEA publication updates.
- Special education program administrators must monitor validated psychometric, nonpsychometric, and "response-to-treatment" methods of identification. They should work with the SEA and universities or colleges to focus attention on the fidelity of the response-to-treatment method on a large scale and its impact on disproportional representation of students from culturally and linguistically diverse backgrounds.

Tips.   The following tips will help special education program administrators think about meeting updated evaluation and eligibility determination requirements and help and evaluate students at risk for or thought to be eligible for special education and related services, pursuant to federal requirements.

- Establish and maintain ongoing professional development activities in the district to help faculty and staff evaluate students with disabilities and students' effective data-monitoring procedures. Encourage teachers and other school personnel to establish and maintain ongoing evaluation data collection techniques on students' progress.
- Be sure to initiate procedures to evaluate district children in a timely and appropriate manner. If parents or guardians do not make a suspected young child or student available in order for the district to conduct a timely and appropriate evaluation, go to the home and approach the parents or guardians directly.
- In order to ensure that a practical method is developed and implemented to determine which children are currently receiving needed special education and related services, and which students are up for reevaluations, keep computerized records on the students. Identify the student and the timing, content, and location of all special education and related services received. Follow established state and local procedures for determining fulltime equivalent numbers of students during peak school times (such as during October or February students' daily attendance counts).
- Work with the local multidisciplinary evaluation and IEP teams to update team members regularly on changes to federal and state laws that pertain to evaluations and eligibility determinations. Hold monthly and bi-monthly in-services and workshops as new clarifications and responses or directives become available to the LEA.
- Distribute an *updated District Policy Handbook* to district parents, teachers, school psychologists, counselors, and other members of the multidisciplinary evaluation and IEP teams. The handbook can describe local, state, and federal procedures that provide new changes to local, state, and federal evaluation and eligibility requirements.

Pitfalls to Avoid.

- Letting slip needed local changes as federal and state laws are updated and or as discrepancy between LEA practices and mandates are noted. Do not let LEA publications become outdated.
- Letting slip monitoring efforts to evaluate district children in a timely and appropriate manner. Be sure to monitor local evaluation and eligibility procedures on a consistent basis.

RESOURCES

The following is a list of national resources that may be helpful when working with others to make appropriate screening, referral, evaluation, and eligibility determination decisions.

Websites

The World Wide Web provides ready access to a variety of resources that contain useful material. Here are some that have been particularly useful to us.

www.aasa.org
This website, offered by the American Association of School Administrators, provides updated legal issues related to FAPE and the IDEA.

www.cec.sped.org/pp/about_pp.html
This website provides important information on Part 300 (Part B Regulations) and Part 303 (Part C Infant and Toddlers). The reader will be able to locate data on federal regulations related to infants, student, and youth with disabilities.

Technical Assistance

There are many forms of technical assistance available for referral, screening, and evaluation requirements. Here are some associations and governmental organizations that provide widespread support.

National Association of Developmental Disabilities Councils
1234 Massachusetts Avenue, NW, Suite 103
Washington, DC 20005
(202) 347-1234
email: naddc@igc.apc.org
URL: www.igc.apc.orc/NADDC/

National Easter Seal Society
230 W. Monroe, Suite 1800
Chicago, IL 60606
1-800-221-6827 or (312) 726-6200
(312) 726-4258 (TTY)
URL: www.easterseals.com

National Parent Network on Disabilities (NPND)
1727 King Street, Suite 305
Alexandria, VA 22314
(703) 684-6763 (voice/TTY)
email: npnd@cs.com

■ ■ ■ ■ ■

CHAPTER SEVEN

MONITORING STUDENTS IN SPECIAL EDUCATION AND RELATED SERVICES

with JOSEPH MERHAUT

OVERVIEW

Many special education program administrators graduate from post-baccalaureate or master's level programs with certification knowledge and skills needed to manage school personnel, programs, and budgets. Typically, these new administrators assume multiple roles and perform multiple tasks. However, pertinent to their roles and tasks is the need for increased, extensive training in the area of special needs students, especially training on ways and means to monitor students actually served in special education and related services. Monitoring students entails accurate counts of students served and data collection activities on the quantity and quality of services and programs within student monitoring systems.

The Individuals with Disabilities Education Improvement Act of 2004 (IDEA 2004) (PL 108-446) mandated important changes to the federal special education law. Further, new changes underscore the importance of aligning the No Child Left Behind Act (NCLB) (PL 107-110) with the IDEA 2004. (President George W. Bush signed the NCLB into law on January 8, 2002. THE NCLB provided for sweeping changes in terms of accountability on the part of the educational system in this country.) As is true with the NCLB, the IDEA 2004 authorized important changes to the federal law that places more emphasis on outcomes, not process.

We define *monitoring* as keeping tabs on the students counted for special education programs or services, while ascertaining from data gathered important age, categorical, graduation–dropout rates, or racial-ethnic variables. Monitoring also entails monitoring student data on the types of programs or services provided, including students' participation and performance on statewide or district assessments, as well as students' opportunities to receive their education in the least restrictive environment.

In this chapter, we examine those sections of the federal law that explain special education program administrators' responsibilities in counting and serving the student population in special education or related services. Additionally, we offer practical strategies that new special education program administrators can use in dealing with the quantitative and qualitative monitoring of special education or related services as students receive services and programs.

Whenever local educational agency (LEA) officials locate, identify, evaluate, place, program, and/or exit students from special education or related services, special education program administrators need to keep student data in an organized and efficient manner. Monitoring guidelines evolve from federal regulations requiring state education agencies (SEAs) to keep up-to-date information on students within state and local jurisdictions.

REGULATIONS

34 CFR §300.750 Annual report of children served: Report requirement

(a) The SEA shall report to the Secretary no later than February 1 of each year the number of children with disabilities aged 3 through 21 residing in the State who are receiving special education and related services.

(b) The SEA shall submit the report on forms provided by the Secretary.

(Authority: 20 U.S.C. 1411(d)(2); 1418(a))

In order to receive funding provided by the federal government, and to provide an accurate national, state, or local picture on the types and qualities of special education or related services provided to whom, it is essential for officials from each state to report to federal authorities by February 1 of each year the number of students in the state who actually receive special education and related services. These students must meet age requirements in order to be counted or monitored. Further, the government mandates that each LEA in every state receiving federal funding must adhere to a specific reporting format using designated forms, in order to ensure consistency of reporting those numbers of students served across age levels.

34 CFR §300.751 Annual reporting of children served: Information required in the report

(a) For any year the SEA shall include in its report a table that shows the number of children with disabilities receiving special education and related services on December 1, or at the State's discretion on the last Friday in October, of that school year—

    (1) Aged 3 through 5;
    (2) Aged 6 through 17; and
    (3) Aged 18 through 21.

(b) For the purpose of this part, a child's age is the child's actual age on the date of the child count: December 1, or, at the State's discretion, the last Friday in October.

(c) Reports must also include the number of those children with disabilities aged 3 through 21 for each year of age (3, 4, 5, etc.) within each disability category, as defined in the definition of "children with disabilities" in §300.7; and

(d) The Secretary may permit the collection of the data in paragraph (c) of this section through sampling.

(e) The SEA may not report a child under paragraph (c) of this section under more than one disability category.

(f) If a child with a disability has more than one disability, the SEA shall report that child under paragraph (c) of this section in accordance with the following procedure:

(1) If a child has only two disabilities and those disabilities are deafness and blindness, and the child is not reported as having a developmental delay, that child must be reported under the category "deaf-blindness."

(2) A child who has more than one disability and is not reported as having deaf-blindness or as having a developmental delay must be reported under the category "multiple disabilities."

(Authority: 20 U.S.C. 1411(d)(2); 1418(a)(b))

In order to keep tabs on the number of students served in special education and related services, the government mandates a specific format across age ranges and disability categories. The government provides to LEA and SEA officials specific directions for counting students identified with more than one disability and for students identified with deaf-blindness or multiple disabilities.

34 CFR §300.752 Annual report of children served: Certification

The SEA shall include in its report a certification signed by an authorized official of the agency that the information provided under §300.751(a) is an accurate and unduplicated count of children with disabilities receiving special education and related services on the dates in question.

(Authority: 20 U.S.C. 1411(d)(2); 1418(b))

School officials must verify the number of students counted in each locale. Thus, special education program administrators must provide written confirmation that all numbers reported to state officials (who then compile data to be forwarded to federal officials) represent a valid representation of students served within each age or disability category. Administrators may count each student only one time, as they verify accuracy of each count in the final submission reported to government officials.

34 CFR §300.753 Annual report of children served: Criteria for counting children

(a) The SEA may include in its report children with disabilities who are enrolled in a school or program that is operated or supported by a public agency, and that—

(1) Provides them with both special education and related services that meet State standards;

(2) Provides them only with special education, if a related service is not required, that meets State standards; or

(3) In the case of children with disabilities enrolled by their parents in private schools, provides them with special education or related services under §§300.452–300.462 that meet State standards.

(b) The SEA may not include children with disabilities in its report who are receiving special education funded solely by the Federal Government, including children served by the Department of Interior, the Department of Defense, or the Department of Education. However, the State may count children covered under §300.184(c)(2).

(Authority: 20 U.S.C. 1411(d)(2); 1417(b))

A student's free appropriate public education (FAPE), under the IDEA as promulgated (20 U.S.C. §§1400–1491), is usually provided either in a public school or in a private school mutually chosen by school officials and the student's parents. However, students unilaterally placed in private schools must also be counted if they receive special education or related services. It is important to be able to locate and follow procedural and substantive requirements on students served not only by public school services, but also those enrolled in and served by private schools. However, within IDEA reporting mandates, it is not necessary to note those students served by other federal departmental programs, such as students served through departments listed above.

34 CFR §300.754 Annual report of children served: Other responsibilities of the SEA

In addition to meeting the other requirements of §§300.750–300.753, the SEA shall—

(a) Establish procedures to be used by the LEAs and other educational institutions in counting the number of children with disabilities receiving special education and related services;

(b) Set dates by which those agencies and institutions must report to the SEA to ensure that the State complies with §300.750(a);

(c) Obtain certification from each agency and institution that an unduplicated and accurate count has been made;

(d) Aggregate the data from the count obtained from each agency and institution, and prepare the reports required under §§300.750–300.753; and reports required under §§300.750–300.753; and

(e) Ensure that documentation is maintained that enables the State and the Secretary to audit the accuracy of the count.

(Authority: 20 U.S.C. 1411(d)(2); 1417(b))

The bottom line important to special education program administrators is to keep accurate and up-to-date data on all students under their jurisdiction requiring special education and related services. By ascertaining accurate and verifiable counts, appropriate auditing on school records can take place. Each student's file can be used to help in the monitoring process of school records.

34 CFR §300.755 Disproportionality

(a) General. Each State that receives assistance under Part B of the Act, and the Secretary of the Interior, shall provide for the collection and examination of the data to determine if significant disproportionality based on race is occurring in the State or in the schools operated by the Secretary of the Interior with respect to—

(1) The identification of children as children with disabilities, including the identification of children as children with disabilities in accordance with a particular impairment described in section 602(3) of the Act; and

(2) The placement in particular educational settings of these children.

(b) Review and revision of policies, practices, and procedures. In the case of a determination of significant disproportionality with respect to the identification of children as children with disabilities, or the placement in particular educational settings of these children, in accordance with paragraph (a) of this section, the state or the Secretary of the Interior shall provide for the review and, if appropriate revision of the policies, procedures, and practices used in the identification or placement to ensure that policies, procedures, and practices comply with the requirements of Part B of the Act.

(Authority: 20 U.S.C. 1418(c))

School officials must be responsive to the growing needs of increasing diversity in our society. A pertinent outcome of monitoring student numbers and correlating such numbers with important variables, such as age, disability category, or race, is to ensure that a FAPE is provided. LEA and SEA officials must keep tabs on the numbers of diverse students placed into special education and related services. A local, state, or national analysis of demographic data on students served can reveal whether a disproportionate number of students are identified, labeled, or placed inappropriately. By monitoring data on students served, government officials can also determine whether state and local jurisdictions provide an equitable resource allocation to ensure an equal educational opportunity to all students.

Disproportionality implies that more ethnic-racial minority students might be served in special education than would be expected based on minorities represented in the general school population. Analyzing trends represented by annual child count figures can reveal whether the number of these students placed in special education programs or services grows at a proportionate or disproportionate rate.

Monitoring accurate records on student counts often guides local and state officials in analyzing age, disability category, or ethnic-racial variables. For instance, in relation to use of demographics, analyses can reveal the LEA's or SEA's (a) treatment of educational assessment and evaluation instruments; (b) programming tendencies; or (c) special education screening, referral, evaluation, or placement trends that underscore educational expectations in this country. In essence, it is important for school officials to be aware of an unduplicated count of students receiving special education and related services on specific yearly dates in order to reflect an accurate picture of educational opportunities available in this country.

Changes in Monitoring Activities through the IDEA 2004

The IDEA 2004, at Section 616, provides more federal direction to state-level activities in monitoring the outcomes of students with disabilities. Accordingly, the IDEA 2004 prioritized specific monitoring outcomes for students with disabilities. These priority areas include monitoring students' graduation and dropout rates; an increased attention to the disproportionality of racial and ethnic students placed into special education and related services; students with disabilities' participation and performance on statewide assessments; and whether students with disabilities actually are receiving a FAPE in their LRE. The new IDEA 2004 established that states must use quantifiable indicators to monitor these priority areas, as well as qualitative indicators to measure performance in the priority areas.

Both federal and state monitoring efforts impose on the secretary of the U.S. Department of Education the duty to perform focus-monitoring oversight of a state's performance plans to enforce corrective action when districts violate the IDEA 2004. The USDE secretary requires the SEA to monitor LEAs and requires states to enforce the federal law.

Thus, SEAs and LEAs must work toward improving educational results and functional outcomes for all students with disabilities. The federal focused monitoring ensures that the SEAs meet program requirements, especially those related to improving educational results for students with disabilities. Special education program administrators will be on the forefront to ensure that districts adhere to federal and state monitoring requirements. Section 616 affects the USDE, all SEAs, and all LEAs by prescribing what is to be monitored, the reporting of findings, and enforcement actions required. Special education program administrators should keep in mind that each SEA performance report receives monitoring, as does each LEA's report.

PUTTING PRINCIPLES INTO PRACTICE

Tips

In order to put principles into practice, new special education program administrators need to get comfortable with the tedious process of creating and maintaining accurate student counts and monitoring activities on those served in special education and related services. The following tips may help new administrators to consider student-counting procedures; they consist of monitoring techniques to maintain accurate, up-to-date records on the numbers of special education students served and the types, numbers, and qualities of programs and services students receive.

- *Get up to date on specific paperwork.* Special education program administrators can monitor students effectively by becoming familiar with special education paperwork. Paperwork forms and formats change as rules and regulations receive updated attention from evolving state or federal mandates. However, effective maintenance of paperwork forms and formats can underscore accurate student records.

    Initially, a new administrator might randomly pull several student files from the special education pupil personnel file and go through a checklist to determine whether all necessary paperwork is in the file and in order. The following are general questions that new administrators may ask as they review paperwork in individual files:

    1. When was the student referred for special education services? Are timelines for screenings, evaluations, IEPs, and services appropriate?
    2. What is contained in his or her IEP? Are data appropriate, up to date, and complete?
    3. Where is the student's educational program located? Does the student have the opportunity to access the general education curriculum? How often? Is the amount of access appropriate based on the student's needs? Is the student served in the LRE? Why or why not?
    4. What are specific comments concerning the student's:
        - Adaptations or modifications to the general education curriculum?
        - Disability category?
        - Native language or mode of communication?

- Racial-ethnic grouping?
- Functional behavioral assessment?
- Instructional strategies?
- Graduation requirements?
- Health issues?
- Behavior management or behavior support?
- Regional and community services?
- Transportation requirements?
- Vocational services?
- Expected graduation date?

Becoming familiar with paperwork requirements will assist new administrators in understanding special education processes and procedures, as well as in familiarizing administrators with the needs of specific students receiving services within their schools.

- *Use a card file system.* By acquiring a 3×5 card file system and color-coding the cards by age, disability category, racial-ethnic grouping, expected graduation date, or student placement, administrators can establish and access an easy system for identifying important student variables within their schools. This color-coded system can provide a quick and efficient visual display of students served and programs provided. Thus, if a student requires emotional support in the LRE, his or her color-coded card might be red. If a student requires learning support in the LRE, the color-coded card might be blue. The administrator can arrange these cards alphabetically by student age, name, grade level, or needs. The cards can act as an easily accessible way for administrators to become familiar with each student and ascertained needs. New administrators may want to have color-coded icons that would advise them when to check students' IEPs, the documentation on phone calls to and from parents, or comments made on meetings attended.

- *Use computerized monitoring systems.* Many schools have purchased student management software packages that assist in monitoring individual variables on students and their families, such as students' academic progress, attendance records, discipline issues, and personalized information pertaining to family interactions or home–school contacts. Typically, software programs have the capability of coding special education services by placing a coded "SE" at the top of each student's database page. Administrators, thus, would be able to access important special education data quickly from all student services provided in the data system. Keeping up to date on available software can assist in student counts and child-monitoring requirements.

- *Keep accurate monitoring records.* Administrators can work with school faculty to develop school record forms that would document data in individual student files for monitoring purposes. Relevant data might target each student's educational program, funding eligibility, grade level, disability category, related services, supplemental aids and services, extended school year eligibility, program location, graduation date, and any other categories.

Administrators can encourage faculty to monitor on an ongoing basis relevant student data on each faculty's caseload. For example, administrators may want to discuss ways and means faculty can readily access relevant sections of students' IEPs that target specially designed instruction. Administrators may want to support faculty and staff attempts to develop, review, revise, or update records on modifications to lessons, tests, progress on state or districtwide assessments, assignments, or required testing modifications by reinforcing faculty who supply anecdotal information in carefully documented, dated student file components.

- *Encourage and document ongoing afterschool meetings to discuss specific needs of individual students.* Meetings titled "Child Study," "Instructional Support," "Student Identification Team," and others share similar purposes and usually are helpful if held at least monthly. Administrators can underscore the need for faculty and staff to use ongoing meetings to brainstorm instructional, behavioral, or extracurricular support students may require. By encouraging faculty and staff to keep relevant and dated documentation of learning or behavioral issues and strategy or support success, both quantifiable and qualitative data can be easily transferred to forms on monitoring accounting systems. For example, counting codes can be established to keep individual data on student's specific classroom performance, such as whether students earn acceptable progress reports, are passing coursework, display problematic curriculum concerns, or require necessary out-of-school services.

- *Develop a strategic plan to monitor students.* It may be helpful to new administrators to work with faculty and staff on developing a strategic plan to monitor and graph student data systemically. Carefully guided discussions during afterschool meetings or in-services on the following questions may generate useful, local monitoring plans, resources, and data-graphing activities:

  - How much time per week do faculty and staff spend on prereferral strategy planning? What are qualitative indicators of planning activities?
  - How much time per week do faculty and staff spend reviewing each student's evaluation or reevaluation data? What are qualitative indicators of evaluation or reevaluation review activities?
  - How much time per week do faculty and staff spend on reviewing each student's IEP? What are qualitative indicators of IEP review activities?
  - How much time per week do students spend in general education courses? What are qualitative indicators of students' access to general education opportunity activities?
  - How much time per week do faculty and staff collaborate with peers on students' needs, instructional strategies, accommodations, and/or behavior support plans? What are qualitative indicators of collaboration activities?
  - How much time per week do faculty and staff collaborate with parents on each student's IEP goals and objectives? What are qualitative indicators of collaboration activities?
  - How much time per week do faculty and staff collaborate with related services providers? What are qualitative indicators of collaboration activities?

Pitfalls to Avoid

- Being slack in keeping track of numbers and data. Be sure to monitor local child counting trends on a consistent basis. Make ongoing changes in local districts as federal and state laws evolve and are updated.
- Getting bogged down by paperwork. Keep district child-count and monitoring data reports current by use of computer technology. Back up all reporting systems in order to avoid losing databases due to computer error or software inadequacies.

Special education monitoring is a tedious, time-consuming process. There are no magic wands out there that can be waved to show new special education program administrators exactly how to conduct all components to the monitoring process. Every school district is different in procedures, but all seem to shoot for the same goals: that is, to obtain accurate numbers on the quantity and quality of student needs and services and to report and maintain valid data.

RESOURCES

There are monitoring sources available online and in each individual community and state that will be helpful to advance student monitoring activities. The following is a list of national resources that may be helpful.

Websites

The World Wide Web provides ready access to a variety of resources that contain useful student monitoring material. Here are some that have been particularly useful to us.

www.cec.sped.org/law_res/doc/law/index.php
Information on the IDEA 2004 is provided along with the latest amendments and final regulations. Articles, general information, speeches, training, and more are also available.

www.dssc.org
This website is created and maintained by the *Disabilities Studies and Services Center* (DSSC). The DSSC is a division of the *Academy for Educational Development* (AED). The website provides information on the many national projects directed by the DSSC such as the *National Information Center for Children and Youth with Disabilities* (NICHY), the *Federal Resource Center* (FRC), and the *Comprehensive School Reform Demonstration* (CSRD).

www.dssc.org/frc/
The *Federal Resource Center* (FRC) for Special Education is a nationwide technical assistance network developed through a five-year contract of several partners at the national level. It offers many resources and information concerning special education.

www.wrightslaw.com
This website provides information for special education at the federal level. The website information is provided by the special education attorney who represents parents. Included in the website are information on IDEA 2004, Section 504 of the Rehabilitation Act of 1973, the Americans with Disabilities Act of 1990, and more.

Technical Assistance

Many forms of technical assistance are available for student monitoring requirements. Here are some associations and governmental organizations that provide widespread support.

Clearinghouse on Disability Information
Office of Special Education and Rehabilitative Services
U.S. Department of Education
Switzer Building, Room 3132
330 C Street, SW
Washington, DC 20202-2524
(202) 205-8241 (voice/TTY)

National Information Center for Children and Youth with Disabilities (NICHCY)
P.O. Box 1492
Washington, DC 20013-1492
1-800-695-0285 or (202) 884-8200 (voice/TTY)
email: nichcy@aed.org

CHAPTER EIGHT

UNDERSTANDING
PLACEMENT ISSUES

OVERVIEW

Placement issues for students with disabilities represent enormous involvement and effort on the part of special education program administrators. Many of these administrators will act as local educational agency (LEA) representatives on behalf of their school districts or educational entities. Special education program administrators must commit to immediate financial or service decisions as they participate in students' educational planning and programming.

The federal law requires educational agencies to provide appropriate programs of special education and related services that are reasonably calculated to provide educational benefits. When special education program administrators work with students' Individualized Education Program (IEP) teams, the teams must initially consider the environments that capitalize on opportunities to interact with nondisabled peers in general education. Only if it is determined that students with disabilities cannot glean educational benefits from general education do IEP teams then consider other placement options. At this point, special education program administrators' knowledge of programs and services in the local area or region is critical. Special education program administrators must be aware of financial obligations and resources their educational agencies are willing to commit on students' behalves.

In this chapter, we examine placement issues in special education programs and services. We start with changes mandated by the new law, the Individuals with Disabilities Education Improvement Act of 2004 (i.e., PL 108-446) in relation to IEPs, including IEP content, IEP team attendance, provisions related to students transferring into the LEA, amending the IEP, and multiyear IEPs.

Next, we examine terms such as *least restrictive environment, continuum of alternative placements, program options, nonacademic settings,* and *private school placements.* We illustrate examples of placement issues to facilitate special education program administrators' understanding of placement benefits and concerns when working with IEP teams.

REGULATIONS: INDIVIDUALIZED EDUCATION PROGRAMS

(1) DEFINITIONS.—In this title:

(A) INDIVIDUALIZED EDUCATION PROGRAM.—

(i) IN GENERAL.—The term "individualized education program" or "IEP" means a written statement for each child with a disability that is developed, reviewed, and revised in accordance with this section and that includes—

(I) a statement of the child's present levels of academic achievement and functional performance, including— H.R. 1350-62 (aa) how the child's disability affects the child's involvement and progress in the general education curriculum; (bb) for preschool children, as appropriate, how the disability affects the child's participation in appropriate activities; and (cc) for children with disabilities who take alternate assessments aligned to alternate achievement standards, a description of benchmarks or short-term objectives;

(II) a statement of measurable annual goals, including academic and functional goals, designed to— (aa) meet the child's needs that result from the child's disability to enable the child to be involved in and make progress in the general education curriculum; and (bb) meet each of the child's other educational needs that result from the child's disability;

(III) a description of how the child's progress toward meeting the annual goals described in subclause (II) will be measured and when periodic reports on the progress the child is making toward meeting the annual goals (such as through the use of quarterly or other periodic reports, concurrent with the issuance of report cards) will be provided;

(IV) a statement of the special education and related services and supplementary aids and services, based on peer-reviewed research to the extent practicable, to be provided to the child, or on behalf of the child, and a statement of the program modifications or supports for school personnel that will be provided for the child— (aa) to advance appropriately toward attaining the annual goals; (bb) to be involved in and make progress in the general education curriculum in accordance with subclause (I) and to participate in extracurricular and other nonacademic activities; and (cc) to be educated and participate with other children with disabilities and nondisabled children in the activities described in this subparagraph;

(V) an explanation of the extent, if any, to which the child will not participate with nondisabled children in the regular class and in the activities described in subclause (IV)(cc);

(VI) (aa) a statement of any individual appropriate accommodations that are necessary to measure the academic achievement and functional performance of the child on State and district-wide assessments consistent with section 612(a)(16)(A); and H.R. 1350-63 (bb) if the IEP Team determines that the child shall take an alternate assessment on a particular State or district-wide assessment of student achievement, a statement of why— (AA) the child cannot participate in the regular assessment; and (BB) the particular alternate assessment selected is appropriate for the child;

(VII) the projected date for the beginning of the services and modifications described in subclause (IV), and the anticipated frequency, location, and duration of those services and modifications; and

(VIII) beginning not later than the first IEP to be in effect when the child is 16, and updated annually thereafter—(aa) appropriate measurable postsecondary goals based upon age appropriate transition assessments related to training, education, employment, and, where appropriate, independent living skills; (bb) the transition services (including courses of study) needed to assist the child in reaching those goals; and (cc) beginning not later than 1 year before the child reaches the age of majority under State law, a statement that the child has been informed of the child's rights under this title, if any, that will transfer to the child on reaching the age of majority under section 615(m). (ii) RULE OF CONSTRUCTION.—Nothing in this section shall be construed to require— (I) that additional information be included in a child's IEP beyond what is explicitly required in this section; and (II) the IEP Team to include information under component of a child's IEP that is already contained under another component of such IEP.

IEP Content

The IDEA 2004 mandates new changes to IEP content. An IEP must include a statement of the student's present levels of academic achievement and functional performance, including how the student's disability affects his or her involvement and progress in the general education curriculum. An IEP must include a statement of measurable annual goals, including academic and functional goals, designed to meet the student's need to enable him or her to be involved in and make progress in the general education curriculum and meet each of the student's educational needs that result from the student's disability.

Short-term objectives/benchmarks are not required for most students with disabilities. Benchmarks and short-term objectives are required only for those students who take alternative assessments aligned to alternate achievement standards. An IEP must include a description of how the student's progress toward meeting annual goals will be measured and when reports on progress (such as quarterly or other reports made concurrently with the issuance of report cards) will be provided.

A new IDEA 2004 requirement focuses on the statement of the special education and related services and supplementary aids and services in the IEP, based on peer-reviewed research where practicable, to be provided to the student or on behalf of the student. Peer-reviewed research is open to interpretation.

However, included in the IEP is a statement of the program modifications or supports for school personnel to be provided to the student so the student will appropriately advance toward attaining the annual goals, be involved in and progress in the general curriculum, participate in extracurricular and nonacademic activities, and be educated and participate with both disabled and nondisabled students. The list of related services has been expanded to include interpreting services and school nurse services.

An IEP must contain an explanation of the extent, if any, to which the student will not participate with nondisabled students in general education, a statement of any individual appropriate accommodations ("modifications" removed in the new IDEA 2004) necessary to measure the student's academic achievement and functional performance on assessments, and the projected start date, frequency, location, and duration of services and modifications.

If the IEP team determines that the student shall take an alternate assessment, the student's IEP must state why he or she cannot participate in the regular assessment and the particular assessment the student will take. A specific change in the newly reauthorized law is that the IEP team must consider the student's need for assistive technology. A medical device that is surgically implanted or replaced is not included in the term "assistive technology device."

The former transition services requirement of the identification of transition needs be-ginning at age 14 has been deleted from the IDEA 2004. Transition services and measurable postsecondary goals are to be included in the IEP not later than the first IEP in effect when the student is 16 and updated annually. While transition planning may begin at any age for a stu-dent with a disability, the "course of study" at age 14, as in the existing IDEA, is no longer re-quired. Further, by one year before the student reaches the age of majority, the IEP must contain a statement that the student has been informed of the rights, if any, that will transfer to the student upon majority.

(B) INDIVIDUALIZED EDUCATION PROGRAM TEAM.—The term "individualized edu-cation program team" or "IEP Team" means a group of individuals composed of— (i) the par-ents of a child with a disability; (ii) not less than 1 regular education teacher of such child (if the child is, or may be, participating in the regular education environment); (iii) not less than 1 special education teacher, or where appropriate, not less than 1 special education provider of such child; (iv) a representative of the local educational agency who— (I) is qualified to pro-vide, or supervise the provision of, specially designed to meet the unique needs of children with disabilities; (II) is knowledgeable about the general education curriculum; and H.R. 1350–64; (III) is knowledgeable about the availability of resources of the local educational agency; (v) an individual who can interpret the instructional implications of evaluation results, who may be a member of the team described in clauses (ii) through (vi); (vi) at the discretion of the parent or the agency, other individuals who have knowledge or special expertise re-garding the child, including related services personnel as appropriate; and (vii) whenever ap-propriate, the child with a disability.

(C) IEP TEAM ATTENDANCE.—(i) ATTENDANCE NOT NECESSARY.—A member of the IEP Team shall not be required to attend an IEP meeting, in whole or in part, if the parent of a child with a disability and the educational agency agree that the attendance of such mem-ber is not necessary because the member's area of the curriculum or related services is not be-ing modified or discussed in the meeting. (ii) EXCUSAL.—A member of the IEP Team may be excused from attending an IEP meeting, in whole or in part, when the meeting involves a modification to or discussion of the member's area of the curriculum or related services, if— (I) the parent and the local educational agency consent to the excusal; and (II) the member submits, in writing to the parent and the IEP Team, input into the development of the IEP prior to the meeting. (iii) WRITTEN AGREEMENT AND CONSENT REQUIRED.—A parent's agreement under clause (i) and consent under clause (ii) shall be in writing.

(D) IEP TEAM TRANSITION.—In the case of a child who was previously served under part C, an invitation to the initial IEP meeting shall, at the request of the parent, be sent to the part C service coordinator or other representatives of the part C system to assist with the smooth transition of services.

(B) ADDITIONAL REQUIREMENT.—If a child with a disability is convicted as an adult under State law and incarcerated in an adult prison, the child's IEP Team may modify the child's IEP or placement notwithstanding the requirements of sections 612(a)(5)(A) and para-graph (1)(A) if the State has demonstrated a bona fide security or compelling penological in-terest that cannot otherwise be accommodated.

(e) EDUCATIONAL PLACEMENTS.—Each local educational agency or State educational agency shall ensure that the parents of each child with a disability are members of any group that makes decisions on the educational placement of their child.

IEP Team Attendance

Changes in IEP development concern IEP meetings. Parents and school officials may agree not to convene an IEP meeting to make changes to the IEP after the annual meeting. Instead, the parents and school officials may develop a written document to modify the current IEP. Upon request, the parents must receive the revised copy of the IEP. For a student who was previously served under Part C, the new bill requires that an invitation to the initial IEP meeting, at the request of the parents, be sent to the Part C service coordinator or other representatives of the Part C system to assist with the smooth transition of services.

For a student convicted as an adult or incarcerated in an adult prison, the IEP team may decide to modify the student's IEP or placement. As with all students with disabilities, however, the parents are vital to the IEP team.

(C) PROGRAM FOR CHILDREN WHO TRANSFER SCHOOL DISTRICTS.—

(i) IN GENERAL.—

(I) TRANSFER WITHIN THE SAME STATE.—In the case of a child with a disability who transfers school districts within the same academic year, who enrolls in a new school, and who had an IEP that was in effect in the same State, the local educational agency shall provide such child with a free appropriate public education, including services comparable to those described in the previously held IEP, in consultation with the parents until such time as the local educational agency adopts the previously held IEP or develops, adopts, and implements a new IEP that is consistent with Federal and State law.

(II) TRANSFER OUTSIDE STATE.—In the case of a child with a disability who transfers school districts within the same academic year, who enrolls in a new school, and who had an IEP that was in effect in another State, the local educational agency shall provide such child with a free appropriate public education, including services comparable to those described in the previously IEP, in consultation with the parents until such time as the local educational agency conducts an evaluation pursuant to subsection (a)(1), if determined to be necessary by such agency, and develops a new IEP, if appropriate, that is consistent with Federal and State law.

(ii) TRANSMITTAL OF RECORDS.—To facilitate the transition for a child described in clause (i)—(I) the new school in which the child enrolls shall take reasonable steps to promptly obtain the child's records, including the IEP and supporting documents and any other records relating to the provision of special education or related services to the child, from the previous school in which the child was enrolled, pursuant to section 99.31(a)(2) of title 34, Code of Federal Regulations; and (II) the previous school in which the child was enrolled shall take reasonable steps to promptly respond to such request from the new school.

Provisions Related to Students' Transferring into the LEA

In the case of students transferring into preschool special education from the Part C program, the IDEA 2004 requires IEP teams to consider the individualized family service plans that contain the material described in Section 636. In the case of an eligible student with an IEP who transfers school districts within the same academic year within the same state, the IDEA

2004 requires the LEA to provide the student with FAPE, including services comparable to those described in the previous IEP, in consultation with the parents until the LEA adopts the previous IEP or develops, adopts, and implements a new IEP. However, for a student with a disability who transfers within the same academic year, who had an IEP that was in effect in another state, the LEA must provide the student with FAPE, including services comparable to those described in the previous IEP, in consultation with the parents until the LEA conducts an evaluation, if determined to be necessary by the LEA, and develops a new IEP, if appropriate.

(f) ALTERNATIVE MEANS OF MEETING PARTICIPATION.—When conducting IEP team meetings and placement meetings pursuant to this section, section 615(e), and section 615(f)(1)(B), and carrying out administrative matters under section 615 (such as scheduling, exchange of witness lists, and status conferences), the parent of a child with a disability and a local educational agency may agree to use alternative means of meeting participation, such as video conferences and conference calls.

Amending the IEP

Parents and school officials may agree to use alternative means of meetings, such as through videoconferences and conference calls. The schools district should encourage the consolidation of reevaluation and IEP meetings.

(4) REVIEW AND REVISION OF IEP.—H.R. 1350-67

(5) MULTI-YEAR IEP DEMONSTRATION.—

(A) PILOT PROGRAM.—(i) PURPOSE.—The purpose of this paragraph is to provide an opportunity for States to allow parents and local educational agencies the opportunity for longterm planning by offering the option of developing a comprehensive multi-year IEP, not to exceed 3 years, that is designed to coincide with the natural transition points for the child.

(B) REPORT.—Beginning 2 years after the date of enactment of the Individuals with Disabilities Education Improvement Act of 2004, the Secretary shall submit an report to the Committee on Education and the Workforce of the House of Representatives and the Committee on Health, Education, Labor, and Pensions of the Senate regarding the effectiveness of the program under this paragraph and any specific recommendations for broader implementation of such program, including— (i) reducing— (I) the paperwork burden on teachers, principals, administrators, and related service providers; and (II) noninstructional time spent by teachers in complying with this part; (ii) enhancing longer-term educational planning; (iii) improving positive outcomes for children with disabilities; (iv) promoting collaboration between IEP Team; and (v) ensuring satisfaction of family members.

(C) DEFINITION.—In this paragraph, the term "natural transition points" means those periods that are close in time to the transition of a child with a disability from preschool to elementary grades, from elementary grades H.R. 1350-69 to middle or junior high school grades, from middle or junior high school grades to secondary school grades, and from secondary school grades to post-secondary activities, but in no case a period longer than 3 years.

Multiyear IEP Demonstration

The IDEA 2004 authorizes the secretary to approve up to fifteen proposals from states to allow LEAs, with written consent of the parent, to develop comprehensive multiyear IEPs, not to exceed three years. Multiyear IEPs must include measurable goals coinciding with natural transition points for the student that will enable the student to be involved in and make progress in the general education curriculum and that will meet the student's other needs that result from the disability. Also included are measurable annual goals for determining progress toward meeting the goals and a description of the process for the review and revision of the multiyear IEP, including a review by the IEP team of the student's multiyear IEP at each of the student's natural transition points. In years other than a student's natural transition points, an annual review of the student's IEP must be made to determine the student's current levels of progress and whether the annual goals for the student are being achieved, as well as a to amend the IEP, as appropriate, to enable the student to continue to meet the measurable goals set out in the IEP.

If the IEP team determines on the basis of a review that the student is not making sufficient progress toward the goals described in the multiyear IEP, the LEA must ensure that the IEP team conducts a thorough review of the IEP in accordance with IEP review requirements within thirty calendar days. In addition, at the request of the parents, the IEP team is to conduct a review of the student's multiyear IEP rather than or subsequent to an annual review. A report will be issued on the effectiveness of multiyear IEPs two years after the new law is enacted.

EXISTING REGULATIONS

In the next sections, we explain existing regulations to federal law, maintained by the IDEA 2004.

34 CFR §300.550 Least Restrictive Environment

General requirements.

An educational placement for a student with a disability must be considered individually and made on the basis of the "least restrictive environment" (LRE) requirements in statutes and regulations at the state and federal level. The Individuals with Disabilities Education Act, 20 U.S.C. §1412(a)(5), and federal regulations at §300.550(b) require:

> (1) That to the maximum extent appropriate, children with disabilities, including children in public or private institutions or other care facilities, are educated with children who are nondisabled; and

> (2) The special classes, separate schooling or other removal of children with disabilities from the regular educational environment occurs only if the nature or severity of the disability is such that education in classes with the use of supplementary aids and services cannot be achieved satisfactorily.

(Authority: 20 U.S.C. 1412(a)(5))

The federal law specifies that the student with a disability must be educated in the LRE. This means that states must have policies and procedures in place to ensure that all students with disabilities, including those in public or private institutions or other care facilities, are educated with students without disabilities, that students are removed from the regular education environment (i.e., the general education setting) only when the severity of a disability is such that instruction in general education classes with the use of supplementary aids and services is not effective. Special education program administrators must work with other team members to follow IDEA procedures and develop an IEP that can support the student with a disability in an appropriate educational setting so that the student can make educational progress.

The LRE provisions reflect the belief that the student is better off and demonstrates increased gains in educational progress when he or she spends as much time as possible interacting with neighbors and peers. And it is a generally held belief that if a student can learn in an environment that is relatively nonrestrictive, then that student can live and interact in such an environment as an adult. Another generally held belief is that the student's neighbors and peers also benefit from LRE participation. Opportunities to participate with diverse students most likely increase acceptance and understanding of differences by all students.

However, if the individual student cannot do well interacting with neighbors and peers in a relatively nonrestrictive setting, LEA officials must work with IEP team to make other educational placements available. Thus, special education program administrators must work with the student's IEP team to consider a continuum of alternative placements.

34 CFR §300.551 Continuum of alternative placements

General requirements.

(a) Each public agency shall ensure that a continuum of alternative placements is available to meet the needs of children with disabilities for special education and related services.

(b) The continuum required in paragraph (a) of this section must—

> (1) Include the alternative placements listed in the definition of special education under §300.26 (instruction in regular classes, special classes, special schools, home instruction, and instruction in hospitals and institutions); and

> (2) Make provision for supplementary services (such as resource room or itinerant instruction) to be provided in conjunction with regular class placement.

(Authority: 20 U.S.C. 1412(a)(5))

Having available a continuum of alternative placements assumes that a variety of service delivery options should be available to meet the specific educational needs of individual students. The ultimate goal strived for by effective special education program administrators, as members of IEP teams, is to tailor instructional programs and settings to meet the educational requirements of individual students. Most students receive their education in the general education environment. However, for the student with more intense ability, behavior, language, learning, mental health, physical or sensory needs, other educational settings and service options must be made available. The following examples illustrate decisions made by IEP teams with regard to the LRE and placement options for students with varying intensity of educational requirements, based on the existing IDEA.

- *Full-time residential school:* Educational services are provided directly to the student in his or her place of residence on hospital or institutional grounds. For example, Tonya has been diagnosed as severely mentally disabled, is deaf-blind, and is nonambulatory. She requires full-time medical assistance. Her IEP team has determined that Tonya's LRE is the Sandpiper Shores Residential School and Treatment Center.
- *Special day school:* Students with disabilities receive their education in a special school with other students with disabilities. For example, diagnosed with spastic quadriplegia due to cerebral palsy since birth, Felicity has been found to be functioning at a profound level of cognitive impairment. In addition to the assistance of a wheelchair and feeding tubes during lunch, her educational program relies on assistive technology in the form of a computer and a commercially available switch used to support the control of her environment. Her teachers program an interface and switch to activate Felicity's software. Her IEP team has determined that Felicity's LRE is the Ruth Ann Special Day Care Center.
- *Full-time special class:* Students with disabilities are educated in a special class located on the grounds of a general education school. For example, Martin functions at a profound level of functioning although he displays no major problems with self-help skills or motor skills. He has no known medical difficulties. Martin's IEP team has determined that his LRE is a full-time special class at Forrest Grove High School.
- *Part-time general education class and part-time special class:* Students with disabilities spend some part of the instructional week with general education peers. For example, Karl displays problem behaviors, specifically inattention to tasks, during his academic instruction time. However, Karl displays excellent language skills and is especially proficient in mathematics class. His IEP team has determined that Karl's LRE is a part-time special class in which he divides his time between instruction with his general education peers and instruction with students with disabilities. Johnson Elementary School houses both programs.
- *General education class with supportive instructional services:* The majority of the academic program is provided during the general education class, but, for a portion of the time, education is provided in a resource-room setting. For example, Rodriquez displays excellent reading skills but requires assistance by his special education teacher in the resource room for spelling and handwriting. Rodriquez functions in his general education curriculum. However, his IEP team has determined that his LRE is the resource-room model at Madison Junior High School. Rodriquez's special education teacher has been working on a consulting basis with his general education class teachers to monitor Rodriquez's progress in his general education classes.
- *General education class with consulting services for general education class teacher:* Resource room teachers and itinerant teachers consult with general education class teachers about modifications in the general education curriculum. Prereferral strategies may be implemented for students who can profit by instruction with general education class peers. For example, Mariah demonstrates adequate comprehension skills but has trouble reading the text. Teachers at the Barbison Elementary School have consulted about the use of a CD-ROM and computer-assisted text for Mariah's general education reading curriculum. When she is allowed to hear stories read from the computer, Mariah has little difficulty following the written discourse. Her IEP team has deter-

mined that Mariah's LRE is the general education class with consulting services. Her teachers through prereferral conferences have continued to monitor use of her computer-assisted instruction.

- *General education class:* The LRE for education of most students with disabilities is the general education class. For example, Bobby requires speech therapy for a diagnosed articulation problem although he displays no educational difficulties other than an articulation problem. Bobby is 5 years old. His IEP team has determined that Bobby's LRE is the general education class at Morehead Elementary School.

Special education program administrators working with IEP teams cannot place students with disabilities outside of general education classrooms if educating the students in general education classrooms with supplementary aids and support services can be achieved satisfactorily. This means that the administrators must do everything within their jurisdictions to provide help to special needs students (such as through adaptations or modification to the curriculum, use of paraprofessionals, application of specialized amplifiers or programmed texts, or other supplementary aids and services), so that removal from the general education class does not have to take place. Further, placement or service within a particular setting is not permanent. Students should be able to "move" from the placements or levels of service based on their educational performance. Additionally, an emphasis should be on returning students to a less restrictive setting as soon as is feasible; educational changes in placement or movement to more restrictive settings should occur only when necessary. When a more restrictive setting is necessary, students should continue to receive a variety of program options.

34 CFR §300.305 Program options

General requirements.

Each public agency shall take steps to ensure that its children with disabilities have available to them the variety of educational programs and services available to nondisabled children in the area served by the agency, including art, music, industrial arts, consumer and homemaking education, and vocational education.

(Authority: 20 U.S.C. 1412(a)(2); 1413(a)(1))

As noted above, LRE concepts establish a preference for educating students with disabilities with their nondisabled peers to the extent possible in the general education class. Consideration of the general education class must be the starting place for any decision making about the placement of the student with diverse learning needs, problem behaviors, or ability levels. However, only if it is objectively determined that no set of services can feasibly be provided to allow the student to succeed in the general education class should the student's IEP team recommend a placement change. Thus, for students such as Tonya, Felicity, and Martin, described above, their LRE is not the general education class. Nonetheless, once a decision is made to change the educational programs and services available to the student with a disability, he or she must still be afforded opportunities that are afforded to other students. Thus, to the extent appropriate, extracurricular activities, such as art or music opportunities, must be made available to Tonya, Felicity, and Martin, and other students requiring special education and/or related services, if their peers have such opportunities. Such opportunities to participate extend to nonacademic settings.

34 CFR §300.306 Nonacademic settings

General requirements.

(a) Each public agency shall take steps to provide nonacademic and extracurricular services and activities in the manner necessary to afford children with disabilities an equal opportunity for participation in those services and activities.

(b) Nonacademic and extracurricular services and activities may include counseling services, athletics, transportation, health services, recreational activities, special interest groups or clubs sponsored by the public agency, referrals to agencies that provide assistance to individuals with disabilities, and employment of students, including both employment by the public agency and assistance in making outside employment available.

(Authority: 20 U.S.C. 1412(a)(1))

Special education program administrators need to ensure that once a decision is made to change the educational programs and services available to the student with a disability, the student must still be afforded nonacademic and extracurricular services and activities in the manner necessary to provide an equal opportunity to participate. Thus, as the LEA representative, many special education program administrators will work with the students' IEP teams to ensure opportunities are available to students with disabilities in counseling services, athletics, transportation, health services, recreational activities, special interest groups or clubs, referrals to agencies, or employment. If other students without disabilities have such opportunities, to the extent appropriate, opportunities to participate in nonacademic and extracurricular services and activities (e.g., the swimming team, the Key Club, the Debate Panel) must be available to students such as Karl, Rodriquez, Mariah, or Bobby.

Some parents of students with disabilities and other IEP team members may decide that even when opportunities are provided for nonacademic and extracurricular services and activities, other service placements or options might be more suitable. For instance, many parents choose to send their children to private schools. The LEA representative may endorse the private school placement because the IEP team makes the determination that a free appropriate public education (FAPE) is not available and/or cannot be provided in the public setting.

34 CFR §300.349 Private school placements by public agencies

(a) Developing IEPs.

    (1) Before a public agency places a child with a disability in, or refers a child to, a private school or facility, the agency shall initiate and conduct a meeting to develop an IEP for the child in accordance with §§300.346 and 300.347.

    (2) The agency shall ensure that representative of the private school or facility attends the meeting. If the representative cannot attend, the agency shall use other methods to ensure participation by the private school or facility, including individual or conference telephone calls.

(b) Reviewing and Revising IEPs.

(1) After a child with a disability enters a private school or facility, any meetings to review and revise the child's IEP may be initiated and conducted by the private school or facility at the discretion of the public agency.

(2) If the private school or facility initiates and conducts these meetings, the public agency shall ensure that the parents and an agency representative— (i) are involved in any decision about the child's IEP; and (ii) agree to any proposed changes in the IEP before those changes are implemented.

(c) Responsibility. Even if a private school or facility implements a child's IEP, responsibility for compliance with this part remains with the public agency and the SEA.

(Authority: 20 U.S.C. 1412(a)(10)(B))

Special education program administrators work with IEP teams, including students' parents, to facilitate appropriate educational placements within the public school setting. However, an IEP team may determine that the local school or district does not have the appropriate placement or service options available, based on what a particular student needs. Therefore, the team locates and secures placement or services for the student in a private school placement, such as an approved private school, hospital setting providing educational service, and/or therapeutic setting offering therapy and school services. Thus, Tonya's IEP team, for example, may work with Tonya's parents to determine that Tonya's LRE is a private hospital setting providing educational service. Tonya has such intense needs that her local school district recognizes it cannot meet her educational needs locally. However, in order to provide Tonya a FAPE, the LEA agrees with Tonya's IEP team to secure her educational services at the Sandpiper Shores Residential School and Treatment Center.

Importantly, special education program administrators need to work with the students' IEP team to ensure a FAPE. Thus, prior to Tonya's private school placement in the hospital setting, her IEP team must meet and develop her IEP. As the representative from Tonya's public school district, the special education administrator may attend the meeting and help to develop Tonya's appropriate IEP. During Tonya's enrollment at the private facility, the special education administrator represents Tonya's public school district to update and revise her IEP as necessary, encouraging participation by Tonya's parents, as well as public and private agency personnel, in Tonya's educational decisions.

Nonetheless, some parents of children with disabilities choose private schools and then claim that a FAPE has been denied to their child. In cases where a FAPE is at issue, the federal law has designated responsibilities of the local and state educational agencies. Such responsibilities are important to special education program administrators, especially as mistakes in the provision of a FAPE can cost local school districts a great deal of time, money, and resources.

34 CFR §300.401 Children with disabilities enrolled by their parents in private school when FAPE is at issue

Each SEA shall ensure that a child with a disability who is placed in or referred to a private school or facility by a public agency—

(a) Is provided special education and related services—

(1) In conformance with an IEP that meets the requirement of §§300.340–300.350; and

(2) At no cost to the parents;

(b) Is provided an education that meets the standards that apply to education provided by the SEA and LEAs (including the requirements of this part); and

(c) Has all of the rights of a child with a disability who is served by a public agency.

(Authority: 20 U.S.C. 1412(a)(10)(B))

All IEP team members, including the student's parents and the special education administrator, work together to ensure all the educational rights afforded to a privately enrolled child. If that particular private school student has a disability, he or she must still be guaranteed a FAPE by the school district. However, parents questioning whether a FAPE has been provided, or whether the LEA has offered appropriate services, may receive tuition reimbursement in the decision to enroll their child in a private school.

34 CFR §300.403 Placement of children by parents if FAPE is at issue

General Requirements.

(a) This part does not require an LEA to pay for the cost of education, including special education and related services, of a child with a disability at a private school or facility if that agency made FAPE available to the child and the parents elected to place the child in a private school or facility. However, the public agency shall include that child in the population whose needs are addressed consistent with §§300.450–300.462.

(b) Disagreements about FAPE. Disagreements between a parent and a public agency regarding the availability of a program appropriate for the child, and the question of financial responsibility, are subject to the due process procedures of §§300.500–300.517.

(c) Reimbursement for private school placement. If the parents of a child with a disability, who previously received special education and related services under the authority of a public agency, enroll the child in a private preschool, elementary, or secondary school without the consent of or referral by the public agency, a court or a hearing officer may require the agency to reimburse the parents for the cost of that enrollment if the court or hearing officer finds that the agency had not made FAPE available to the child in a timely manner prior to that enrollment and that the private placement is appropriate. A parental placement may be found to be appropriate by a hearing officer or a court even if it does not meet the State standards that apply to education provided by the SEA and LEAs.

(d) Limitation on reimbursement. The cost of reimbursement described in paragraph (c) of this section may be reduced or denied—

(1) If— (i) At the most recent IEP meeting that the parents attended prior to removal of the child from the public school, the parents did not inform the IEP team that they were rejecting the placement proposed by the public agency to provide FAPE to their child, including stating their concerns and their intent to enroll their child in a private school at public expense; or (ii) At least ten (10) business days (including any holidays that occur on a business day) prior to the removal of the child from the public school, the

parents did not give written notice to the public agency of the information described in paragraph (d)(1)(i) of this section;

(2) If, prior to the parents' removal of the child from the public school, the public agency informed the parents, through the notice requirements described in §300.503(a)(1), of its intent to evaluate the child (including a statement of the purpose of the evaluation that was appropriate and reasonable), but the parents did not make the child available for the evaluation; or

(3) Upon a judicial finding of unreasonableness with respect to actions taken by the parents.

(e) Exception. Notwithstanding the notice requirement in paragraph (d)(1) of this section, the cost of reimbursement may not be reduced or denied for failure to provide the notice if—

(1) The parent is illiterate and cannot write in English;

(2) Compliance with paragraph (d)(1) of this section would likely result in physical or serious emotional harm to the child;

(3) The school prevented the parent from providing the notice; or

(4) The parents had not received notice, pursuant to section 615 of the Act, of the notice requirement in paragraph (d)(1) of this section.

(Authority: 20 U.S.C. 1412(a)(10)(C))

If the parents of a student with a disability, who previously received special education and related services under the authority of a school district/public agency, enroll the student in a private preschool, elementary, or secondary school *without* the consent of or referral by the local public agency officials, a court or a hearing officer may require the LEA to reimburse the parents for the cost of that enrollment if the court or hearing officer finds that the LEA had not made FAPE available to the student in a timely manner prior to that enrollment and that the private placement is appropriate. It is important for school administrators to note that a parental placement may be found to be appropriate by a hearing officer or a court even if it does not meet the state standards that apply to education provided by the SEA and LEAs.

Thus, if Felicity's parents claim that Felicity has not received a FAPE and decide to enroll Felicity in the Ruth Ann Special Day Care Center without the consent of or referral by the Avalon School District (i.e., Felicity's home school district), a court or hearing officer may order the Avalon School District to reimburse Felicity's parents for the cost of her enrollment if it is determined legally that the Avalon School District had not made a FAPE available to Felicity in a timely manner prior to her Ruth Ann Special Day Care Center enrollment and that this private placement is appropriate.

Special education program administrators should note that a student with a disability is entitled to tuition reimbursement when a FAPE is denied, and the parents or guardians have sought out appropriately a privately secured placement. The three-pronged process for determining tuition reimbursement has been interpreted by the Federal Regulations at 34 CFR §300.403. The first consideration entails whether the local educational agency provided a FAPE. If it is determined in the affirmative that the LEA has provided a FAPE, the LEA does not have to pay for the cost of education, including special education and related services.

When the parents and the school district disagree over whether the LEA provided a FAPE, however, the availability of a program appropriate for the student, and the question of financial responsibility, is subject to the due process procedures. Important for special education program administrators' consideration is whether the parents decided to place their student *unilaterally* (i.e., without consent by the LEA). If the parents made a unilateral placement decision, the parents may have to pay. The following considerations require special attention.

- Special education program administrators need to analyze carefully whether the student's IEP team has followed mandated procedures and regulations. Did the IEP team work to ensure appropriate procedures and regulations? For example, did the IEP team provide adequate notice to the parents or guardians regarding the IEP team meeting location? Had the LEA fostered the appropriate makeup of participants on the IEP team? Were evaluations or services provided in a timely manner?
- Special education program administrators also need to analyze carefully whether the student's IEP team followed mandated substantive issues. For example, were IEP implementations and service delivery appropriate and timely? Did the IEP make careful determinations in planning, implementing, managing, and evaluating the instructional setting? Did the IEP team monitor the student's progress to ensure instructional effectiveness regarding the provision of the student's FAPE?

The trigger for consideration of the above regulations in all of their complexity is denial of FAPE. FAPE is the end result of the offer of an appropriate IEP. In order to ensure a FAPE, special education program administrators work closely with their faculty and staff to provide appropriate educational opportunities so that special education students can make meaningful educational progress.

PUTTING PRINCIPLES INTO PRACTICE

Based on the previous discussions, what should special education program administrators be prepared to deal with as "most likely" placement and program option issues? What advice can we provide based on our analysis of placement and program issues? We offer practical suggestions below. These tips will help special education program administrators think about ways and means to determine appropriate placement and program option decisions based on individual students' needs. The following tips consist of ideas to help special education program administrators to work as effective members of the IEP placement decision team pursuant to federal requirements.

Tips

- When functioning as the LEA, strive to assess whether an appropriate education can be provided in the general education class. Consider what the environment offers now and what it might be able to offer the student when augmented with supplementary aids and services. Assume that the general education setting is the student's LRE, unless proven otherwise by substantive factors based on the individual student's needs.

- Lead the IEP team to examine what services can be provided to the student without the student's having to undergo a change in educational placement. In all placement decisions, recognize that an effective IEP team, including the student's parents, consults and collaborates before deciding. Base team decisions on a collaborative, communication model that considers all team members' input into every placement or program decision.
- Operate on the principle that students with disabilities should receive their education in the general education classroom whenever possible. However, maintain a full continuum of alternative placements and options for those cases in which students cannot succeed even in enhanced general education classes. Remain current on local services and programs to seek more effective and efficient ways of delivering special education programs and service options to students who need them. Consider time and transportation factors, such as the number of miles from home and access to the location, when considering placement or program options.
- Work toward disseminating data promoting effective public relations so that relevant community members are familiar with available program options and services offered in the local area. Seek out a willing partnership with local school board members, administrators, educators, and family members in building a collaborative orientation to serve students with disabilities in their neighborhood schools and general education classrooms whenever possible. However, be familiar with what other services can offer.
- Seek out technical support and training opportunities for educators and paraprofessionals under the special education supervisor's jurisdiction so that faculty and staff are aware of available and effective aids, services, and modifications to enable students with disabilities to succeed in general education classes, without having to change students' placements.
- Work with fellow educators to lessen the effects of such challenges as ameliorating paperwork overloads; improving early intervention services; and reducing the over- or misidentification of nondisabled children, especially those from diverse families. Help faculty and staff under the special education administrator's jurisdiction to receive ongoing professional development and training in data collection techniques, instructional tactics, discipline strategies, and behavior supports. Seek out relevant and timely professional development so that a highly qualified teaching force teaches all students with disabilities—no matter what the placement option or location.

Pitfalls to Avoid

- Letting record keeping impinge on individualized planning and teaming for placement decisions of all students with disabilities. Monitor dates and timelines of all students' evaluation and IEP processes to ensure appropriate placement decisions.
- Irrelevant and untimely use of materials and resources, even if faculty or staff demonstrates resistance to change. Work to create, implement, and maintain school and building organization, underscoring the training and support required by general education,

special education teachers, paraprofessionals, or classroom aids and assistants. Seek out updated placement materials and resources to disseminate to faculty or staff on the educational, social, and communications needs of individual students within the local school entity.

- Losing sight of effective record keeping. Keep accurate records and make data-based decisions on an analysis of needed services, for the purpose of determining whether those services are sufficiently "portable" to be included as part of a general education class placement.
- Not monitoring where private enrolled students receive their education and programs or services. Remember to include these children in child accounting activities, updating required evaluations and IEPs on time and as warranted. Ensure privately enrolled children receive a FAPE by staying in regular communication with their parents or guardians and their private school educators and administrators.

RESOURCES

The following list of national resources may be helpful when working with others to determine appropriate placement decisions.

Websites

The World Wide Web provides ready access to a variety of resources that contain useful placement decision material. Here are some that have been particularly useful to us.

www.aasa.org/NewsManager/anmviewer.asp?a+3962&z+3
This website, offered by the American Association of School Administrators, provides updated legal issues related to FAPE and the IDEA.

CFR Titles on GPO Access—Part 300–Part 399
www.access.gpo.gov/nara/cfr/waisidx_99/34cfrv2_99.html
This website provides important information on Part 300 (Part B Regulations) and Part 303 (Part C Infant and Toddlers). The reader will be able to locate data on federal regulations related to infants, student, and youth with disabilities.

Federal Register Online
www.access.gpo.gov/su_docs/aces/aces140.html
(Daily publication of Federal Register. Search back issues of Federal Register.) This website provides an update on relevant components of the Federal Register relating to important national legislation.

www.wrightslaw.com/news/2003/idea.house.sidebyside.napas.pdf
This website, offered by the National Association of Protection and Advocacy Systems (NAPAS), has developed an analysis of IDEA changes.

Technical Assistance

Many forms of technical assistance are available for placement decision requirements. Here are some associations and governmental organizations that provide widespread support.

National Association of Developmental Disabilities Councils
1234 Massachusetts Avenue, NW, Suite 103
Washington, DC 20005
(202) 347-1234
email: naddc@igc.apc.org
URL: www.igc.apc.orc/NADDC/

National Information Center for Children and Youth with Disabilities (NICHCY)
P.O. Box 1492
Washington, DC 20013-1492
1-800-695-0285 or (202) 884-8200 (voice/TTY)
email: nichcy@aed.org

DEALING EFFECTIVELY WITH TRANSITION SERVICES IN THE INDIVIDUALIZED EDUCATION PROGRAM (IEP)

MICHAEL DUNSMORE

OVERVIEW

An IEP must include (a) a statement of the transition service needs of the student (under the applicable components of the student's IEP) that focuses on the student's courses of study (such as participation in advanced-placement courses or a vocational education program) for each student with a disability beginning at age 14 (or younger, if determined appropriate by the IEP team), and updated annually or (b) a statement of needed transition services for the student, including, if appropriate, a statement of the interagency responsibilities or any needed linkages for each student beginning at age 16 (or younger, if determined appropriate by the IEP team) [§300.347(b)].

Transition services are intended to prepare students to move from the world of school to the world of adult life outside of school. In planning what type of transition services a student needs, the IEP team should consider areas such as postsecondary education or vocational training, employment, independent living, and community participation. Transition services are a coordinated set of activities directly based on the specific needs of the student. These should be based on the student's needs and take into account their preferences, goals, and interests. Transition services should include direct instruction, community experiences, the development of employment, and other postschool adult living objectives. Again, determination of what is best is based on the student's needs. This can be enhanced and refined with the use of needs assessments done by teaching staff and parents, functional vocational assessments, and assessment of daily living skills and needs.

IDEA regulations now require that the IEP team "work with each student with a disability and the family to select courses of study that will be meaningful to the student's future and motivate the student to complete his or her education" (Bateman, 1994). IDEA requires transition services, and planning is part of a student's IEP starting at the age of 14. However, prior to this age the IEP team must consider instruction and experiences that will prepare the student for postsecondary training or education, employment, and independent living. At age 14 and thereafter every student with a disability must have an IEP containing specific transition-related goals and objectives that reflect the specific student's postschool goals.

In this chapter we explain the important issue of transition. We review federal requirements related to transition and key aspects of IEP meetings for a student who is over the age of fourteen. Our focus is on providing a practical understanding of special education services that facilitate the transition from school to adult life outside of school.

REGULATIONS

34 C.F.R. §300.29 Transition services

(a) As used in this part, *transition services* means a coordinated set of activities for a student with a disability that—

(1) Is designed within an outcome-oriented process, that promotes movement from school to postschool activities, including postsecondary education, vocational training, integrated employment (including supportive employment), continuing and adult education, adult services, independent living, or community participation:

(2) Is based on the individual student's needs, taking into account the student's preferences and interests; and

(3) Includes—

(i) Instruction;

(ii) Related services;

(iii) Community experiences;

(iv) Development of employment and other postschool adult living objectives; and

(v) If appropriate, acquisition of daily living skills and functional vocational evaluation.

(b) Transition services for students with disabilities may be special education, if provided as specially designed instruction, or related services, if required to assist a student with a disability to benefit from special education.

(Authority: 20 U.S.C. 1401(30))

The state is responsible for ensuring that districts provide students with disabilities 14 years of age and older a coordinated set of activities to facilitate transition. These activities must be:

- Designed within an outcome-oriented process to promote the movement from school to postschool activities.
- Based on a student's needs, taking into account the student's preferences and interests.

Secondary teachers *must* work with students and their families to identify specific interests, preferences, and needs before transition planning takes place. This exploration and identification process can take many forms. Ideally, transition planning needs to start as early as possible. Elementary teachers should be encouraged to start discussing transition with students and their parents. They can start the thought process and lay the groundwork for later transition activities. Activities can include:

- Career education activities.
- Exploration of work sites through job shadowing, internships, or paid competitive jobs.
- Exploration of vocational-technical offerings at the school, vocational school, or community college level.
- Interest and vocational inventories.
- Service learning projects, including projects using Internet research.

Someone in the school system should be assigned responsibility for collecting, analyzing, and systematically displaying this assessment data to be used in transition planning. The classroom teacher will be the point person in collecting data and coordinating direct instruction for transition planning. Often service learning and outside community-based projects will require the assistance of other personnel. This can be coordinated with the work-study or school-to-work coordinator. This person may already have needed contacts to develop job shadowing and other employment-related needs. Many districts are finding it useful to include a transition portfolio as part of the student's IEP. This makes it part of the yearly evaluation as well as a method to document the student's progress. The portfolio then can then go with the student upon graduation to be used by the outside agencies. This also documents when and where the student registers with outside, county, state, and federal agencies, which streamlines the enrollment process.

The IDEA Amendments of 1997 also require that a student of *any age* be invited to IEP planning if transition services are going to be discussed. Further, regulations state that throughout a student's education, IEPs must focus on providing instruction and experiences to enable the child/student to prepare for postschool activities. Accordingly, students need to learn what to do at their IEP meetings. Without previous instruction in terminology, roles, expectations, and the many other aspects of what occurs at these meetings, students often opt not to attend these meetings. Moreover, if they do attend, they are uninvolved and say little. This also is consistent with the parents. The process of how each student's plan of study is developed is almost as important as the plan itself. Simply developing a plan or course of study that lists grade-by-grade classes that a student needs to complete to graduate does not meet IDEA's intent nor help the student and or the parents in this process. The better prepared and informed the student and parents are, the better the meeting and the better the outcome. The earlier this process is started and better documented the sooner the student will receive needed services.

PUTTING PRINCIPLES INTO PRACTICE

A three-step process should be followed in the development of the transition plan. First, students need to discuss their interests with the IEP team. This discussion should include their skills and their limits. This process should include the family. Again, this should be started as early as possible. The earlier that the students' needs are recognized, the more instruction and preparation can be provided through the school and outside agencies. Assessing students' capabilities and needs should be an ongoing process. Next, the discussion must relate to the student preferences for possible postschool outcomes, including postschool educational opportunities. Finally, the student and IEP team must develop a course of study showing agreed-upon classes for each grade, as well as other school experiences that facilitate transition into the desired postschool outcome.

Planning Stages

As the student nears graduation, his or her transition plan should drive the IEP. It is important for the special education administrator to designate a "point" person within the staff who will oversee the transition steps. The following suggestions provide guidance in doing this.

Step One

- Officially introduce parents and families to the transition process when student turns 13 or moves from eighth to ninth grade.
- Begin to discuss what directions to explore for careers and other postschool activities.
- Begin to discuss what outcomes mean for transition.
- Prepare to survey parents and students as to their future goals.
- Introduce new key players to transition process (e.g., inside and outside agencies and representatives).
- Start gathering assessment information for planning.
- Develop a timeline and complete profile as information is gathered.
- Keep parents and student informed and current on goals and objectives of plan.

Step Two

- Continue to add information to profile throughout ninth and tenth grade, especially regarding assessment information such as career, vocational, skills, and personality inventories that are used to build IEP outcomes.
- Have needed releases signed by parents, student, and involved agencies to include personnel and visa versa.
- Bring agency representatives to school as class speakers.
- Offer agency information to parents.
- Continue to explore career options, including vocational assessment, training, work-based learning projects, community-based learning opportunities, job shadowing, service learning, and volunteering.
- Begin to explore postsecondary options, including support services, independent living skills, case management services, and self-advocacy.
- Address personal and social skills, self-advocacy, work readiness, and citizenship.
- Encourage open cases with the state mental health or mental retardation agencies where applicable.

During Step Two, many districts have case meetings where they bring all the local agencies together and discuss the students. This is an excellent method to develop relationships between the school and outside agencies. This is also a good time to invite parents and teachers to listen to presentations from the agencies. Most states have either state, regional, or county base service units that coordinate mental health/mental retardation services. The base service agencies are the primary point of contact for outside agency support to our students. Any discussions regarding the students will need to be done anonymously unless the parent is present.

Step Three
- Develop a Multi-Action Plan (MAP) as a blueprint for developing final IEP, utilizing all information to date.
- Follow through with all specific district actions needed for a successful transition from school to the real world.
- Encourage and monitor the student and follow up with the family.
- Review and update student and parental information regarding any changes with abilities, interest, aptitudes, and living arrangements.
- Continue to emphasize employability skills, independent living skills, self-advocacy skills, and social skills where needed.
- Provide assessment and evaluations as to ability and level in the previous areas.

To improve transition results for students with disabilities, you need to develop a cohesive transition team. Your team will require creativity and everyone's working together. There are many services in every community, and you will need to know what these are and how to access them. If team members cultivate relationships with their community resources and combine successful teamwork methods with the services available, transition planning can be easy and effective. Further, there is a variety of vocational and skill assessment instruments available that can be used to assist you and your staff in assessing student needs and abilities. Your school psychologist and/or guidance office should have these available. If not, your state department of education would be a starting point to getting any needed assessments.

Tips

- Evaluate transition services in your system/district.
- Look into establishing or strengthening your community transition team (i.e., public relations are important).
- Designate a staff person to make phone calls to develop new community agency contacts.
- Explore the potential of extra state or even foundation funding to share across agencies or for service development. This can include scholarship and grant money for both educational and technical postsecondary training.
- Set a meeting with staff members to learn each person's experience in transition.
- Develop a cooperative agreement with another agency or staff member specifying how to coordinate transition and to lead the team.

- Talk to other districts with successful transition programs.
- Encourage your staff to be creative in problem solving.
- Determine and use a variety of assessment tools that will help identify needs and document development and future goals.
- Distribute a student handbook to district parents. The handbook can describe local efforts and guidelines for transition. It can also include contact names and numbers for adult services providers. Most state, regional, or county agencies have these already completed. Contact your local, regional/county, or state agency.
- Distribute a student support services handbook to district staff members, helping to increase the staff members' awareness of various district transition services. Include a key contact person that can field staff questions about transition.
- Establish and maintain ongoing professional development activities in the district to help faculty and staff become aware of the continually changing need for transition services for students with disabilities. Network with service providers and other transition coordinators.

Pitfalls to Avoid

- Not monitoring the implementation of the transition components of the IEP. Ensure that the staff are provided the time and support to network with the appropriate agencies.
- Waiting until the "last minute" to assure that proper instruction can be provided as needed and determined in the student's IEP.
- Waiting too long to register the student is registered with the mental health and/or mental retardation agency (if they qualify). The earlier this is done, the easier it will be to coordinate community agency providers. If a student does not qualify, he or she can be referred to state rehabilitation and training agencies. These agencies are designed for employment placement and training and usually will not actively work with students until they graduate or leave school. However, they will start the process during the student's last year of school. A reminder when dealing with state employment agencies: Their goal is competitive employment or training that leads to competitive employment and is usually based on need.
- Waiting too long to address housing issues. Group homes or assisted living programs are extremely overcrowded and have long waiting lists as well as being very competitive for their open slots. Waiting until the student's last year in school almost assures that he or she will not have a slot once leaving the school setting. Again, starting the identification and need process earlier will enable the proper referrals to be done in a timely manner to assure the student gets the needed service.
- Not ensuring that the staff is providing the appropriate components of the transition IEP to the student. Proper documentation assures that all student needs have been provided and gives needed information to service providers. This assures the student will not repeat steps, causing a delay in service implementation.
- Not following up with adult services providers to ensure that the parents are getting the information they need to make informed decisions, as well as assuring that parents are also following through.

- Based on the previous bullet's responses, not making ongoing changes to how transition is implemented to ensure the appropriate steps are in place when necessary, for both parents and outside agencies.

Frequently Asked Questions about Transition Services

Addressing transition needs of students with disabilities requires knowledge of a wide range of service options. A review of the following frequently asked questions will illustrate this variety and provide answers for future use.

1. *How do the general education curriculum demands fit in with transition goal?*

The two are not mutually exclusive. Once the postschool outcomes are identified and the activities outlined, the student's needed instruction should come from applicable curriculum, whether that be general education curriculum or a specialized curriculum. *Example:* A high school sophomore has identified his career goal as that of an auto mechanic. With that long-term goal in mind, and based on his current academic skills, he is taking a consumer math course focusing on personal budgets, mortgages, insurance costs, calculating sales tax, calculating discounts, and other appropriate skills. His language arts course is also career oriented and includes emphasis on writing resumes, business letters, composing letters of introduction, and letters of complaint. Each of these courses is included in the general education curriculum, but his specially designed instructions include the methods, support services, and strategies needed for him to be successful in the career he has targeted.

2. *Why should we begin the IEP process with transition?*

For students ages 14 and older, or younger if the IEP team determines it to be appropriate, transition planning drives the IEP. The identified postschool outcomes then drive the instruction needed for the student. The overall document becomes a detailed plan for the student, describing his or her present levels and designing goals and objectives. This should be individualized for each specific student need. The need should be based on the goals of the student and his or her family and be data driven based on the results of student/family inventories and assessment testing. The idea is to prepare the student for success after high school.

3. *What about elementary students and agency involvement?*

To incorporate career awareness and exploration activities in an elementary setting, it is important to plant the seeds early and then build year to year. Take advantage of community resources and invite guest speakers from community businesses or organizations into the classroom. Independent living skills can be introduced at an elementary level through beginning activities such as cooking, meal planning, shopping, and home maintenance skills. When speaking with your student's parents, encourage them to promote their child's participation in community activities, such as scouts and community sports teams.

   If a child is already involved in an agency or support service, someone from the agency should be invited to the IEP meeting. Oftentimes agencies are not apt to be involved with elementary-age students; however, this is still a good time to start communication with various agencies in regard to anticipated needs. It is important to take every opportunity to inform parents of elementary-age students about the transition planning that will begin when their child approaches 14 years of age. Demonstrate the links between their children's current goals, objectives, your instruction/curriculum, and the eventual transition planning. This is also an ideal time, if applicable, to open a case with appropriate agencies such as those providing mental health or developmental disabilities services and to introduce families to community agencies and representatives. Start the networking process.

4. *How do you get the students to be more realistic about their futures?*

The primary recommendation is begin transition planning early. Teachers need to provide career awareness and career exploration activities, as well as personal exploration instruction, which will allow students to learn the needed skills, level training, and job availability for themselves. As the student grows and matures, the goal would be for his or her ability to realistically match personal strengths and preferences to the job requirements to increase as well. When we create a learning environment that enables students to come to this understanding on their own, we empower them to make more choices that are appropriate about their future. This also helps the students move beyond unrealistic employment expectations (i.e., professional athlete, pro wrestler). The student's personal growth and/or continued focus on long-term goals provide the opportunity for him or her to come to recognize the important role they play in their own IEPs and their educational programs. If students grow to understand their own impact on the IEP process, they are empowered to self-advocate and lead the direction of their education and future. Student/parent inventories and assessment help narrow the student interests, as well as assess limitations and capabilities. This helps guide the student through high school preparation and instruction. Also, this will help build a database of information if there are problems or pitfalls.

5. *How do we get the parents and students to be realistic about future goals?*

Some students and their families will have unrealistic expectations in regard to their abilities and future. Start early. Make transition an active component of your district's curriculum. If you begin when the student is middle-school age, there is time and instructional opportunities to not only allow him or her to personally research various careers, but to grow in awareness and understanding of his or her own interests, strengths, limitations, and preferences. Numerous tools can be utilized throughout the middle school years, such as vocational interest inventories, the followup activities included in the student's vocational evaluation report, community tours that focus on careers, job shadowing experiences, community members as classroom speakers, and web-based assignments. All of these activities will enable the student and his or her parents to gain better understanding of his or her own interests and strengths as well as learn detailed information about the requirements of specific career areas. And, as stated earlier, it will provide the student a database of information and resources that opens future doors.

6. *How are we to better involve the parents?*

One advantage of transition planning is that it enables all the team members to focus on where the student wants to be on completion of high school. This is an important marker in a child's life and often times triggers more parental involvement. Many IEP teams have had success with previously marginally involved parents when they see the advantages of transition planning and the possibilities for their children after graduation because of good transition planning and development. Another unfortunate reality is this is an opportunity for parents to separate from their children. Even this can be a positive with a creative team.

It is important that transition planning is essential if students in your district are going to be successful. This in itself breeds continued and future successes. Developing an effective team that develops maintains and follows the district policy and procedure will assure a quality and successful program for you and your students.

RESOURCES

An example of a transition plan is presented in this section. Organizations that will be helpful in building effective transition services for students with disabilities are also listed.

Example of a Transition Plan

III. TRANSITION PLANNING:

1. Will the student be 14 years of age or older during the term of this IEP?

    ____ No—(not necessary to complete this section)

    ____ Yes—Team must address the student's courses of study and how the course of study applies to components of the IEP.

    Student's courses of study:

    ____ Student will graduate based on district graduation requirements (attach student transcript).

    ____ Student will graduate based on IEP goals (attach student transcript)

    ____ Student will be enrolled in a Career and Technical program: _____

2. Will the student be 16 years of age or older during the term of this IEP, or is the student younger and in need of transition services as determined by the IEP team?

    ____ No—(not necessary to complete this section)

    ____ Yes—Team must address and complete this section.

DESIRED POSTSCHOOL OUTCOMES: Define and project the desired postschool outcomes as identified by the student, parent, and IEP team in the following areas. State how the services will be provided and person(s) responsible for coordinating these services.

(continued)

Example of Transition Plan *(continued)*

SERVICE	*HOW SERVICE IS PROVIDED*	*PERSON RESPONSIBLE*
Postsecondary Education/Training		
Employment		
Community Living **a) Residential**		
b) Participation		
c) Recreation/ Leisure		

STATEMENT OF COORDINATED TRANSITIONAL SERVICES AND ACTIVITIES NEEDED TO SUPPORT DESIRED POSTSCHOOL OUTCOMES:

The instructional areas should support the desired postschool outcomes. The following instructional areas should appear in the IEP as annual goals, short-term instructional objectives or benchmarks, and/or specially designed instruction. *For example (if appropriate): Instruction and Related Services, Community Experiences, Work-Based Training, Acquisition of Daily Living Skills, Functional Vocational Evaluation, and Adult Living.*

D. LINKAGES

List agencies that may provide services/support (before the student leaves the school setting):

_____   _____
Agency Name   Phone Number

_____   _____
Responsibilities/Linkages

Agency Name   Phone Number

Responsibilities/Linkages

Agency Name   Phone Number

Responsibilities/Linkages

Organizations

Alliance for Technology Access (ATA)
2175 East Francisco Blvd., Suite L
San Rafael, CA 94939
(415) 455-4575
email: atainfo@ataccess.org
URL: www.ataccess.org

**Americans with Disabilities Act Disability and Business Technical Assistance
Centers (DBTACs)**
1-800-949-4232
The DBTACs provide information, referral, TA, and training on the ADA.

The ARC National Employment Training Program
500 East Border, Suite 300
Arlington, TX 76010
1-800-433-5255 or (817) 277-0553
URL: www.thearc.org

Association of Higher Education and Disability (AHEAD)
P.O. Box 21192
Columbus, OH 43221-0192
(614) 488-4972
email: ahead@postbox.asc.ohio-state.edu
URL: www.ahead.org

**Council for Exceptional Children, Division on Career Development
and Transition**
1920 Association Drive
Reston, VA 20191-1589
(703) 620-3660 or (703) 264-9446
URL: www.cec.sped.org

Easter Seals National Headquarters
230 West Monroe, Suite 1800
Chicago, IL 60606
1-800-221-6827 or (312) 726-6200
email: webmaster@seals.com
URL: www.easterseals.org

HEATH Resource Center (National Clearinghouse on Postsecondary Education for Individuals with Disabilities)
One Dupont Circle, NW, Suite 800
Washington, DC 20036-1193
1-800-544-3284 or (202) 939-9320
email: heath@ace.nche.edu
URL: www.acenet.edu/programs/heath/home.html

Job Accommodation Network (JAN)
918 Chestnut Ridge Road, Suite 1, P.O. Box 6080
Morgantown, WV 26506-6080
1-800-526-7234 or (304) 293-7186
email: jan@jan.icdi.wvu.edu
URL: janweb.icdi.wvu.edu

Mobility International USA (MIUSA)
P.O. Box 10767
Eugene, OR 97440
(541) 343-1284
email: info@miusa.org

National Council on Independent Living (NCIL)
1916 Wilson Boulevard, Suite 209
Arlington, VA 22201
(703) 525-3406 or (703) 525-4153
email: neil@tsbbs08.tnet.com

National Information Center for Children and Youth with Disabilities (NICHCY)
P.O. Box 1492
Washington, DC 20013
1-800-695-0285 or (202) 884-8200
URL: www.nichcy.org

National Rehabilitation Information Center (NARIC)
8455 Colesville Road, Suite 935
Silver Springs, MD 20910-3319
1-800-346-2742 or (301) 588-9284 or (301) 495-5626
email: naric@capaccess.org
URL: www.cais.com/naric

National Transition Alliance for Youth with Disabilities
Transition Research Institute, University of Illinois
113 Children's Research Center, 51 Gerty Drive
Champaign, IL 61820
(217) 333-2325
email: nta@aed.org
URL: www.dssc.org/nta

President's Committee on Employment of People with Disabilities
1331 F Street, NW, Suite 300
Washington, DC 20004
(202) 376-6200 or (202) 376-6205
email: info@pcepd.gov
URL: www.pcepd.gov

Project Action
700 Thirteenth Street, NW, Suite 200
Washington, DC 20005
1-800-659-6428 or (202) 347-3066
email: project_action@nessdc.org
URL: www.projectaction.org

Research and Training Center on Independent Living
University of Kansas
4089 Dole Building
Lawrence, KS 66045-2930
(913) 864-4095
email: rtcil@kuhub.cc.ukans.edu
URL: www.lsi.ukans.edu/rtcil/rtcil.htm

School-to-Work Learning and Information Center
400 Virginia Avenue, SW, Suite 150
Washington, DC 20024
1-800-251-7236
email: stw-1c@ed.gov
URL: www.stw.ed.gov/index.htm

Technical Assistance Alliance for Parent Centers (PACER)
PACER Center
4826 Chicago Avenue
South Minneapolis, MN 55417-1098
1-888-248-0822 or (612) 827-7770
email: alliance@taalliance.org
URL: www.taalliance.org

U.S. Equal Employment Opportunity Commission
1801 L Street, NW
Washington, DC 20507
1-800-669-4000 or (202) 663-4900
URL: www.eeoc.gov

REFERENCES

Bateman, D. F. (1994). Transitional programming: Definitions, models, and practices. In A. Rotatori & J. O. Schwenn (Eds.), *Advances in special education* (Vol. 8, pp. 109–136). New York: JAI Press.

CHAPTER TEN

WORKING EFFECTIVELY WITH PARENT GROUPS

OVERVIEW

Shared parental participation and decision making is one the fundamental principles of IDEA 2004. Parents have many traditional rights that they can exercise on behalf of their children with disabilities. These rights are documented in the sections on major principles of the law, evaluation procedures, individualized education programs, least restrictive placement, and procedural due process; however, the expanded opportunities for shared decision making, as granted in IDEA 97 and reinforced in IDEA 2004, include offering parents the right to participate in discussions and join with educators in making decisions about the general improvement of the education of their children. This chapter will review information on forming and maintaining parent groups.

PUTTING PRINCIPLES INTO PRACTICE

It is a wise special education administrator who seeks to establish and maintain parent advisory groups that are proportionally representative of the special education population. How better to build positive parent/school relationships then by providing and sharing knowledge, experiences, training, and support to interested parents? "Okay," we can hear you wondering, how do I start a parent group? If one already exists when I start my administrative position, how can I build a relationship with the group? The following implementation plan consists of ideas to help you prepare to *establish* or *maintain* an active parent advisory group and facilitate its members' participation in improving education for their children.

Organizing New Groups

Organizing a new parent group can be a positive task for the special education administrator. It provides an opportunity to meet parents using a collaborative approach and build positive relationships. A good rule for organizing a parent group is to view it as an opportunity to connect with the parents you will be working with and to provide a positive forum for parent training and workshops. Many questions arise, including which parents to invite, what types of meetings or programs to offer, where the meetings will take place, and the list goes on. To begin, invite a core group of parents who are interested in the idea; then move on to more involved meetings once you get a group started.

Each school district or agency has different needs for parent groups; however, the following tips and ideas will help you to think about how to get a group started regardless of the size of the district or the purpose of the group.

Tips

- Ask your special education teachers to supply names of parents who may be interested in participating in the group.
- Contact those parents personally by phone and follow up with a written invitation for an "organizational meeting."
- Ensure that you invite parents that represent all grade levels and exceptionality categories. If possible, invite parents that represent students with exceptionalities at the early intervention level.
- Plan the first meeting with an agenda that focuses on establishing the goals/mission of the group and provides participants with clear objectives.
- Form specific committees that can address the varied needs of the group (e.g., invited speakers, needs assessment, public relations, etc.).
- Establish a specific monthly date, time, and meeting place.
- Provide the group with a comfortable and accessible meeting space.
- Provide light refreshments (coffee/punch, cookies).
- Provide babysitting services.
- Encourage special education teachers and a few administrators to attend. This will help give the parents the impression that school personnel are interested in parent projects and ideas.
- Strive to elect a parent leader(s) by the end of the first year.
- Help the group decide how they will be organized; review PTO governmental structures for a model.
- Fade your involvement in the overall organization and implementation of the group, as needed.
- Keep the meetings productive and positive.

Working with Existing Groups

When you are new to an administrative position or new to a school district, it is wise to acquaint yourself with how an existing group operates by contacting a group leader and setting an appointment to discuss the goals and functions of the group as it already operates. Whichever of the following tips seem the most relevant to you, begin addressing them as soon as possible. You want to make a good impression with the parent leadership contingent.

Tips

- Attend the first meeting to show your support and interest.
- Prepare a list of questions that will help you determine the "pulse" of the group and gain a sense of group dynamics.

- Ask what you can do to facilitate group goals at the district level.
- *Listen* to the tone of group and do not offer suggestions unless your opinion is directly solicited.
- Even if the group asks your opinion, defer until you have time to think about the question and get a sense of the district as a whole.
- Ask to see a list of activities the group sponsored or offered during the previous year or two to get a sense of its goals.
- Talk with district teachers and administrators about the parent group and its involvement in any programs or committees.
- Plan a trust-building activity (or getting-to-know-you activity) so that parents in the group get to know who you are as a person and as a supervisor. They want to know how you will deal with their children and if you have their best interests at heart.
- Do not attempt to "take over" the meeting, even if you have great ideas about programs or training for the group; during the first few meetings work at understanding the group.

Pitfalls to Avoid
- Not *budgeting* for special mailings, refreshments, speakers, babysitters, and any other possible expenses.
- Taking over the group. Although the need may vary from group to group, try not to take over; be visible and helpful, not overpowering.
- Not allowing time for parents to meet *without* school personnel. Perhaps set up a time (30 minutes) before or after the meeting for parents to meet without your presence.
- Not keeping yourself open and positive to parent ideas.

RESOURCES

Many parent resources are available online and in each individual *community and state* that will be helpful to you and your parent groups; however, the following is a list of national parent resources that may be helpful when forming parent advisory groups.

Advocates for Special Kids
www.advocatesforspecialkids.org
The Advocates for Special Kids (ASK) website is focused on special education issues and advocacy for children with special needs. ASK is a nonprofit organization dedicated to helping parents with special education. ASK believes parents need, and are entitled to, accurate and complete information that will allow them to make informed decisions about their children's education. ASK's goal is to ensure that parents are fully informed and empowered to advocate on behalf of their children; that educators are fully informed, well trained, and empowered to take appropriate steps to address the needs of ALL children in their classrooms; and that school districts are aware that parents and the community insist on equal partnership in ensuring that our schools are the best they can be—for ALL our children.

Disability Resources Monthly (DRM)

www.disabilityresources.org

This website provides access to the DRM WebWatcher, an easy-to-use online subject guide to disability resources on the Internet and the DRM Regional Resource Directory, a guide to state and local agencies and organizations.

Families and Advocates Partnership for Education (FAPE)

www.fape.org

The Families and Advocates Partnership for Education (FAPE) project aims to improve educational outcomes for children with disabilities. It links families, advocates, and self-advocates, communicating the new focus of the Individuals with Disabilities Education Act (IDEA 2004) and represents the needs of six million children with disabilities and their families. FAPE is one of four projects funded by the U.S. Department of Education to reach parents, administrators, service providers, and policymakers nationwide with information about implementing IDEA. Because a primary goal of the IDEA is to ensure that children with disabilities receive a quality education, this website provides information on IDEA legislation and accompanying laws, relevant publications, partnership information, and a news line that supports families of children with disabilities.

Family Village

www.familyvillage.wisc.edu

Family Village is a global website community that integrates information, resources, and communication opportunities on the Internet for persons with cognitive and other disabilities, for their families, and for those that provide them with service and support. The website, sponsored in part by The Joseph P. Kennedy, Jr., Foundation and Mitsubishi Electric America Foundation, includes informational resources on specific diagnoses, communication connections, adaptive products and technology, adaptive recreational activities, education, worship, health issues, disability-related media and literature to name a few.

Family Voices

www.familyvoices.org

Family Voices is a national, grassroots clearinghouse for information and education concerning the health care of children with special health needs. Family Voices believes that children with special health care needs face common problems caused by fundamental inadequacies in the health care system. The Family Voices website provides member families with advocacy information focused on the following goals: (1) Every child deserves quality primary and specialty health care that is affordable and within geographic reach; (2) families are the core of this nation's health system; (3) quality health care is family centered, community based, coordinated, and culturally competent; (4) health benefits must be flexible and guided by what children need; (5) strong family–professional relationships improve decision making, enhance outcomes, and assure quality; and (6) families practice cost-effectiveness and expect the same in health care. Links to ten regional coordinators are available through the website as well as other pertinent health care links.

LD On-Line

www.ldonline.org

LD On-Line asserts itself as the leading website on learning disabilities, dyslexia, attention deficit disorder, attention deficit hyperactivity disorder, special education, learning differences, and other related issues for parents and teachers of children and youth with learning disabilities. LD Online is a service of the Learning Project at WETA, Washington, DC, and other partners that include the Eisner Foundation, Inc., Schwab Learning, The Emily Hall Tremaine Foundation, The Law Firm of McKenna Long & Aldridge, and The Charles Lafitte Foundation. This interactive website includes recent news on learning disabilities and related issues, parent and teacher-friendly links, ask Dr. Larry Silver, legal briefs, first person essays, and ask the teaching expert, to name a few. LD Online also features artwork and writing selections from children and youth with learning disabilities.

National Dissemination Center for Children and Youth with Disabilities (NICHCY)

www.nichcy.org

The National Information Center for Children and Youth with Disabilities is the national information and referral center that provides information on disabilities and disability-related issues. Anyone can use the free NICHCY services, including families, educators, administrators, journalists, and students. The NICHCY website offers information about specific disabilities, special education and related services for children in school, individualized education programs (IEPs), parent materials, disability organizations, professional associations, education rights and what the law requires, early intervention services, transition to adult life and much more. In addition, the website provides information specialists who are available to answer questions in English and Spanish about areas of interest or concern via email. The website offers publications and fact sheets on specific disabilities that can be downloaded at no cost, and experts can put interested parties in touch with disability organizations around the country that can offer additional assistance and information.

National Parent Network on Disabilities (NPND)

www.npnd.org

The National Parent Network on Disabilities is a nonprofit organization dedicated to empowering parents. NPND is located in Washington, DC, and has the unique capability to provide members with the most up-to-date information on the activities of all three branches of government that affect individuals with disabilities and their families. After subscribing, the NPND website supplies members with *The Friday Facts,* a publication dedicated to the "inside scoop" on key legislative news, which NPND asserts is "quick, easy, and informative to read." In addition, the NPND is the first national-level umbrella organization designed to unite individual parents, family members, grassroots parents groups, statewide parent centers, and coalitions from across the nation, state, and local levels that represent the interests of individuals with disabilities.

Parent Advocacy Coalition for Educational Rights (PACER)

www.pacer.org

Founded in 1977, the mission of PACER is to expand opportunities and enhance the quality of life of children and young adults with disabilities and their families based on the idea of *parents helping parents.* The organization offers assistance to individual families, workshops and materials for parents and professionals, and leadership in securing a free appropriate public education for ALL students across the nation. The website provides legislative information and updates, relevant articles, advocacy training information, technology links, and transition to work and employment strategies for youth with disabilities. Whether a parent suspects his or her toddler needs special assistance or his or her teenager needs support in preparing for the workplace, the PACER website can help parents identify the resources and services available to help families learn and grow through all phases of childhood and all disabilities.

Parent Training and Information Centers

www.parentpals.com

Parent Pals/Special Education Guide is a special education community sponsored by Ameri-Corp Speech and Hearing whose goal is to provide special education and gifted information, continuing education, support, weekly tips, games, book resources, and news and views for parents and professionals. Therapists, audiologists, teachers, nurses, and physicians contribute information on ALL disability categories.

Technical Assistance Alliance for Parent Groups

www.taalliance.org

The Alliance is an innovative project that focuses on providing technical assistance for establishing, developing, and coordinating Parent Training and Information Projects and Community Parent Resource Centers under the Individuals with Disabilities Education Act (IDEA). Parent Training and Information Centers (PTIs) and Community Parent Resource Centers (CPRCs) in each state provide training and information to parents of infants, toddlers, children, and youth with disabilities and to professionals who work with these children and assists in helping parents to participate more effectively with professionals in meeting the educational needs of children and youth with disabilities. The goal of the Parent Centers is to work to improve educational outcomes for ALL children and youth with disabilities. The website offers federal news, provides IDEA alerts, centers of expertise, web links and resources, data collections and surveys, and a directory of resources as listed below:

> **Alliance Coordinating Office**
> PACER Center
> 8161 Normandale Blvd.
> Minneapolis, MN 55437-1044
> (952) 838-9000 (voice)
> (952) 838-0190 (TTY)
> (952) 838-0199 (fax)
> 1-888-248-0822

email: alliance@taalliance.org
URL: www.taalliance.org

Region 1
Statewide Parent Advocacy Network (SPAN)
35 Halsey Street, 4th Floor
Newark, NJ 07102
(973) 642-8100
www.spannj.org

Region 2
Exceptional Children's Assistance Center (ECAC)
907 Barra Row, Suite 102/103
Davidson, NC 28036
(704) 892-1321
www.ecac-parentcenter.org

Region 3
Family Network on Disabilities of Florida, Inc.
2735 Whitney Road
Clearwater, FL 33760
(727) 523-1130
www.fndfl.org

Region 4
Ohio Coalition for the Education of Children with Disabilities
Bank One Building
165 West Center Street, Suite 302
Marion, OH 43302
(740) 382-5452
www.ocecd.org

Region 5
PEAK Parent Center, Inc.
611 North Weber, Suite 200
Colorado Springs, CO 80903
(719) 531-9400
www.peakparent.org

Region 6
Matrix Parent Network and Resource Center
94 Galli Drive, Suite C
Novato, CA 94949
(415) 884-3535
www.matrixparents.org

......

CHAPTER ELEVEN

EFFECTIVELY SUPPORTING WITHIN DISTRICT AND SCHOOL TRANSITIONS

MARY BETH ROTH

OVERVIEW

During a typical educational career, most students transition within and between schools many different times (Queen, 2002). All students experience several transitions as part of going to school (e.g., leaving home for preschool or kindergarten and moving from elementary to middle school, middle school to high school, and high school to postschool opportunities) and some experience many more (e.g., students with disabilities, students from diverse backgrounds living in areas of high mobility). Often, transitions are marked by a variety of special events as each level welcomes incoming students with programs and orientations. For example, elementary teachers invite rising kindergartners and parents to Beginners' Day each spring. Middle school teachers welcome field trips of rising sixth graders. High school teachers and staff conduct Open House and Registration Night for rising ninth graders. And all schools—preschools, elementary, middle, high schools, and universities—mark the completion of the terminal grade with pomp, circumstance, and ceremony in varying degrees. Parents, students, and the school community celebrate the conclusion of the students' success at one level and promotion to the next by partaking in activities marked by symbolism and tradition. This chapter will address transitions specific to students with disabilities within and between schools as a part of children's school careers. Supporting transitions within and between schools is important for special education administrators; thus, specific recommendations for facilitating smooth transitions for students with disabilities will be addressed.

WHAT WE KNOW ABOUT WITHIN DISTRICT AND SCHOOL TRANSITIONS

A variety of interpretations exist as to the meaning of transition in the educational process. To some, transition reflects a one-time set of activities undertaken by programs, families, and children at the end of the year. To others, transitions reflect ongoing efforts to link children's natural environments to school environments. Last, others define grade or school transition as the manifestation of the developmental principles of continuity; that is, creating pedagogical, curricular, and/or disciplinary approaches that transcend and continue between programs (Kagan & Neuman, 1998). Kraft-Sayre and Pianta (2000) describe transitions as the process that all partners experience as students move from one level to the next rather than a single event that happens to a child. Regardless of the focal point, transitions from classroom to classroom or school to school are increasingly being recognized as critical periods in the movement through public education in the United States, especially for students with disabilities who often require prolonged transition periods to meet both academic and social success (Brolin & Loyd, 2004).

Due to the noted decrease in achievement, motivation, and self-esteem at the entry grade of each educational level, researchers have taken a closer look at the transition and transfer process. Typically, they have found losses, at all levels, of academic achievement as students move into their first year in the new school (Alspaugh, 1998; Perry & Weinstein, 1998). Academic achievement at the kindergarten level is widely attributed to early intervention programs; however, initial gains sometimes fade as students move through the primary grades. In the National Head Start Demonstration study, Bohan-Baker and Little (2002) suggested that local commitments to effective transition between local sites appeared to combat the "fade-out effect" with respect to student achievement. Also, Ramey and Ramey (1999) found that children who received additional environmental support as they moved into and through kindergarten and the early elementary grades performed better in reading and math. For students with disabilities, any loss of academic or social/emotional gains must be minimized by special education administrators; thus a smooth transition through the early elementary years is critical (Patton, Cronin, & Jairrels, 1997).

Losses in academic achievement have been especially prominent at the entry grade to middle school and in the ninth grade of high school. Alspaugh (1998) found achievement losses in students who transitioned to sixth grade from elementary school. These losses were more significant in students who attended a large middle school that pulled sixth graders from multiple elementary schools rather than students who made a linear transition to one middle school. At the high school level, achievement losses were more significant for those ninth-grade students who came from middle schools rather than K-8 schools. The experience of making a previous transition did not moderate achievement loss during the transition to high school, and thus these students encountered a double-jeopardy situation. Many teachers of students with disabilities report a more serious loss of achievement during the transition to high school (Brolin & Loyd, 2004).

At the middle school level, Mullins and Irvin (2000) discovered that initially student self-concept and self-esteem decreases as students make the adjustment to new friends and surroundings. Researchers have documented the lowest self-esteem ratings and highest self-consciousness ratings from subjects between the ages of 12 and 14. As students transition into high school, low self-esteem often results from the stress of rigorous academic demands and social pressures. This can lead to further problems that include alcohol and drug abuse, poor attendance, and dropping out of school (Berliner, 1993; Mullins & Irvin, 2000).

Student motivation and behavior are two additional factors that transition researchers have studied. At all school levels, student motivation and behavior become even more of a problem if the welcoming school does not implement strategies and techniques to assist these students. Eccles and colleagues (1993) found that classroom environmental factors such as teacher discipline and control practices, teacher–student relations, teachers' sense of efficacy, opportunities for student decision making, and ability grouping have an effect on student motivation and behavior. Schools that address these issues through transition programs that involve students, staff, and parents have demonstrated gains in student performance and have reduced dropout rates by 20 percent (Smith, 1999).

School transitions in education are important to the academic and social-emotional growth of the individual. Researchers have offered a variety of explanations for the negative changes that occur as a result of these transitions. Many attribute this to the lack of effective transition programs that involve communication and planning between the sending and receiving agencies (Kagan & Neuman, 1998; Weldy, 1995). Others suggest that the changing nature of educational environments experienced by children could be responsible for the declines associated with transition. Children who arrive at school to find developmentally appropriate, child-centered, and well-managed classrooms are more likely to like school and attend regularly, grow academically, and involve their families in their education (Eccles et al., 1993; Ramey & Ramey, 1999).

As a result of the negative aspects of student transitions, many transition researchers over the past decade have called for more comprehensive approaches to these times of change. The more comprehensive approach is built upon a commitment to teamwork and collaboration where educators, parents, and students work together in designing and implementing transition programs. Successful transition programs include the following attributes:

1. A sensitivity to the anxieties accompanying a move to a new school setting.
2. The importance of parents and teachers as partners in this effort.
3. The recognition that becoming comfortable in a new school setting is an ongoing process not a single event (Bohan-Baker & Little, 2002; Cooke, 1995; NMSA, 2002).

How Transferring Affects Students

Both young adolescents and parents experience a wide variety of emotions, behaviors, and concerns during the elementary to middle school transition period. The middle school transition is considered a major stepping-stone to adulthood as students enter adolescence and develop their own identity in a more mature and demanding environment (Elias, 2002; National Middle School Association, 2002). The transition from elementary to middle school may be especially challenging because it often involves both significant school and personal change. These personal physical, emotional, and social changes that occur in puberty are often associated with heightened emotionality, conflict, and defiance of adults. Adolescent children experience these changes at different times and at varying rates, thus making the middle school transition difficult both externally and internally (Akos, 2002).

Fear.   Students experience a variety of fears even before they enter the middle school doors. Researchers have found that new middle school students' greatest fear is getting lost, followed by difficulties finding and opening lockers, and bringing materials to the right class at the right time. Transitioning middle school students are also worried about finding bathrooms and getting on the right bus when it is time to go home (Akos, 2002; Elias, 2002; Shumacher, 1998). Additionally, Akos discovered that students were concerned about getting bullied by older students and doing well in classes. These concerns are often compounded by the fact that students must adjust to traveling longer distances to school, eating in a larger cafeteria, and changing clothes in a locker room (Elias, 2002).

Akos (2002) surveyed sixth graders at mid-year to determine what they perceived to be the most difficult aspects of middle school. Twenty-six percent of the participants responded with the fear of getting lost and 13 percent responded that making friends was difficult. Other answers included learning your class schedule and getting to class on time. Students also indicated in the survey results those who helped them the most with the transition to middle school. The top response was friends, followed by teachers and parents.

Friendship.   Friendship functions as an important social support when students face stressful events such as making the transition from elementary to middle school. As indicated by Akos (2002), making friends and receiving their help was critical in the students' perception of a successful transition. Forgan and Vaughn (2000) found that friendships played an important role in the middle school transition. Students were able to make more friends in middle school due to having different class periods and having the opportunity to participate in extracurricular activities. Students viewed the opportunity to make new friends as a positive experience and indicated that this helped them in adjusting to the new school. It has also been noted that students who perceived themselves as more capable of making friends prior to the school transition were indicated to be less vulnerable to the potentially damaging effects of peer strain (difficulty with peers) during the early part of the transition. Young adolescents' abilities to negotiate the challenges of the middle school peer environment and to view difficulties in peer relationships as temporary are important assets in making a smooth adjustment to middle school (Fenzel, 2000).

Academic Factors.   Researchers have found that student achievement, motivation, self-esteem, and behavior are most often negatively affected after students transition to middle school. As reported earlier, significant losses in academic achievement have been found at sixth grade as compared to students who attended K-8 schools. An additional study compared students with and without a learning disability (LD) at traditional middle schools and at K-8 schools. Anderman (1998) found achievement differences in math and science between eighth-grade adolescents with and without LD are much smaller in schools where students do not experience transition until at least the ninth grade. Thus, students placed in relatively small cohort groups for long spans of time tend to experience more desirable educational outcomes (Alspaugh, 1998; Anderman, 1998).

In a study on the transition effects of school grade-level organization upon student achievement as students make the transition from self-contained to departmentalized classes, Alspaugh and Harting (1995, 1997) discovered consistent achievement losses for grade-level transitions. Schools with configurations of K-4, K-5, K-6, K-7, and K-8 were studied. However, schools tended to recover from the achievement losses in years following the transition. Also, middle schools that grouped students into interdisciplinary teams performed significantly better on standardized achievement tests overall than schools that were departmentalized.

The decline in academic achievement appears highly related to academic motivation (Mullins & Irvin, 2000). In considering motivation, researchers have asked two questions to capture the most important motivational constructs: "Can I succeed on this task?" and "Do I want to succeed on this task?" Constructs relevant to the first question include students' self-concepts of ability, expectancies for success, efficacy beliefs, and perceived control. The second question relates to students' valuing of achievement, goals or purposes for achievement, and anticipated effort (Eccles et al., 1993). Anderman and Midgley (1998) found that as students moved to middle school there was an increased focus on ability goals in both math and English rather than the task-oriented focus of the elementary level. This resulted in a significant decrease in academic efficacy across the transition from fifth to sixth grade with some improvement in seventh grade.

Interactions.   Eccles and colleagues (1993) have determined that the quality of the teacher–student relationship is associated with students' academic motivation and attitudes toward school. Students who moved from a supportive elementary teacher to a low supportive teacher in middle school showed a decline in ratings of intrinsic value, perceived usefulness, and value of subject matter. Low-achieving students were particularly at risk for declining motivation when they moved to less facilitative middle school environments. Eccles also suggests that declines in motivation, which often are associated with the early adolescent period, are more due to the mismatch between students' needs and the opportunities afforded them in traditional middle schools.

Students at the middle school level have the need for autonomy and making their own decisions. Researchers in this area indicate that students often do not have these opportunities (Mullins & Irvin, 2000). Midgley and Feldlaufer (1987) studied student decision making at the transition from sixth grade to junior high and found that teachers and students differed in their perceptions about the extent to which students were allowed to make decisions in the classroom. Students actually indicated that they had more decision-making ability at the elementary level. Eccles and colleagues (1993) found that both teachers and students felt students had fewer decision-making opportunities at the middle school level, demonstrating a growing lack of congruence between students' desires and the opportunities available to them. Students who perceived their teachers as putting constraints on their preferred level of participation showed the largest and most consistent declines in their interest in math between elementary school and seventh grade. If the design of the classroom environment is conducive to the developmental level of the students, the declines often seen in early adolescents' decline in academic motivation can be avoided (Eccles et al., 1993; Mullins & Irvin, 2000). Teachers throughout the middle school years can provide opportunities for every child to experience social and academic success by utilizing classroom strategies that promote social development as well as those that address individual learning needs (NMSA, 2000).

Self-Esteem.   Many educational researchers have also been interested in the development of self-esteem through the adolescent period. Self-esteem has been defined as the individual's overall evaluation of himself or herself or how one feels about oneself (Harter, 1990). Self-esteem is an additional factor that can be negatively impacted by the transition to middle school. Wigfield and Eccles (1994) reported that children's self-esteem decreased significantly as students transitioned from elementary school to seventh grade in junior high school. However, students' self-esteem increased during the seventh-grade year, and the drop in self-esteem in the fall of the seventh-grade year was not long lasting. This drop could be attributed to the students' reaction to a new and different environment and adjusting to being the youngest students in the school rather than the oldest.

Researchers have also revealed that students who have positive self-concepts in academic and social domains at the end of their elementary year have a more positive adjustment period in junior high. Predictors in these domains include math ability, physical attractiveness, and peer social skills. Feelings of self-worth are enhanced by social support from close friends, which indicates that developing close relationships as resources for students to draw on benefits the process of adapting to a new school. Finally, students who showed increases in self-esteem gains in the seventh grade, also indicated that their parents were attuned to them and that they felt autonomous in decision-making situations. As students transition throughout the school year and face additional school strains related to academic demands, the role of the parent becomes important as a support resource for coping. Parents have been shown to exert a strong influence on adolescents with respect to issues surrounding the environment and attainment (Fenzel, 2000; Lord & Eccles, 1994).

Behavior.   Student behavior is also a factor that can negatively affect the student transition process to middle school. Meekos (1989) found that students who were reported as the most aggressive and disruptive in elementary school recorded more negative attitudes toward their new school, and the responses became even more negative as the year progressed. Students new to middle school are faced with learning new school rules and routines and must function in different physical and social environments. While some students reportedly enjoy the additional freedom acquired in middle schools, others have difficulty following the rules and procedures that accompany it (Akos, 2002; Perkins & Gelfer, 1995).

It is evident that as students transition from elementary to middle school, social, developmental, and academic experiences are affected. Students are required to adjust to what they see as new settings, structures, and expectations. This occurs conjunctively with the changes students are experiencing both physically and emotionally as they transition from childhood to adolescence. Therefore, this complicated period of adjustment often results in declines in achievement, performance motivation, and self-perceptions (NMSA, 2002). While little research has focused on within-district and school transfer experiences of students with disabilities, there is no reason to believe that their experiences will be different than their peers without disabilities.

PUTTING PRINCIPLES INTO PRACTICE

The middle years are the most critical in the overall transition process for students. This adjustment is not only difficult because of the early adolescent years, but also because of the importance of receiving and sending students successfully on both sides of the middle level (Weldy, 1995). A great deal of literature as well as transition studies exist that have stated a need for comprehensive approaches to help facilitate the transition process from elementary school to middle school. The National Middle School Association in conjunction with the

National Association of Elementary School Principals have developed a position statement that urges principals, teachers, school counselors, parents, and students from both levels to work together in the planning and implementing of strategies that will directly address students' concerns and ease the transition to middle school (NMSA, 2002).

Critical Elements

In a three-year transition study sponsored by the National Association of Secondary School Principals (NASSP), the American Association of College Registrars and Admissions Officers, and National Association of College Admissions Counselors, four elements were named and defined as being critical to the transition. These critical elements are communication, cooperation, consensus, and commitment (Weldy, 1995).

Communication. Communication is defined as the process of meeting with and talking to the various groups of people involved in the transition process (Weldy, 1995). One component of this process is the transmission of information between the sending and receiving schools. A planning team made up of teachers, administrators, specialists, and parents from both groups should be developed. This team should meet several times to acquire information about the best procedures for transition planning and to generate strategies for implementation. Researchers have recommended a variety of practices that involve communication. These include:

1. The sending schools should provide receiving schools with comprehensive information about each student, including subject area achievement, special needs, and behavior problems.
2. Both sending and receiving should provide several activities that will involve students, parents, teachers, and staff that enhance collaboration and the sharing of information in the transition process.
3. The receiving schools should provide feedback to the sending schools regarding the success of students at the new schools in terms of achievement and social adjustment (Perkins & Gelfer, 1995; Schumaker, 1998; Weldy, 1995).

Cooperation. It is essential that key people on both sides of the transition process plan together the activities that are designed to help students navigate through the transition process. These people include administrators, teachers, counselors, parents, and students (Weldy, 1995). In order for the goals and objectives to be accomplished, these individuals must work together as a team. Each member brings a different perspective and acts as a source of expertise for the development of the transition plan (Perkins & Gelfer, 1995). The following guidelines have been developed and identified to ensure that the cooperation element is included in the transition planning process:

1. Planning the transition should be conducted in a systematic, timely, and collaborative style. For students with disabilities and their parents, this plan should begin earlier than nondisabled peers (Brolin & Loyd, 2004).
2. Meetings should have planned agendas that are concise and structured, with nothing hidden or predetermined.

3. Meeting times should be convenient and not infringe on participants' other duties and responsibilities.
4. Incentives should be provided for committee participants in the form of release time, recognition, amenities, and professional rewards.
5. Family members should receive information to help their children adapt and be given opportunities to provide input to the transition team.
6. The current and subsequent programs should collaborate and provide the necessary experiences for the new year (Gallagher, Maddox, & Edgar, 1984; Weldy, 1991).

Including these guidelines in the transition planning process will ensure that cooperation takes place between constituents and results in a transition plan that best meets the needs of the adolescent child.

Consensus. In order to provide strong transitions for students, it is necessary for the key people involved to agree on the goals and objectives of the program and what strategies and activities should be undertaken. Participants must come to consensus on what will be changed, how and when activities will be implemented, and who will responsible (Weldy, 1995). The planning team should meet first to develop a written strategic transition plan that includes the identification of goals and objectives of the transition process (Perkins & Gelfer, 1995). Potential problems should also be included when addressing the goals. This leads to the next step in the process, which is the formulation of specific activities, procedures, individual responsibilities, and timelines of the transition plan. Weldy (1995) found that consensus was not difficult to accomplish when site-based management principles were used in the determination of goals, objectives, and strategies. Support and agreement from top-level administration is necessary for continued success; however, the planning and execution of the plan will depend on parents, teachers, counselors, and parents.

Commitment. The first three elements will fall short of the strength needed in transition programs if those who have communicated and planned do not have the commitment to carry out the plans. Once the transition team has developed a written plan, the team must gain school support and commitment from the participating teachers. The written strategies should be shared with all those in the school community involved in the transition process. Staff development for teachers, administrators, and counselors should take place to discuss the goals, potential problems, activities, procedures, and significance of the program (Perkins & Gelfer, 1995; Weldy, 1991). Commitment also requires that the transition program include an evaluation component. This gives those involved in the transition process the opportunity to assess program goals and strategies with continuous improvement as the ultimate focal point.

Transition Tips

Researchers have recommended a variety of transition activities that can ease the process of students acclimating to a new school environment. Jones (2001) suggests that the following activities be implemented in the spring of the fifth-grade year before students start sixth grade at the middle school level, although these tips can also apply to many grade-level transitions:

1. Establish a buddy system or mentoring program between elementary and middle school students.
2. Send student letters from team teachers for next year.
3. Plan one or more visits with the team including the counselor, administrator, teachers, and middle school students to the feeder school.
4. Send copies of yearbook, school newspapers, and any other informative background materials to feeder schools.
5. Plan a field trip to middle school for fifth graders to tour the school and participate in an orientation program.

During the summer additional activities can take place to continue the spring transition efforts including:

1. Sending home letters and updates welcoming students and families and inviting them to school activities.
2. Parent Teacher Organizations making welcome calls to each new family.
3. Contacting the local cable company about airing a segment about the middle school.
4. Hosting a summer open house or school visitation. (Jones, 2001; Schumacher, 1998)

Jones (2001), Elias (2002), and Cooke (1995) recommend that these activities occur during the first few days of sixth grade:

1. Stagger school opening so that only one grade is in the building on the first day. This allows the entire staff to help that grade level.
2. Address logistics such as lockers and schedules immediately and practice with students with disabilities.
3. Be sure students know the guidance counselors and how to contact them.
4. Schedule early and periodic individual and/or group counseling visits for new students.
5. Distribute the school handbook and review information (rules, cafeteria procedure, schedules, etc.). Students with disabilities would benefit from frequent reviews throughout the first month of school.

To ensure that students continue to feel comfortable throughout the year, these activities are recommended for the fall semester:

1. Guidance counselors should conduct one full period of group guidance with each class by the end of the first month of school.
2. The librarian should conduct orientation sessions for the media center.
3. The administration or guidance office should conduct special sessions for parents on related middle school topics. (Cooke, 1995; Schumacher, 1998)

A Dozen Facts to Know about Transitions

Most students in the United States progress through at least four transitional periods during the academic cycle. Transitions typically occur as students move into kindergarten, middle school, high school, and postsecondary study. A plethora of research studies have been undertaken, and researchers have found that transitions can have a negative impact on student achievement, motivation, self-esteem, and behavior. Students initially demonstrate declines in developmental areas in the early part of the transition process; however, most rebound at a later point and eventually show gains in both achievement and self-esteem. Researchers have reported similar results at all transition levels; however, effects are particularly pronounced for students moving into middle grades.

Students entering middle school arrive with a variety of uncertainties and fears. Students were found to be particularly worried about getting lost, dealing with a lock or locker, making new friends, and being bullied by older students. Several factors affect the ease of the transition including the students' self-esteem level before the transition, peer support, parent support, and the nature of the middle school environment. Schools and classrooms should be supportive to students and administrators, and teachers should acknowledge the impact of peer relationships as well as the nature of student/teacher relationships on ongoing performance. Schools organized by teams and composed of teachers that are nurturing and supportive, demonstrate better academic growth and achievement across transition years than schools that do not (Queen, 2003).

Educators have developed transition models that included specific recommendations for implementing transition programs. Elements that are essential to successful implementation include communication, consensus, cooperation, and commitment between all parties involved. The transition process from elementary to middle school should be ongoing and include specific goals, objectives, and strategies that meet the developmental and academic needs of the adolescent child. Incorporating these components into the process eases the transition and reduces the risk for losses in achievement, motivation, and self-esteem.

Students with and without disabilities entering a new school look forward to having more choices and making new and more friends; however, they also are concerned about being picked on and teased by older students, having harder work, making lower grades, and getting lost in a larger, unfamiliar school. As they make the transition into high school, many experience a decline in grades and attendance (Barone, Aguirre-Deandreis, & Trickett, 1991; Queen, 2002; U.S. Department of Education, 2002; Ysseldyke, Algozzine, & Thurlow, 2000), and they view themselves more negatively and experience an increased need for friendships. By the end of tenth grade, as many as 6 percent drop out of school (Herzog, Morgan, Diamond, & Walker, 1996; Queen, 2002). For middle school students, including those who have been labeled "gifted" or "talented and high-achieving," the transition into high school can be an unpleasant experience (Phelan, Yu, & Davidson, 1994; Queen, 2002; Ysseldyke et al., 2000).

When middle school students participate in high school transition programs with diverse activities, generalized benefits are observed and administrators report that they expect fewer of their students to drop out before graduation when the school provided supportive advisory group activities or responsive remediation programs (cf. Queen, 2002). On balance, evidence supporting the need for transition programs is straightforward and knowing a few facts goes a long way in effectively supporting transitions for all students (cf. Queen, 2003):

- Fact 1: The lower the students' grades drop during ninth-grade transition, the higher the students' probability of dropping out of school.

- Fact 2: Students who fail during the transition and drop out of school experience life-long difficulties physically, socially, emotionally, and economically.
- Fact 3: The larger the high school, the greater the negative impact of transition on ninth-grade students.
- Fact 4: Students, once in school, who experience two or more transitions prior to ninth grade have a greater probability of quitting high school.
- Fact 5: High school dropout rates are higher for students who attend middle schools than for students who attend K–8 schools.
- Fact 6: Ninth-grade students' adjustments to high school are complicated by their perceptions of a bigger school, different environment, changed class schedule, and smaller classes.
- Fact 7: Fear of getting lost in the high school building is by far the number one fear of ninth-grade students.
- Fact 8: Ninth-grade students view high school teachers as being less helpful than middle school teachers.
- Fact 9: Ninth-grade students must have at least one adult in their lives for genuine support in order to become academically and socially successful.
- Fact 10: Ninth-grade students who have negative experiences during the transitional period have poor attendance, low grades, and fewer friends. They tend to become behavior problems and have greater vulnerability to negative peer influence.
- Fact 11: Dropout rates increase for poorly transitioned students, especially minority students, in schools using high stakes testing.
- Fact 12: Social and economic factors negatively impact graduation rates, especially in large urban areas.

REFERENCES

Akos, P. (2002, June). Student perceptions of the transition to middle school. *Professional School Counseling, 5*(5), 339–346.

Alspaugh, J. W. (1998, September/October). Achievement loss associated with the transition to middle school and high school. *Journal of Educational Research, 92*(1), 20–26.

Alspaugh, J. W., & Harting, R. D. (1995). Transition effects of school grade-level organization on student achievement. *Journal of Research and Development in Education, 28*(3), 145–149.

Alspaugh, J. W., & Harting, R. D. (1997). Effects of team teaching on the transition to middle school. *Spectrum, 15,* 9–14.

Anderman, E. M. (1998, March/April). The middle school experience: Effects on the math and science achievement of adolescents with LD. *Journal of Learning Disabilities, 31*(2), 128–139.

Anderman, L. H., & Midgley, C. (1998). *Motivation and middle school students.* (EDO-PS-98-5). Washington, DC: Office of Educational Research and Improvement. (ERIC Document Reproduction Service No. ED421281).

Barone, C., Aguirre-Deandreis, A. I., & Trickett, E. J. (1991). Mean-ends problem-solving skills, life stress, and social support as mediators of adjustment in the normative transition to high school. *American Journal of Community Psychology, 19*(2), 207–225.

Berliner, D. (1993). Mythology and the American system of education. *Phi Delta Kappan, 632–640.*

Bohan-Baker, M., & Little, P. M. (2002). *The transition to kindergarten: A review of current research and promising practices to involve families.* Cambridge, MA: Harvard Family Research Project.

Brolin, D. E., & Loyd, R. J. (2004). *Career development and transition services* (4th ed.). Upper Saddle River, NJ: Pearson.

Cooke, G. J. (1995). Choice, not chance: Strengthening school transitions. *Schools in the Middle, 4*(3), 8–12.

Eccles, J., Wigfield, A., Midgley, C., Reuman, D., MacIver, D., & Feldlaufer, H. (1993). Negative effects of traditional middle schools on students' motivation. *The Elementary School Journal, 93*(5), 553–574.

Elias, M. J. (2002, April). Transitioning to middle school. *Education Digest, 67*(8), 41–44.

Fenzel, L. M. (2000). Prospective study of changes in global self-worth and strain during the transition to middle school. *Journal of Early Adolescence, 20*(1), 93–117.

Frogan, J., & Vaughn, S. (2000, January/February). Adolescents with and without LD make the transition to middle school. *Journal of Learning Disabilities, 33*(1), 33–44.

Gallagher, J., Maddox, M., & Edgar, E. (1984). *Early childhood interagency transition model.* Seattle: Edmark.

Harter, S. (1990). Causes, correlates, and the functional role of global self-worth. In R. J. Sternberg & J. Kolligan, Jr. (Eds.), *Competence considered* (pp. 67–97). New Haven, CT: Yale University Press.

Hertzog, C. J., Morgan, P. L., Diamond, P. A., & Walker, M. J. (1996). Transition to high school: A look at student perceptions. *Becoming, 7*(2), 6–8.

Jones, J. P. (2001). Engineering success through purposeful articulation. In T. S. Dickinson (Ed.), *Reinventing the middle school* (pp. 287–301). New York: Routledge Falmer.

Kagan, S. L., & Neuman, M. J. (1998). Lessons from three decades of transition research. *The Elementary School Journal, 98*(4), 365–379.

Kraft-Sayre, M. E., & Pianta, R. C. (2000). *Enhancing the transition to kindergarten: Linking children, families, and schools.* Charlottesville: University of Virginia.

Lord, S. E., & Eccles, J. S. (1994). Surviving the junior high transition. *Journal of Early Adolescence, 14*(2), 162–199.

Meekos, D. (1989). *Students' perceptions of the transition to junior high: A longitudinal perspective.* Paper presented at the Biennial Meeting of the Society for Research Development, Kansas City, MO.

Midgley, C., & Feldlaufer, H. (1987). Student and teachers decision-making fit before and after school transition to junior high school. *Journal of Early Adolescence, 7*(2), 225–241.

Mullins, E. R., & Irvin, J. K. (2000). Transition into middle school: What research says. *Middle School Journal, 31*(3), 57–60.

National Middle School Association (NMSA). (2002). *Supporting students in their transition to middle school: A position paper jointly adopted by the National Middle School Association and The National Association of Elementary School Principals.* (Retrieved from www.nmsa.org/news/transitions.html.)

Patton, J. R., Cronin, M. E., & Jairrels, V. (1997). Curricular implications of transition: Life skills instruction as an integral part of transition education. *Remedial and Special Education, 18,* 294–306.

Perkins, P. G., & Gelfer, J. I. (1995, January/February). Elementary to middle school: Planning for transition. *Clearing House, 68*(3), 171–174.

Perry, K. W., & Weinstein, R. S. (1998). The social context of early schooling and children's school adjustment. *Educational Psychologist, 34*(4), 177–197.

Phelan, P., Yu, H. C., & Davidson, A. L. (1994). Navigating the psychosocial pressures of adolescence: The voices and experiences of high school youth. *American Educational Research Journal, 31*(2), 415–447.

Queen, J. A. (2002). *Student transitions from middle to high school: Improving achievement/safer environment.* Larchmont, NY: Eye on Education.

Queen, J. A. (2003, August 29). Making the leap: Dr. Queen's 12 factors for successful transitions. ABCNews.com. Retrieved January 25, 2004, from http://abcnews.go.com/sections/WNN/DailyNews/transitions030821.html.

Ramey, C. T., & Ramey, S. L. (1999). Beginning school for children at risk. In *The transition to kindergarten.* Baltimore, MD: Paul H. Brookes.

Schumacher, D. (1998). *The transition to middle school.* (EDO-PS-98-6). Washington, DC: Office of Educational Research and Improvement. (ERIC Document Reproduction Service No. ED422119).

Smith, D. R. (1999). Middle school transition: The strength of ties. Unpublished doctoral dissertation, Oklahoma State University.

U.S. Department of Education. (2002). *Twenty-Fourth Annual Report to Congress on the Implementation of the Individuals with Disabilities Education Act.* Washington, DC: Office of Special Education Programs.

Weldy, G. R. (1991). *Stronger school transitions to improve student achievement: A final report on a three-year demonstration project: Strengthening school transitions for students K–13.* Reston, VA: National Association of Secondary School Principals. (ERIC Document Reproduction Service No. EJ499102).

Weldy, G. R. (1995). Critical transitions. *Schools in the Middle, 4*(3), 3–7.

Wigfield, A., & Eccles, J. S. (1994, May). Children's competence beliefs, achievement values, and general self-esteem: Change across elementary and middle school. *Journal of Early Adolescence, 14*(2), 107–126.

Ysseldyke, J. E., Algozzine, B., & Thurlow, M. L. (2000). *Critical issues in special education.* Boston: Houghton Mifflin.

CHAPTER TWELVE

MANAGING FEDERAL FUNDS

OVERVIEW

Obviously, managing federal funds for special education is an important concern to local administrators, perhaps more so for special education program administrators and central office personnel. Although local educational agencies (LEAs) have continuously lobbied for the federal legislature to live up to its promise to provide funding for 40 percent of the excess cost of special education services, they have little direct impact on how much federal funding they receive. The focus of LEAs is to know the rules for using federal funds in order to use them effectively to support programs and to protect local taxpayers' contributions to special education funding.

The *Individuals with Disabilities Education Improvement Act of 2004 (IDEA 2004)* (i.e., Public Law 108-446) provided for important changes to the funding formula that will affect the way special education program administrators work with the LEAs' respective shares of IDEA 2004 funds, based on school district child counts. Special education program administrators should be cognizant of IDEA 2004 mandates.

In this chapter, we examine the key funding provisions of the federal regulations related to LEAs and changes established by the IDEA 2004. We will review concepts such as *commingling, supplanting versus supplementing, excess cost, maintenance of effort, permissive use of funds, equitable participation* and *allocations.* We will also discuss tips for using funds effectively as well as pitfalls that can lead to unnecessary audit exceptions and possible sanctions.

REGULATIONS

IDEA 2004 Funding

H.R. 1350-32

(i) IN GENERAL.—A State funding mechanism shall not result in placements that violate the requirements of subparagraph (A), and a State shall not use a funding mechanism by which the State distributes funds on the basis of the type of setting in which a child is served that will result in the failure to provide a child with a disability a free appropriate public education according to the unique needs of the child as described in the child's IEP.

(18) MAINTENANCE OF STATE FINANCIAL SUPPORT.—

(A) IN GENERAL.—The State does not reduce the amount of State financial support for special education and related services for children with disabilities, or otherwise made available because of the excess costs of educating those children, below the amount of that support for the preceding fiscal year.

(B) REDUCTION OF FUNDS FOR FAILURE TO MAINTAIN SUPPORT.—The Secretary shall reduce the allocation of funds under section 611 for any fiscal year following the fiscal year in which the State fails to comply with the requirement of subparagraph (A) by the same amount by which the State fails to meet the requirement.

(C) WAIVERS FOR EXCEPTIONAL OR UNCONTROLLABLE CIRCUMSTANCES.—The Secretary may waive the requirement of subparagraph (A) for a State, for 1 fiscal year at a time, if the Secretary determines that—

(i) granting a waiver would be equitable due to exceptional or uncontrollable circumstances such as a natural disaster or a precipitous and unforeseen decline in the financial resources of the State; or (ii) the State meets the standard in paragraph (17)(C) for a waiver of the requirement to supplement, and not to supplant, funds received under this part.

(D) SUBSEQUENT YEARS.—If, for any year, a State fails to meet the requirement of subparagraph (A), including any year for which the State is granted a waiver under subparagraph (C), the financial support required of the State in future years under subparagraph (A) shall be the amount that would have been required in the absence of that failure and not the reduced level of the State's support.

(20) RULE OF CONSTRUCTION.—In complying with paragraphs (17) and (18), a State may not use funds paid to it under this part to satisfy State-law mandated funding obligations to local educational agencies, including funding based on student attendance or enrollment, or inflation. (ii) STATE PLAN.—The State educational agency shall develop, not later than 90 days after the State reserves funds under this paragraph, annually review, and amend as necessary, a State plan for the high cost fund. Such State plan shall—

(I) establish, in coordination with representatives from local educational agencies, a definition of a high need child with a disability that, at a minimum— (aa) addresses the financial impact a high need child with a disability has on the budget of the child's local educational agency; and (bb) ensures that the cost of the high need child with a disability is greater than 3 times the average per pupil expenditure (as defined in section 9101 of the Elementary and Secondary Education Act of 1965) in that State;

(II) establish eligibility criteria for the participation of a local educational agency that, at a minimum, takes into account the number and percentage of high need children with disabilities served by a local educational agency;

H.R. 1350-24

(III) develop a funding mechanism that provides distributions each fiscal year to local educational agencies that meet the criteria developed by the State under subclause (II); and

(IV) establish an annual schedule by which the State educational agency shall make its distributions from the high cost fund each fiscal year.

(iii) PUBLIC AVAILABILITY.—The State shall make final State plan publicly available not less than 30 days before the beginning of the school year, including dissemination of such information on the State website.

(F) ASSURANCE OF A FREE APPROPRIATE PUBLIC EDUCATION. Nothing in this paragraph shall be construed— (i) to limit or condition the right of a child with a disability who is assisted under this part to receive a free appropriate public education pursuant to section 612(a)(1) in the least restrictive environment pursuant to section 612(a)(5); or (ii) to authorize a State educational agency or local educational agency to establish a limit on what may be spent on the education of a child with a disability.

The IDEA 2004 established a six-year path to reach the 40 percent goal of the excess cost of special education services. However, the U.S. Department of Education estimated only a small percentage increase for each state's LEAs. For example, in Pennsylvania, intermediate units, as the state's LEAs, should expect a 2 to 3 percent increase in their IDEA 2004 allocated funding during the 2005–2006 school year. Based on already established child count activities, each intermediate unit will work with districts and public charter schools within its locale to "flow through" respective shares of federal funds. The December 2004 child count will be the basis for the 2005–2006 IDEA 2004 funding. If that child count dropped, however, the pass-through funding allocation could be less than the estimated amount.

The IDEA 2004 also established that each state may use up to 10 percent of state-level activity funds to establish "risk pools." The purpose of the risk pools is to reimburse the LEA for "high-need; low incidence, catastrophic or extraordinary aid."

34 CFR §300.152 Prohibition against commingling

(a) The State must have on file with the Secretary an assurance satisfactory to the Secretary that the funds under Part B of the Act are not commingled with State funds.

(b) The assurance in paragraph (a) of this section is satisfied by the use of a separate accounting system that includes an audit trail of the expenditure of the Part B funds. Separate bank accounts are not required. (See 34 CFR 76.702 (Fiscal control and fund accounting procedures).)

(Authority: 20 U.S.C. 1412(a)(18)(B))

The prohibition of commingling is primarily an auditing issue. The regulations guard against the blending of funds in ways that make it difficult to track the federal revenues and the corresponding expenditures. Although there is no requirement to maintain separate banking accounts, the LEA must use an accounting system that can separate federal from state or local revenues. This provision is necessary in order for LEAs to demonstrate that they maintain local effort (i.e., are appropriating the same amount of local dollars toward special education during fiscal periods when the federal appropriations are increasing). Also, this provision assists LEAs to ensure that federal revenues are not used to supplant local or state revenues.

34 CFR §300.184 Excess cost requirement

(a) General. Amounts provided to an LEA under Part B of the Act may be used only to pay the excess costs of providing special education and related services to children with disabilities.

(b) Definition. As used in this part, the term excess costs means those costs that are in excess of the average annual per-student expenditure in an LEA during the preceding school year for an elementary or secondary school student, as may be appropriate. Excess costs must be computed after deducting—

   (1) Amounts received—

      (i) Under Part B of the Act;

      (ii) Under Part A of title I of the Elementary and Secondary Education Act of 1965; or

      (iii) Under Part A of title VII of that Act; and

   (2) Any State or local funds expended for programs that would qualify for assistance under any of those parts.

(Authority: 20 U.S.C. 1401(7); 1413(a)(2)(A))

The intent of the IDEA is to provide supplemental funding to local school districts to assist in covering the costs of special education services. The excess cost provision requires LEAs to provide the same level of basic education funding for all students, including students with disabilities. Beyond this basic education, students with disabilities require additional supplemental aides and services. Therefore, LEAs can only use IDEA funds to cover the excess cost above the basic education funds. The exception to the requirement is in the case of students with disabilities between the ages of 3 and 5 and 18 and 21 years. If LEAs do not provide educational services to nondisabled students in these age groups, then the IDEA funds can be used to support the entire educational program for students with disabilities in these age groups. Section §300.185, "Meeting the excess cost requirement," provides further guidance regarding the excess cost provisions.

34 CFR §300.231 Maintenance of effort

(a) General. Except as provided in §§300.232 and 300.233, funds provided to an LEA under Part B of the Act may not be used to reduce the level of expenditures for the education of children with disabilities made by the LEA from local funds below the level of those expenditures for the preceding fiscal year.

(b) Information. The LEA must have on file with the SEA information to demonstrate that the requirements of paragraph (a) of this section are met.

(c) Standard.

   (1) Except as provided in paragraph (c)(2) of this section, the SEA determines that an LEA complies with paragraph (a) of this section for purposes of establishing the LEA's eligibility for an award for a fiscal year if the LEA budgets, for the education of children with disabilities, at least the same total or per-capita amount from either of the fol-

lowing sources as the LEA spent for that purpose from the same source for the most recent prior year for which information is available:

    (i) Local funds only.

    (ii) The combination of State and local funds.

(2) An LEA that relies on paragraph (c)(1)(i) of this section for any fiscal year must ensure that the amount of local funds it budgets for the education of children with disabilities in that year is at least the same, either in total or per capita, as the amount it spent for that purpose in—

    (i) The most recent fiscal year for which information is available, if that year is, or is before, the first fiscal year beginning on or after July 1, 1997; or

    (ii) If later, the most recent fiscal year for which information is available and the standard in paragraph (c)(1)(i) of this section was used to establish its compliance with this section.

(3) The SEA may not consider any expenditures made from funds provided by the Federal Government for which the SEA is required to account to the Federal Government or for which the LEA is required to account to the Federal Government directly or through the SEA in determining an LEA's compliance with the requirement in paragraph (a) of this section.

(Authority: 20 U.S.C. 1413(a)(2)(A))

As discussed earlier, the intent of Congress is to provide supplemental support to LEAs for covering the excess costs of special education. LEAs are required, as are SEAs, to ensure that IDEA funds are not used to *supplant* state and local funds. Instead, IDEA funds are to be used to *supplement* state and local funds directed toward providing FAPE to students with disabilities. Accordingly, the maintenance of effort (MOE) provision is included to assure that LEAs continue to provide at least the same level of support as they have done in prior years. Usually this is not an issue for LEAs because the costs of providing special education have continually risen since the inception of IDEA. The costs of personnel salaries and fringe benefits alone typically offset reductions in costs due to retirements of more costly personnel. Nonetheless, LEAs need to be cognizant of this provision.

LEAs have been concerned about the ramifications of this provision in cases when state legislatures have increased their share of revenue for special education. This is particularly an issue when states are trying to not only increase their share of revenues, but are also trying to reduce the local share in order to relieve LEAs of some of the fiscal burden of special education. In such cases, if the LEAs can show that the combination of state and local support is at least the same as in prior years, then they have met the requirements of the MOE provision.

There are legitimate circumstances that cause the local and state dollar amount for a total special education program to decrease while the MOE provision is still met. Section §300.232, "Exception to maintenance of effort," provides for four mitigating circumstances:

1. The voluntary departure, by retirement or otherwise, or departure for just cause, of special education or related services personnel, who are replaced by qualified, lower salaried staff.

2. A decrease in the enrollment of children with disabilities.
3. The termination of the obligation of the agency to provide a program of special education to a particular child with a disability that is an exceptionally costly program.
4. The termination of costly expenditures for long-term purchases, such as the acquisition of equipment or the construction of school facilities.

LEAs that explain their decrease in total contribution under any of the above circumstances should be able to demonstrate their compliance with the MOE provision.

The regulations provide another helpful condition for LEAs to meet the MOE provision. That is, a LEA can count as local funds up to 20 percent of the amount of funds it receives under Section 611 of IDEA that exceeds the amount received for IDEA in the prior year. This provision went into effect when the regulatory trigger was activated at a federal allocation to states of 4.1 billion dollars in fiscal year 1999. The federal allocation has steadily increased well above the trigger amount ever since.

34 CFR §300.235 Permissive use of funds

(a) General. Subject to paragraph (b) of this section, funds provided to an LEA under Part B of the Act may be used for the following activities:

(1) Services and aids that also benefit nondisabled children. For the costs of special education and related services and supplementary aids and services provided in a regular class or other education-related setting to a child with a disability in accordance with the IEP of the child, even if one or more nondisabled children benefit from these services.

(2) Integrated and coordinated services system. To develop and implement a fully integrated and coordinated services system in accordance with §300.244.

(b) Non-applicability of certain provisions. An LEA does not violate §§300.152, 300.230, and 300.231 based on its use of funds provided under Part B of the Act in accordance with paragraphs (a)(1) and (a)(2) of this section.

(Authority: 20 U.S.C. 1413(a)(4))

The permissive use of funds provision was incorporated into the IDEA regulations in order to clarify how funds can be used for students who receive services in the regular classroom. Often, students with disabilities are provided itinerant instructional or supplemental aides and services as they are interacting with their nondisabled peers. For instance, a speech and language clinician may be working with a student on the use of language. Often the most appropriate way to develop skills is in naturally occurring interactions among peers. The speech and language clinician engages not only the students with disabilities but also the nondisabled peers. In other cases a paraprofessional paid through IDEA funds may be assigned to a student in a regular classroom. From time to time the paraprofessional may work with the student with disabilities as well as other students in some group activity. The intent of this provision is to avoid creating an unintentional effect of deterring special education services from being delivered in an integrated classroom environment. Nonetheless, the services that are being provided must be documented in the student's IEP and the activities of the personnel must be focused on carrying out the IEP.

34 CFR §300.453 Expenditures [Equitable participation]

(a) Formula. To meet the requirement of §300.452(a), each LEA must spend on providing special education and related services to private school children with disabilities—

(1) For children aged 3 through 21, an amount that is the same proportion of the LEA's total subgrant under section 611(g) of the Act as the number of private school children with disabilities aged 3 through 21 residing in its jurisdiction is to the total number of children with disabilities in its jurisdiction aged 3 through 21; and

(2) For children aged 3 through 5, an amount that is the same proportion of the LEA's total subgrant under section 619(g) of the Act as the number of private school children with disabilities aged 3 through 5 residing in its jurisdiction is to the total number of children with disabilities in its jurisdiction aged 3 through 5.

(b) Child count.

(1) Each LEA shall—

(i) Consult with representatives of private school children in deciding how to conduct the annual count of the number of private school children with disabilities; and

(ii) Ensure that the count is conducted on December 1 or the last Friday of October of each year.

(2) The child count must be used to determine the amount that the LEA must spend on providing special education and related services to private school children with disabilities in the next subsequent fiscal year.

(c) Expenditures for child find may not be considered. Expenditures for child find activities described in §300.451 may not be considered in determining whether the LEA has met the requirements of paragraph (a) of this section.

(d) Additional services permissible. State and local educational agencies are not prohibited from providing services to private school children with disabilities in excess of those required by this part, consistent with State law or local policy.

(Authority: 20 U.S.C. 1412(a)(10)(A))

Equitable participation is a complex construct of the IDEA funding parameters. Its purpose is to assure that all students with disabilities, regardless of where they receive their education, are given the opportunity to participate in FAPE. The provision applies to students with disabilities *enrolled by their parents* in private, including parochial, schools or facilities. This provision does not apply to students with disabilities who are placed in private schools or facilities *by the LEA*. The equitable participation provision mandates that LEAs demonstrate that they provide services to students with disabilities enrolled by their parents in private schools or facilities that are monetarily proportionate to the number of students with disabilities attending private schools and the per pupil allocation the LEA receives. The actual funds used to provide such services do not have to be IDEA funds. They may be paid for through other federal, state, or local funds as long as the expenditures are *proportionate* to the number of students with disabilities in private schools or facilities. Also, the funds cannot be used in a way that benefits the private school or facility or the general needs of students in the private school or facility. For instance, if equipment is purchased for students with disabilities, such as a computer or some assistive technology device, the equipment is only allowed to be used for purpose of IDEA and must remain under the administration of the LEA.

Once a student is identified as being eligible for services under the provisions of the IDEA, a school district must offer a free and appropriate public education to that student. If the parents or the child decline the offer of FAPE and subsequently elect to attend a private school or facility, then the student is eligible under the equitable participation provision for a limited set of services. The LEA does not have to make available the full breadth of services that are provided to students who are placed in public or private facilities by the LEA. The student does not have an individual right to specific services even if such services were a part of the initial offer of FAPE. Instead, the student and parents may elect to receive, if appropriate and agreed to by the LEA, a limited set of services provided by the LEA to be used in private schools or facilities. To determine which services are to be offered, the LEA must survey the private schools and facilities in which students are placed by their parents and determine which services will and will not be made available. For example, the LEA and the private schools and facilities may agree that speech and language services are to be provided, but not occupational (OT) or physical therapy (PT). If a student enrolled by his or her parents in a private facility after being offered FAPE is in need of OT, but not speech or language therapy, then the LEA is not required to provide OT.

34 CFR §300.712 Allocations to LEAs [for preschool and school-age programs]

(a) Interim procedure. For each fiscal year for which funds are allocated to States under §300.703(b) each State shall allocate funds under §300.711 in accordance with section 611(d) of the Act, as in effect prior to June 4, 1997.

(b) Permanent procedure. For each fiscal year for which funds are allocated to States under §§300.706–300.709, each State shall allocate funds under §300.711 as follows:

(1) Base payments. The State first shall award each agency described in §300.711 the amount that agency would have received under this section for the base year, as defined in §300.706(b)(1), if the State had distributed 75 percent of its grant for that year under section §300.703(b).

(2) Base payment adjustments. For any fiscal year after the base year fiscal year—

(i) If a new LEA is created, the State shall divide the base allocation determined under paragraph (b)(1) of this section for the LEAs that would have been responsible for serving children with disabilities now being served by the new LEA, among the new LEA and affected LEAs based on the relative numbers of children with disabilities ages 3 through 21, or ages 6 through 21 if a State has had its payment reduced under §300.706(b)(2), currently provided special education by each of the LEAs;

(ii) If one or more LEAs are combined into a single new LEA, the State shall combine the base allocations of the merged LEAs; and

(iii) If, for two or more LEAs, geographic boundaries or administrative responsibility for providing services to children with disabilities ages 3 through 21 change, the base allocations of affected LEAs shall be redistributed among affected LEAs based on the relative numbers of children with disabilities ages 3 through 21, or ages 6 through 21 if a State has had its payment reduced under §300.706(b)(2), currently provided special education by each affected LEA.

(3) Allocation of remaining funds. The State then shall—

(i) Allocate 85 percent of any remaining funds to those agencies on the basis of the relative numbers of children enrolled in public and private elementary and secondary schools within each agency's jurisdiction; and

(ii) Allocate 15 percent of those remaining funds to those agencies in accordance with their relative numbers of children living in poverty, as determined by the SEA.

(iii) For the purposes of making grants under this section, States must apply on a uniform basis across all LEAs the best data that are available to them on the numbers of children enrolled in public and private elementary and secondary schools and the numbers of children living in poverty.

(Authority: 20 U.S.C. 1411(g)(2))

34 CFR Part 301 Preschool Grants for Children with Disabilities (Section 619 of Part B of the Individuals with Disabilities Education Act)

34 CFR §301.31 Allocations to local educational agencies

(a) Base payments. The State shall first award each agency described in Sec. 301.30 the amount that agency would have received under section 619 of the Act for fiscal year 1997 if the State had distributed 75 percent of its grant for that year under section 619(c)(3), as then in effect.

(b) Base payment adjustments. For fiscal year 1998 and beyond—

(1) If a new LEA is created, the State shall divide the base allocation determined under paragraph (a) of this section for the LEAs that would have been responsible for serving children with disabilities now being served by the new LEA, among the new LEA and affected LEAs based on the relative numbers of children with disabilities ages 3 through 5 currently provided special education by each of the LEAs;

(2) If one or more LEAs are combined into a single new LEA, the State shall combine the base allocations of the merged LEAs; and

(3) If for two or more LEAs, geographic boundaries or administrative responsibility for providing services to children with disabilities ages 3 through 5 changes, the base allocations of affected LEAs shall be redistributed among affected LEAs based on the relative numbers of children with disabilities ages 3 through 5 currently provided special education by each affected LEA.

(c) Allocation of remaining funds. After making allocations under paragraph (a) of this section, the State shall—

(1) Allocate 85 percent of any remaining funds to those agencies on the basis of the relative numbers of children enrolled in public and private elementary and secondary schools within the agency's jurisdiction; and

(2) Allocate 15 percent of those remaining funds to those agencies in accordance with their relative numbers of children living in poverty, as determined by the SEA.

(3) For the purpose of making grants under this section, States must apply on a uniform basis across all LEAs the best data that are available to them on the numbers of children enrolled in public and private elementary and secondary schools and the numbers of children living in poverty.

(Authority: 20 U.S.C. 1419(g)(1))

During the legislative review of the IDEA in 1997, political pressure was mounting for full funding of IDEA. Appropriations to states were about to increase significantly (i.e., from 8 to 19 percent of the excess cost of special education services), albeit not to the level authorized in the original 1975 legislation (i.e., 40 percent of the excess cost of special education services). Additionally, the IDEA amendments included provisions for states to distribute funds in a manner that does not encourage or discourage the identification of students with disabilities. In order to deal with the neutral distribution provisions and mindful of the potential problems of radically changing how states distributed funds to its LEAs, the legislature delineated provisions for distributing the amount of funds in the base year in the same way as had been done in the past (i.e., the number of students with disabilities). Therefore, the legislature would not adversely affect the LEAs in a dramatic way. However, any funds appropriated by the legislature above the $4.1 billion benchmark are to be distributed based on total school enrollment and poverty level of students. Accordingly, 85 percent of new funds are distributed based upon total student population of the LEA and 15 percent on a poverty index (e.g., number of students on free and reduced lunches). This formula was applied to section 611 (i.e., programs for students 5 to 21 years of age) and section 619 (i.e., programs for students 3 to 5 years of age). However, funding for section 619 programs has been frozen for the past several years.

One concern that was raised during the public review of the regulations was that some LEAs may lose funds as a result of the new formula. There is no explicit "hold harmless" provision to ensure that LEAs will receive at least the amount provided in the base year. However, SEAs are permitted to in effect hold harmless the effects of the formula by using their portion of the allocation to assist LEAs if their funding is reduced.

TIPS AND PITFALLS TO AVOID

1. *When in doubt, use the federal funds for clearly allowable expenditures and transfer questionable expenditures to local or state funding budget accounts.* The general rule is that federal funds are to supplement state and local programs and funds. Whatever an LEA has traditionally provided is the core set of programs and services. Any expansion of existing services (e.g., adding a new teacher or therapist at full time equivalent ratio) or creation of new programs or services (e.g., travel training) are typically allowable expenditures under IDEA funding. Costs that are allowed can include, but may not be limited to, the following:

- Extended year programs.
- Training programs for teachers of students with disabilities.
- Training programs for other professionals or paraprofessionals who work with students with disabilities.
- Training programs for parents of students with disabilities.
- Assistive devices.
- Supplies and materials.
- Program monitoring and evaluation activities.
- Work experience coordinators and job coaches.
- Special education teachers.
- Teachers' aides.
- Psychologists.
- Psychiatric services (for evaluation purposes).
- Occupational and physical therapy.
- Speech therapy.
- Audiological services for evaluation and maintenance of equipment.
- Social work services.
- Bus aides.
- IEP specified nursing services.

Costs that are not allowed can include, but may not be limited to, the following:

- Any expenditure made before the beginning date or after the ending date of an approved project.
- Salaries for general education teachers.
- Operational costs for school-owned property (e.g., rent, heat, telephones).
- Salaries for school administrators not associated with special education programs.
- Construction.
- Business costs.
- Travel expenses for staff whose salaries and fringe benefits are not paid by the IDEA grant.

There are numerous categories of expenditures for which you can use federal funds. If you are unsure about a specific expenditure, investigate if the expenditure can be covered using state or local funds. Then transfer an allowable expenditure(s) of an equivalent amount paid for using state or local funds to the federal funds account.

2. *Spend your federal funds first; usually you have greater flexibility with state and local funds.* Federal funds cannot be carried forward from one fiscal year to another. State and local funds may not have the same restriction. You do not want to have to return any of the federal funds for at least two reasons. First, it sends a message that you don't need the federal assistance or you are unable to manage your funds properly. The U.S. Congress continues to renege on its financial commitment to LEAs. Currently, the federal government pays approximately 19 percent of the excess cost of special education programs and services. Under the original legislation in 1975 (i.e., PL 94-142), the legislature committed to paying for 40 percent of excess costs. Although substantial strides

have been made in the last several years (i.e., increasing the level of funding from 8 to 19 percent), federal funding remains far below its promise from nearly thirty years ago. Secondly, you want to reduce, as much as possible, the financial burden on local resources to the maximum extent, particularly if your LEA's tax base is limited. In such cases it usually requires a significant effort to generate tax revenues. For instance, in southwestern Pennsylvania, one mil of property tax can generate as little as $15,000 and as much as $250,000. The effort at both ends of this range is the same; however, the revenue generated is significantly different. Federal dollars are generated from a larger collective and represent a more equalized effort.

3. *Be aware of your obligations to charter schools.* LEAs must be able to demonstrate that they are carrying out the provisions of the IDEA for students who attend charter schools for whom the district has granted the charter. The same funding provisions and restrictions apply to programs and services to students with disabilities attending charter schools. The LEA must make available to charter schools the same level of funding as it does to other schools.

4. *Be aware of other obligations under the IDEA.* There is a variety of other financial responsibilities that LEAs bear. First, students can and are placed in residential facilities as a layer of the continuum of service options available under the concept of least restrictive environment. For a very small percentage of students who have extensive educational needs, a residential placement is the least restrictive placement. LEAs are responsible for providing for the costs of such placement regardless of the extreme cost typical of such programs. LEAS are also responsible for the provision of educational services to students with disabilities who are incarcerated. The rules for which school district is responsible or even the state vary across the country. You may need to consult with your state department of education and/or the regional educational service agency (i.e., intermediate unit, BOCES) to determine who is responsible for funding such services.

Additionally, LEAs are responsible for providing assistive devices such as augmentative communication devices, computers, braillers, hearing aids, and closed circuit televisions for students with visual impairments. The cost of some of these devices can be very high. LEAs need to budget for these potential expenditures, every year although they may not expend these line items. Federal funds through IDEA are good sources because they are appropriate expenditures and local funds can be reserved for other core expenses. If in a given year the LEA has budgeted more federal funds than expended for assistive devices, the LEA can transfer expenses from state or local accounts to the federal account. The unexpended revenues in the state or local accounts can be carried over via a reserve account or fund balance to the succeeding fiscal year.

Another area of expenditure is extended school year (ESY) expenses. For a growing number of students, ESY services are being prescribed in order that they do not regress over long educational breaks or for whom recoupment of skills after a long break from educational services is onerous or negates the progress over the regular school term. In most case, students who qualify for ESY are students with extensive needs. Therefore, their ESY programs tend to be expensive. The most extreme examples are services for students who are in residential placements. However, there may be other students with relatively mild to moderate levels of disability who qualify or for whom the LEA elects to provide ESY services. The criteria for qualifying tend to be vague, requiring sound professional judgments about exactly for which areas of a student's IEP ESY services are necessary. Due to the ambiguity of criteria and assertiveness of some parents, LEAs in some cases may provide services to more students or more services to qualifying services than are absolutely required. LEAs must be prudent in their decision making regarding ESY.

RESOURCES

The following is a list of national resources that may be helpful when working with others to making decisions regarding the use of federal funds.

American Association of School Administrators (AASA)
1801 North Moore Street
Arlington, VA 22209-1813
(703) 875-0738
(703) 528-2146 (fax) (TTY)

Center for Special Education Finance (CSEF)
American Institutes for Research
P.O. Box 1113
Palo Alto, CA 94302
(650) 843-8136
(650) 858-0958 (fax)

The Council for Exceptional Children
IDEA Local Implementation by Local Administrators Partnership (ILIAD)
ASPIIRE IDEA Partnership
1110 North Glebe Road
Suite 300
Arlington, VA 22201-5704
(877) CEC-IDEA
(703) 264-1637 (fax)
(866) 915-5000 (TTY) (toll free)

Council of Chief State School Officers (CCSSO)
Resource Center on Educational Equity
1 Massachusetts Avenue, NW, Suite 700
Washington, DC 20001
(202) 336-7007
(202) 408-8072 (fax)

The Education Commission of the States
700 Broadway
Suite 1200
Denver, CO 80203-3460
(303) 293-8905
(303) 299-3600 (fax)

National Association of State Directors of Special Education (NASDSE)
1800 Diagonal Road
Suite 320
Alexandria, Virginia 22314
(703) 519-3800
(703) 519-3808 (fax)
(703) 519-7008 (TDD)

CHAPTER THIRTEEN

MANAGING SPECIAL EDUCATION BUDGETS

OVERVIEW

Once a special education administrator learns how the federal funding of IDEA is organized (Chapter 12), he or she can focus on budgeting and managing expenses at the LEA level. In this chapter, we discuss budget preparation activities and accounting codes that special education program administrators will implement in their employment. We offer guidelines and tips to ensure appropriate budgets and accountability of expenses. We suggest tips for avoiding inappropriate budgeting or expenses and we offer resources on managing special education budget activities.

BUDGETING CYCLE

Budgeting and the management of expenses and revenues is an ongoing process that will be faced by new special education program administrators early in their assignments. Both tasks occur in a distinctive cycle. Typically, the cycle is defined by the fiscal year. In most local education agencies (LEAs), the fiscal year begins July 1 and ends June 30. In others, the fiscal year runs concurrently with the calendar year, January 1 through December 31.

The federal government has a fiscal year that runs from October 1 to September 30. It was changed over two decades ago because Congress consistently failed to pass all of its thirteen appropriation bills prior to the beginning of the old fiscal calendar (i.e., June 1). The solution was to push the fiscal calendar back to October 1. However, the problem was not resolved. Currently, Congress consistently continues to miss the October 1 deadline for passage of its appropriation bills. The point here is that LEAs are dependent on other governmental bodies for their appropriations. If all entities at the federal, state, and local levels are not in synchronization, budgeting and the management of expenses and revenues become even more challenging.

BUDGET PREPARATION ACTIVITIES

Of course, the budgeting cycle in reality begins months in advance of the beginning of the fiscal year (see Table 13.1). Business managers and administrators meet to project program and financial needs for the upcoming year. For capital outlay projects (i.e., school construction or renovation), the planning process will start a year or more prior to construction.

By January of the prior year, budget preparation activities are underway. Special education program administrators will work with superintendents to examine enrollment projections and anticipate new or existing program needs based upon federal- or state-imposed educational initiatives or local initiatives. Discussions will take place with the members of the board of directors to begin gathering their input. Data will be gathered from frontline administrators and compiled by central office staff. Depending on the degree of participatory management used in an organization, school-based and central office staff will begin to identify program priorities.

Once the priorities are identified, then the resources (human and material) to carry out the activities associated with the priorities are identified. With this information the business staff can begin to translate resource needs into dollar amounts. With the projected cost data, administrators typically reexamine the priority programs and reassess the level of priority and the affordability. In cases where initiatives are imposed, such as the No Child Left Behind Act, there is little debate as to whether associated initiatives will be implemented. Instead, the discussion is about how to achieve efficacious adequate yearly progress (AYP) with very limited funding. Once the mandatory priorities are reviewed, optional priorities are reviewed with cost data, and decisions are made about what an LEA can afford during the upcoming fiscal year.

With these decisions unfolding, superintendents and business managers, along with other administrators or special education program administrators, will again meet with their board of directors to discuss program costs. Usually, in the early part of the process, expenses exceed expected revenues. Administrators with board direction will begin to cut entire programs or pare down programs in order to align expenditures with revenues. When administrators and boards of directors are satisfied that they have cut all unnecessary expenses from the budget and there remains a revenue shortfall, then the board of directors will discuss if and how to increase revenues.

While there are no specific Individual with Disabilities Education Act (IDEA) budget regulations, and thus no resulting changes occurring as a result of the Individuals with Disabilities Education Improvement Act of 2004 (IDEA 2004) concerning special education

TABLE 13.1 Budget Cycle

- Fiscal Year: July 1–June 30.
- Planning begins in spring.
- Budgets are prepared and finalized in June.
- Submitted to state department of education by June 30.
- Monitoring is ongoing.
- Budget revisions are made in January.

budgeting and the management of expenses and revenues, there are important accounting codes and functions that new administrators or special education program administrators should understand.

ACCOUNTING CODES: FUNCTIONS AND OBJECTS

Generally Accepted Accounting Principles (GAAP)

Financial Accounting for Local and State School Systems (Handbook 2R2). To enable effective auditing of finances, budget items are categorized by a standard set of defined *functions* and *objects* for expenses and revenues. The budget functions define broad program areas of the budget, while objects define more specific areas of expenses and revenues. Each function and object has a narrative title and description along with a numeric code. For instance, in a special education budget, a special education program administrator will typically have a function for the expenses of different types of programs based on exceptionality, such as learning disabilities, emotional disturbance, autism, etc. Or, functions may be based on the types of services provided, such as learning support, behavior support, life skills support, etc. Within an expense function, objects are used to delineate the types of expenditures, such as salaries, medical insurance, retirement contributions, social security contributions, or workers' compensation insurance, and so forth.

Each function and object has a numeric code that carries meaning. These numeric *function codes* will vary from state to state but carry out the same purpose. The codes named in this chapter are based on the coding system used in Pennsylvania. For instance, 1100 functions relate to general education expenses, and 1200 functions relate to special education functions. Likewise, *object codes* in the 100–199 range relate to salary, the 200–299 range relates to fringe benefit expenses, the 300–399 range specifies contracted service expenses, the 400–499 range is for rentals and leases, the 500–599 range is for travel expenses, the 600–699 range designates supplies, and the 700–799 range designates equipment expenses. Within these object category ranges, the numeric codes are used to pinpoint even more specific types of expenses (see Tables 13.2 and 13.3).

As with expenses, revenues have associated codes and titles as well. The revenue function codes delineate the sources of the revenue: federal, state, or local. For instance, the 6000 functions reflect estimates of revenue from local sources (e.g., local property taxes); 7000 functions reflect estimates from state sources (e.g., special education subsidy); 8000 codes reflect federal sources; and 9000 codes reflect revenue from incoming budget transfers (i.e., revenues being transferred from another fund operated by the school district or agency to the special education or general operation budget).

Again, the object codes provide more specific information that delineates the source of revenues within a category (see Table 13.4). For example, an LEA may generate earnings from investments coded as 6510, receive social security reimbursement from the state coded as 7810, and receive retirement contribution reimbursement as 7820. The latter two items result from the LEA's paying the full social security and retirement contributions and the state's reimbursing the LEA for its share. In all three of these examples, the function code reflects state funding (i.e., 7000) and the 270, 810, and 820 object codes reflect more specific

TABLE 13.2   Example Budget Sheet with Function and Object Codes and Titles

28-Jan-04   01:10 PM   INTERMEDIATE UNIT #1 FOR BUDGET YEAR 2003-04   PAGE 1
PENDING FUNCTION BY OBJECT EXPENDITURE REPORT - FUND 23 (SPECIAL EDUCATION FUND) JAN '04

	ADJUSTED	YTD	PENDING	UNEXPENDED	ENCUMBERED	UNENCUMBERED
	BUDGET	EXPENDED	EXPENDED	BALANCE	PO	BALANCE
1200 SPECIAL PROGRAMS						
110 OFFICIAL/ADMINISTRATIVE						
120 PROFESSIONAL - EDUCATIONAL						
122 SUBSTITUTE SALARIES						
150 OFFICE/CLERICAL						
190 INSTRUCTIONAL ASSISTANT						
192 SUB AIDES SALARIES						
211 MEDICAL INSURANCE						
212 DENTAL INSURANCE						
213 LIFE INSURANCE						
214 INCOME PROTECTION INSURANCE						
215 VISION INSURANCE						
220 SOCIAL SECURITY CONTRIBUTIONS						
230 RETIREMENT CONTRIBUTIONS						
240 TUITION REIMBURSEMENT						
250 UNEMPLOYMENT COMPENSATION						
260 WORKMENS COMPENSATION						
322 PROFESSIONAL ED SERVICES - IUs						
324 TEACHER INDUCTION						
440 RENTALS						
513 CONTRACTED CARRIERS						
580 TRAVEL & CONFERENCE						
581 CONF & SEMINARS						
610 GENERAL SUPPLIES						
640 BOOKS & PERIODICALS						
760 EQUIP-REPLACEMENT						
2100 SUPPORT SVC PUPIL PERSNL						
2300 SUPPORT SVC ADM						
331 LEGAL FEES						
2400 SUPPORT SVC PUPL HLTH						

TABLE 13.2 Continued

28-Jan-04   01:10 PM   INTERMEDIATE UNIT #1 FOR BUDGET YEAR 2003-04   PAGE 1
PENDING FUNCTION BY OBJECT EXPENDITURE REPORT - FUND 23 (SPECIAL EDUCATION FUND) JAN '04

	ADJUSTED BUDGET	YTD EXPENDED	PENDING EXPENDED	UNEXPENDED BALANCE	ENCUMBERED PO	UNENCUMBERED BALANCE
2500 SUPPORT SVC BUSINESS						
2600 OPERATION-MAINTENANCE						
160 CRAFTS AND TRADES						
170 OPERATIVE						
180 SERVICE WORK & LABORER						
211 MEDICAL INSURANCE						
212 DENTAL INSURANCE						
213 LIFE INSURANCE						
214 INCOME PROTECTION INSURANCE						
215 VISION INSURANCE						
220 SOCIAL SECURITY CONTRIBUTIONS						
230 RETIREMENT CONTRIBUTIONS						
250 UNEMPLOYMENT COMPENSATION						
260 WORKMENS COMPENSATION						
410 CLEANING SVCS						
421 NATURAL GAS						
422 ELECTRICITY (NON HEATING)						
424 WATER/SEWAGE						
430 REPAIRS & MAINTENANCE SERVICES						
440 RENTALS						
444 RENTAL OF VEHICLES						
460 EXTERMINATION SERVICES						
523 GENERAL PROPERTY & LIABILITY INS						
531 POSTAGE						
610 GENERAL SUPPLIES						
620 ENERGY						
750 EQUIP-ORIG/ADDITIONAL						
760 EQUIP-REPLACEMENT						

TABLE 13.3 Example of Expenditure Codes and Corresponding Descriptions Used by the New Jersey Department of Education

INSTRUCTION

Personal Services - Salaries	100-100	• Salaries and stipends for teachers, instructional (full-time, part-time, summer, substitutes). For substitutes for consortium member (not lead agency) staff, use 200-800; • Teachers or aides (full or part-time employees of applicant) nonclerical; • Contracted salary for activities outside the normal work time; and • Compensation for teacher training/professional development activities outside the normal work time.
Purchased Professional & Technical Services	100-300	• Educational consultants working directly with students (includes travel & expenses); • Speakers for students; and • Standardized specific subject exams administered/scored by external testing agency, i.e., Cosmetology/Hairstyling Exam.
Other Purchased Services	100-500	Service costs (not professional or technical) for persons not on LEA/Agency's payroll who interact with students/clients: • Internet access and use charges for instructional purposes; • Leases/rentals of instructional equipment; • Line charges (Internet, videoconferencing, etc.); • Tuition for students; • Shipping and handling charges for the above items; and • Service calls and maintenance contracts for instructional items.
General Supplies	100-600	Classroom supplies and materials (other than textbooks): • Consumable items used by students; • Textbooks and workbooks for student use (textbooks not used in the classroom must be included under 200-600); • Software, instructional, regardless of unit cost (includes site licenses); • Supplies, instructional (for classroom use); • Student testing materials; • CD-ROMs, videocassettes for instruction; and • Shipping and handling charges for the above items.
Other Objects	100-800	Costs for instructional goods and services not included above; i.e.: • Field trip admission fees for students as part of instruction; and • Itemized costs for approved student travel (airfare, meals, lodging, conference registration fees).

SUPPORT SERVICES

Personal Services - Salaries	200-100	• Salaries, noninstructional (full- or part-time); and • Salaries, teachers or aides (full- or part-time employees of applicant), curriculum work.
Personal Services - Employee Benefits	200-200	• Benefits and other necessary deductions.

TABLE 13.3 Continued

Purchased Prof.-Ed. Services	200-300	• Consultants, professional or technical; and • Graphic design—consultant fees, vendor fees.
Purchased Prof.-Ed. Services	200-320	• Consultants, educational.
Purchased Property Services	200-400	• Leases/rentals—noninstructional equipment, vehicles; • Maintenance contracts, vehicles and equipment; and • Repairs and maintenance, vehicles and equipment.
Other Purchased Services	200-500	• Advertising; • Registration fees, staff conferences; • Copying/duplicating; • Field trip transportation (i.e., bus rental); • Food—catering for professional development programs; • Internet access and use charges, noninstructional; • Postage; • Printing; • Telephone; • Tuition, staff; and • Vehicle insurance.
Travel	200-580	• Travel, staff—accommodations, transportation, meals (conferences/workshops).
Supplies and Materials	200-600	• Reference and library books (including shipping and handling); • Food for field trips; • Misc. refreshments; • Software, noninstructional; • Supplies, noninstructional; and • Gas, vehicle.
Other Objects	200-800	• Substitute salaries for consortium member agency, other than lead agency. Consortium *member* agency must keep records of salaries and deductions; and • Other noninstructional items not included above.
Indirect Costs (heating/cooling, lighting, etc.)	200-860	• **Not allowed** for Perkins Vocational Grant applications.
FACILITIES ACQUISITION AND CONSTRUCTION SERVICES		
Buildings	400-720	• Reasonable renovations integral to the use of instructional equipment approved for purchase.
Instructional Equipment	400-731	• Instructional equipment (may include delivery and installation, if included on budget detail form).
Noninstructional Equipment	400-732	• Noninstructional equipment (may include delivery and installation, if included on budget detail form).

TABLE 13.4   Example IDEA Part B Section 611 Budget Sheet for Revenues

BUDGET CODE	BUDGET DESCRIPTION	2003–2004 BUDGET	% INC (DEC)	2002–2003 BUDGET
6000	**Revenue from Local Sources**			
6510	Earnings from Investments	-		-
TOTAL	**FROM LOCAL SOURCES - 6000**	-		-
7000	**Revenue from State Sources**			
7810	State Share Social Security			-
7820	State Share Retirement	52,528	276.0%	13,971
TOTAL	**FROM STATE SOURCES - 7000**	**52,528**	**276.0%**	**13,971**
8000	**Revenue from Federal Sources**			
8512	Subsidy IDEA	9,842,126	19.8%	8,213,565
8515	Subsidy IDEA- Pre School	-		-
TOTAL	**FROM FEDERAL SOURCES - 8000**	**9,842,126**	**19.8%**	**8,213,565**
GRAND TOTAL REVENUES		**9,894,654**	**20.3%**	**8,227,536**

information about the revenues. Note also that the last two digits of the object code carry additional meaning to delineate the revenues further.

CALCULATING AND BUDGETING FOR THE TOTAL COST OF OPERATION

General and special education expenses and revenues are typically contained within the same budget. However, expenses are categorized separately by ascribing different function codes to each. For example, all general education expenses may be ascribed the 1100 function code and special education expenses the 1200 function code. However, on the revenue side, the funds may come under the same function code because of the common source of revenues (e.g., state revenues), but they are delineated by object codes. State revenues for general education may be coded as 7250 and special education as 7270. In any case, the funding sources for programs that support students with disabilities can be from federal, state, and/or local sources.

Additionally, in considering the costs for educating a student with disabilities, consideration must be given to the issue of excess cost. That is, special education expenses are those expenses that are in excess of the financial support an LEA provides to every student. This is referred to as the "per pupil tuition rate." Regardless of whether a student requires special education services, the district expends a certain amount of money on each student. The tuition rate is the total expenditures of general education program operation divided by the LEA's student full-time equivalent (FTE) enrollment. This amount has a broad range within and between states. Nationally, the average per pupil expenditure rate in 1999 was $6,508 and is projected to be between $8,419 and $8,557 in 2005 (Gerald & Hussan, 2001). By using the tuition rate and adding special education costs per special education FTE, an LEA can calculate the total cost on average of educating a student with disabilities.

LEA personnel need to remember that the tuition rate is applied to all students. The true cost of special education programs is comprised of the costs above and beyond the general education tuition rate. Furthermore, federal and state subsidies help to offset the local contribution so that local taxpayers are contributing a fraction of the excess cost of special education programs. Figure 13.1 illustrates the difference between general education and special education funding. The excess cost in this illustration refers to the portion of the excess costs funded from local sources. This percentage will vary depending upon how special and general education programs are funded by individual states. Public education in Hawaii, for instance, is totally funded by the state. However, in the other states, local revenues are used to some extent.

Most service enterprises are labor intensive. Therefore, personnel costs usually account for 80 percent or more of operational expenses. Consequently, how an administration staffs the special education programs and the level of services provided will be the two most important program factors affecting the budget. Obviously, each special education program requires a teacher. In budgeting for programs, consideration must be given to other staffing needs or perceived needs. For example, the number of classroom paraprofessionals and/or one-on-one personal care aides needs to be determined. The amount of time a student spends receiving services from the special education teacher and how many students are on a teacher's class roster are important factors. Also, the extent to which students with disabilities need related services in order to benefit from their special education programs is relevant.

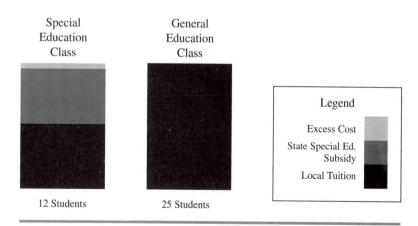

FIGURE 13.1   Comparing Components of General and Special Education Funding

The most prolific example is in the area of speech and language services. The number of students receiving speech and language services is usually one of the largest FTEs for an LEA. Care needs to be given in diagnosing when such services are warranted and at what level. Entrance and exit criteria need to be aligned with developmental standards for the acquisition of articulation and language skills. A number of students begin their formal schooling with articulation patterns that are not perfect, but developmentally appropriate. Such students do not require speech services, or their articulation delays can be ameliorated through consultation services provided to the parents, special education teachers, and general education teachers. On the exit end, care must be given so that students are dismissed from speech and language services (and any other special education or related service) when the need for such services ceases. The reason could be that the students' skills have developed such that they are commensurate with their peers.

In other cases, particularly with students with moderate or severe disabilities, they have progressed as far as possible and further service will not provide benefit. An example is students with moderate cognitive disabilities who are high school age. For most of these students, the educational focus needs to shift away from basic academic and language skills and toward transition skills for postsecondary programs or community living.

Once staffing determinations are made, calculations are made for salary and fringe benefits and other related expenses (i.e., supplies and materials, travel, etc.). Fixed expenses for salary and fringe benefits make calculations relatively easy and predictable. Fringe benefits will include various insurance programs and will vary based on the contracts or collective bargaining agreements with employees. Typically, they include medical, dental, and vision insurance. Medical insurance is by far the most costly and complex. Programs vary widely and range from traditional indemnity programs to preferred patient organizations (PPO), point of service (POS), and health maintenance organization (HMO) programs. Additionally, within any type of insurance program, there are variations in plan designs. Some plans have deductibles and co-payments for doctor visits or drug prescriptions. Additionally, employees may have individual, husband and wife, employee and dependents, or family coverage. Type of plan, plan designs, and level of coverage all factor into the premium rate paid by employers. Consequently, each employee may have a different associated medical insurance cost. Dental and vision insurance rates are usually much less expensive and fewer options may be available. However, there may be plan design and level of coverage differences among employees. Again, a cost must be assigned to each employee. Other fringe benefit costs include employer social security contributions (FICA), which currently entail 7.65 percent of salary, as well as workers' compensation insurance, income protection, life insurance, unemployment compensation, and retirement contributions, whose costs are variable among states and LEAs.

Table 13.5 illustrates using a spreadsheet layout to budget a hearing support program for a regional educational service agency. Expenses under this function code (i.e., 1221 Hearing Support Services) represent the *direct costs* of the program. That is, these are the costs associated with the specific activities involving hearing support services. The staffing pattern for this hearing support program includes teachers, interpreters, and paraprofessionals. Salaries are determined by local collective bargaining agreements, based on a stepped scale for the teachers and paraprofessionals. The interpreters often are not in a collective bargaining group, and salaries are set by the agency based upon the local market. The column for

TABLE 13.5 Budget Worksheet for Hearing Support Services

1221 SPECIAL EDUCATION—HEARING SUPPORT

FX	OBJDETAIL	2002-03 SALARIES	2002-03 BUDGET	2003-04 SALARIES	2003-04 BUDGET	INC/(DEC) PR YR BUD
	120 Salaries Teachers	652,295	658,818	671,895	678,614	**19,796**
	1DAILEY, DANA	27,900		27,700		748.11
	2DENNIS, SHIRLEY	62,255		63,955		999.66
	3EDENFIELD, THERESA	25,400		28,200		803.24
	4ESNO, KATHLEEN	61,455		63,155		999.66
	5JESTER, ANNA LOUISE	61,455		63,155		999.66
	6KIFER, KATHLEEN	62,255		63,955		999.66
	7LORENZO, ROBERTA	62,255		63,955		1,027.59
	8MAMULA, ANNETTE	62,255		63,955		1,027.59
	9PALAISA, MARGARET	62,255		63,955		1,027.59
	10SMITH, THOMAS	62,255		63,955		999.66
	11STEWART-VOGT, PEGGY	40,300		42,000		1,027.59
	12TATRAI, GAI LINN	62,255		63,955		999.66
PRIOR YR = 12						
	121 Interpreters	89,945	90,844	104,750	105,798	**14,953**
	1BALOGA, DANIELLE	19,055		21,550		803.24
	2BARKEY, KIM	19,055		21,550		803.24
	3FLETCHER, MELANIE	17,510		20,050		284.94
	4TAJC, PAUL	19,055		21,550		284.94
	5WEAVER, TRACY	15,270		20,050		284.94
	122 Substitute Teachers					
	190 Salaries Aides	53,153	53,685	55,448	56,002	**2,318**
	1HUNT, MARGARET	12,904		13,602		
	2KNUPSKY, DEBRA	14,302		14,502		803.24
	3MURPHY, CYNTHIA	12,904		13,602		
	4STOLLAR, DARYLANNE	13,043		13,742		
	192 Substitute Aides					
	211 Medical Insurance		154,609		179,091	**24,482**
	212 Dental Insurance		9,140		9,537	**397**
	213 Life Insurance		2,220		1,593	**(627)**
	214 Income Protection		2,330		2,398	**68**
	215 Eye Care		752		784	**32**
	220 Social Security		61,456		64,292	**2,836**
	230 Retirement		9,238		31,684	**22,445**
	240 Tuition Reimbursement		—		—	**—**
	250 Unemployment Compensation	1,607		1,681		
	260 Workers Compensation		11,247		14,287	**3,040**
	320 Contracted Educational Services		—		—	**—**
	330 Contracted Professional Services		—		—	**—**
	440 Classroom Rent		—		—	**—**
	580 Travel regular		20,000		20,000	**—**
	581 Travel Conference		—		—	**—**
	610 General Supplies		14,000		8,000	**(6,000)**
	630 Food		—		—	**—**
	640 Textbooks		4,000		2,000	**(2,000)**
	750 Equipment - New		3,000		2,000	**(1,000)**
	760 Equipment - Replacement		—		—	**—**
	SUBTOTAL 1221	795,393	1,096,946	832,093	1,177,760	**80,815**

medical insurance contains a considerable range in costs. Those staff with family indemnity insurance have monthly premium costs of $1,027.59 or $12,331.08 annually. Those with individual point of service medical insurance have monthly premium costs of $284.94 or $3,419.28 annually. The dental and eye insurance monthly costs reflect family ($49.68/$4.08) or individual coverage ($16.53/$1.39). Income protection and life insurance are uniform programs without plan options.

The other costs reflected in the hearing support program are included in the object code ranges from 300 to 700. These costs represent only $32,000 or less than 3 percent of the total of the direct costs ($1,177,760) of the hearing support program. General supplies, textbooks, and equipment account for $12,000, while travel expenses account for the remaining $20,000. The travel expenses are high because a majority of the hearing support services are provided through an itinerant program. Given the low incidence population, students are spread out over a wide geographic region. Staff is reimbursed for travel expenses incurred from the first work station of the day to the last work station at the annually determined IRS rate (e.g., 36.5 cents per mile).

Other *indirect costs* are not included in the 1221 Hearing Support function. These indirect costs are spread out in some systematic way across all program functions (e.g., speech and language support, learning support, emotional support, vision support, etc.). They include expenses for a program supervisor, business office operations, central administration services, data processing services, equipment repair, and so forth. These items are delineated under other function and object codes in other parts of the budget. Thus, to calculate the *total cost of a particular program,* the indirect and direct costs must be added. In this example, indirect costs are assigned to each hearing support program, which is defined by a set of services headed by a teacher. Consequently, there are twelve hearing support programs. Indirect costs have been calculated as $13,330 per program for a total of $159,960. Therefore, the total cost of hearing support services is calculated a $1,337,720 (see Table 13.6).

TIPS AND PITFALLS TO AVOID

We offer a number of strategies that new special education program administrators need to keep in mind while planning for and preparing a budget. Fundamentally, these have to do

TABLE 13.6   Calculation of the Total Cost of Hearing Support Services for an Educational Service Agency

Direct Costs:			**1,177,760**
	Salary and Fringe Benefits	1,145,760	
	Supplies, equipment, etc.	32,000	
Indirect Costs:			**159,960**
Total Costs:			*1,337,720*

with controlling expenses, increasing revenues, and using the relationships between and among budgets to meet the overall needs of the LEA.

• *Look to consolidate programs by focusing on student needs instead of disability label (single exceptionality v. varying exceptionality).* As mentioned earlier, the most costly parts of a special education budget are salary and fringe benefits. Consequently, managing the use of staff is going to pay benefits. How programs are structured varies from state to state, but one of the major principles underlying IDEA is that programs for individual students should be organized based upon the needs of students, not their disability categories. This means that students who are classified as having mental retardation and learning disabilities can be served in the same programs when their common needs allow. Having this flexibility allows LEAs to maximize the use of staff. For instance, an elementary school has 300 students with eight students with learning disabilities and five with mental retardation in grades 4 and 5 with similar academic and instructional needs. The LEA could serve all thirteen students in one resource program rather than having two resource rooms, one for the students with learning disabilities and one for those with mental retardation. Pennsylvania accommodates such structure under the term learning support programs, while the state of Florida uses varying exceptionalities programs in a similar way.

• *Use competition to drive down contracted service costs.* Many LEAs contract out for various related services, such as discussed in Chapter 15. One way to help drive the costs for such services down is to take advantage of a competitive marketplace. There are a number of national or regional agencies that provide speech and language clinicians, psychologists, occupational therapists, and physical therapists. There are local agencies, as well, that provide these services. All strive to be competitive in the breadth, quality, and cost of their services. Special education program administrators can drive the costs down by issuing a request for proposal (RFP) to multiple providers. They should carefully identify the specifications for each service (e.g., occupational therapy, physical therapy, etc.), including items such as participation in IEP meetings, evaluation services, travel costs, and Medicaid billing. In some professions, there are tiered levels of providers. For instance, an occupational therapist (OT) or a certified occupational therapy assistant (COTA) can provide occupational therapy. Likewise, a physical therapist (PT) or physical therapist assistant (PTA) can provide physical therapy. In the specifications, it is important to require a cost breakdown for both tiers of service. Another strategy is to specify a multiyear contract as part of the proposal. This will encourage more agencies to bid because if they have to add staff, they can guarantee a longer contract term. Also, it will enable providers to bid even lower because of the security of a multiyear contract and they can spread their overhead costs across multiple years.

• *Use the power of consortia to drive down costs.* Costs for a variety of goods and services can be reduced by having a larger presence in the marketplace. LEAs can take advantage of their common needs for goods and services by working together as a purchasing consortium. Some states do this already by negotiating statewide prices for textbooks and other materials. In other states, regional service agencies (e.g., intermediate units, BOCES, etc.) use consortia to negotiate prices for general school supplies, janitorial supplies, computers, natural gas, fuel, electricity, health insurance, and bus services. There are Internet bidding and purchasing programs specifically for school districts, such as eschoolmall.com. Using consortia can result in significant savings to LEAs.

• *Negotiate stability into health insurance costs.* A specific target for the consortia strategy is the procurement of health insurance. The purpose of using a consortium is twofold: (1) to negotiate better rates on premiums and plan designs and (2) to spread risk across a broader base. One issue that needs to be addressed is the current language that the participating members of the consortia include in their collective bargaining agreements. In many cases, not only is the specific type of medical insurance plan specified (e.g., indemnity, PPO, POS, etc.), but the specific provider (e.g., Blue Cross, US Health, AETNA, etc.) is named as well. This may limit the prospects for getting multiple bidders for the consortium. Nonetheless, the consortium can drive the costs down even with only one provider bidding because of the increased size of the group. The second purpose of the insurance consortium is to spread the risk of "shock claims," individual claims greater than $100,000, and high usage rates across more lives. Shock claims and high usage rates absorbed by a single, small, poor school district can be catastrophic. That is, either or both can cause precipitous increases in insurance rates and long-term instability in costs. For example, the Intermediate Unit 1 Insurance Trust (IU1IT) has been able to contain insurance rate increases well below the marketplace average. At a time when average increases have risen to around 35 percent regionally, the IU1IT is able to keep increases at 10 to 12 percent per year. Member districts also are able to spread their risk across 25 school districts, 5 vocational-technical schools, and the intermediate unit. Fifty percent of each school district's premium rates are determined by their own usage during the prior two years and 50 percent of the usage of the entire consortium. Thus, rates are significantly more stable from year to year.

• *Take advantage of Medicaid billing.* Due to what is referred to as the Medicaid loophole, students with disabilities who are in need of special education are eligible for Medicaid. In 1988, Congress clarified this issue by passing the Medicare Catastrophic Coverage Act (PL 100-360). This law mandates that federal Medicaid funds must be available to reimburse for the cost of related services found in a child's IEP, individualized service plan, or individualized family service plan. Therefore, state education agencies are eligible for federal reimbursement for the related services they are providing to children who are eligible for Medicaid. LEAs are eligible to bill Medicaid through their state agencies for certain services that are provided by the LEA as part of the student's individual education plan. Typical services for which LEAS can bill include audiological services, speech and language services, occupational therapy, vision services, interpreter services, physical therapy, nursing services, personal care assistants, orientation and mobility needs, social work services, assistive technology, psychiatric services, and psychological services. Revenues from Medicaid reimbursement can be substantial and are well worth the effort to procure them.

• *Reduce technology costs through e-Rate.* The Telecommunications Act of 1996 was the first comprehensive revision of the federal communications laws in more than sixty years. The universal service section of this law provides assistance to schools and libraries in obtaining access to state-of-the-art services and technologies at discounted rates. LEAs can apply for and receive reimbursements of up to 90 percent of their costs for a wide variety of telecommunication systems and services including phone service, Internet access, wide area networks, wiring, teleconferencing services, distance learning circuits, etc. For more information, visit the Federal Communication Commission website at www.fcc.gov/learnnet or contact your state Department of Education

- *Overestimate expenses and underestimate revenues.* Always overestimate your expenditures in order to provide a cushion against unexpected costs or unexpected cost increases. For example, even though an administrator may not plan to fill a position until three months or so into the fiscal year, it is important to budget the related expenses as though the position were to be filled on the first day of the fiscal year. If the administrator were planning to hire new staff into vacancies, it is wise to budget salaries and fringe benefits at step five or higher on the salary schedule even though the administrator knows he or she will be hiring someone at a lower step. Likewise, it can be helpful to estimate fringe benefit costs higher than reasonably expected. On the other hand, administrators should underestimate revenues. For instance, if one were to collect local property taxes, it is important to underestimate the collection percentage. If the administrator anticipated revenue reimbursements from Medicaid or e-Rate, he or she should only budget a small fraction or budget nothing from these sources. These strategies can help if expenses are higher than expected. If, in fact, at the end of the fiscal year the actual revenues exceed the actual expenses, the administrator will have developed a budget surplus that can be used to increase a fund balance or rainy day fund.

- *Spend federal revenues first.* It is important to always spend down federal revenues before any state or local revenues. If administrators are able to make it through the fiscal year without having to use all of the revenues, typically they can carry over local and state revenues into the next fiscal year. If federal funds are not expended, they must be returned. Additionally, administrators may help to reduce the local tax burden in the community.

RESOURCES

The following is a list of resources for further general information on special education budgeting and budgeting for public agencies.

Center for Special Education Finance (CSEF)
American Institutes for Research
P.O. Box 1113
Palo Alto, CA 94302
(650) 843-8136
(650) 858-0958 (fax)

Education Commission of the States
700 Broadway, #1200
Denver, CO 80203-3460
(303) 299-3600
(303) 296-8332 (fax)
www.ecs.org

Financial Accounting Standards Board (FASB)
401 Merritt 7
P.O. Box 5116
Norwalk, CT 06856-5116
(203) 847-0700
(203) 849-9714 (fax)
URL: www.fasb.org

Governmental Accounting Standards Board (GASB)
401 Merritt 7, P.O. Box 5116
Norwalk, CT 06856-5116
(203) 847-0700
URL: www.gasb.org

REFERENCES

Gerald, D. E., & Hussar, W. J. (2001). *Projections of education statistics to 2011.* Washington, DC: National Center for Education Statistics, U.S. Dept. of Education.

CHAPTER FOURTEEN

INDEPENDENT EDUCATIONAL EVALUATION (IEE)

OVERVIEW

IDEA 2004 continues to assure parents of students with disabilities the opportunity to obtain an independent educational evaluation (IEE) if they disagree with the LEA's evaluation results or believe the LEA's evaluation is inadequate. Despite federal regulations that clearly specify parent rights and the conditions under which an IEE is warranted at *public expense,* special education administrators often struggle negotiating the *process,* which is evidenced in the increasing number of due process hearings or court decisions regarding IEEs (Freedman, 1996). This chapter will define IEE, provide guidelines and tips for avoiding inadequate LEA evaluations, and highlight steps to assure that an IEE, provided at public expense, is appropriate.

REGULATIONS

§300.302 Independent educational evaluation

(a) **General.**

(1) The parents of a child with a disability have the right under this part to obtain an independent educational evaluation of the child, subject to paragraphs (b) through (e) of this section.

(2) Each public agency shall provide to parents, upon request for an independent educational evaluation, information about where an independent educational evaluation may be obtained, and the agency criteria applicable for independent educational evaluations as set forth in paragraph (e) of this section.

(3) For the purposes of this part—

(i) **Independent educational evaluation** means an evaluation conducted by a qualified examiner who is not employed by the public agency responsible for the education of the child in question; and

(ii) **Public expense** means that the public agency either pays for the full cost of the evaluation or ensures that the evaluation is otherwise provided at no cost to the parent, consistent with §300.301.

(b) **Parent right to evaluation at public expense.**

(1) A parent has the right to an independent educational evaluation at public expense if the parent disagrees with an evaluation obtained by the public agency.

(2) If a parent requests an independent educational evaluation at public expense, the public agency must, without unnecessary delay, either—

(i) Initiate a hearing under §300.507 to show that its evaluation is appropriate; or

(ii) Ensure that an independent educational evaluation is provided at public expense, unless the agency demonstrates in a hearing under §300.507 that the evaluation obtained by the parent did not meet agency criteria.

(3) If the public agency initiates a hearing and the final decision is that the agency's evaluation is appropriate, the parent still has the right to an independent educational evaluation, but not at public expense.

(4) If a parent requests an independent educational evaluation, the public agency may ask for the parent's reason why he or she objects to the public evaluation. However, the explanation by the parent may not be required and the public agency may not unreasonably delay either providing the independent educational evaluation at public expense or initiating a due process hearing to defend the public evaluation.

(c) **Parent-initiated evaluations.** If the parent obtains an independent educational evaluation at private expense, the results of the evaluation—

(1) Must be considered by the public agency, if it meets agency criteria, in any decision made with respect to the provision of FAPE to the child; and

(2) May be presented as evidence at a hearing under this subpart regarding that child.

(d) **Requests for evaluations by hearing officers.** If a hearing officer requests an independent educational evaluation as part of a hearing, the cost of the evaluation must be at public expense.

(e) **Agency criteria.**

(1) If an independent educational evaluation is at public expense, the criteria under which the evaluation is obtained, including the location of the evaluation and the qualifications of the examiner, must be the same as the criteria that the public agency uses when it initiates an evaluation, to the extent those criteria are consistent with the parent's right to an independent educational evaluation.

(2) Except for the criteria described in paragraph (e)(1) of this section, a public agency may not impose conditions or timelines related to obtaining an independent educational evaluation at public expense.

(Authority: 20 U.S.C. 1415(b)(1))

An IEE is an evaluation conducted by a qualified examiner(s) who is NOT employed by the LEA (or public agency) responsible for the education of the student in question and is provided at public expense as long as all criteria for obtaining an IEE are met.

After analysis of recent court cases, Etscheidt (2003) determined that the *crux* of the IEE issue balances primarily on the *adequacy* of the LEA's evaluation; specifically, is it in *compliance* with the IDEA evaluation criteria? Second, the *scope* of the LEA's evaluation must assess all areas of suspected disability to validate or contest a diagnosis of a disability. Here, the LEA must conduct an in-depth evaluation in all areas of expressed concern rather than a cursory or standard review. Third, does the LEA evaluation focus the IEP team in *useful education planning?* In other words, if the LEA's evaluation does not yield information that identifies specific educational needs to develop interventions, parents are on solid ground for requesting an IEE.

PUTTING PRINCIPLES INTO PRACTICE

So, where do you begin? Because an IEE is not a condition of the law that needs to be implemented as such, it is important for the special education administrator to develop an implementation plan in the event of an IEE request or the presentation of an IEE. The following tips are organized around the three areas discussed above: (1) appropriate evaluation, (2) scope of evaluation, and (3) utility of evaluation.

Appropriateness of Evaluation

According to Etscheidt's (2003) research, the *primary* legal criterion used in hearings and court decisions for IEE is to determine the *appropriateness* of the district's evaluation; in other words, did the district: (a) use a variety of assessment tools and strategies, (b) use more than a single procedure as the sole criterion for determining exceptionality and subsequent programming, and (c) use technically sound instruments that are nondiscriminatory, valid, reliable, and administered by trained personnel? Assuming a parent signs the permission to evaluate or reevaluate the following guidelines should be followed to ensure that the evaluation is "appropriate":

Tips.
- Develop evaluation questions. Depending on the prereferral system used in your school, this can be determined by the prereferral team WITH INPUT from the parents, teachers, and other personnel. At the very least, the evaluation questions MUST be determined prior to requesting parent consent to evaluate so that all team members understand the *purpose of the evaluation.* In addition, evaluation questions serve as a *framework* for all team members; including parents.
- Once the evaluation questions are developed, determine what team members will conduct each part of the evaluation. It helps to keep a detailed team evaluation checklist with calculated timelines for management purposes. Many current IEP tracking tools can be used for tracking of specific management timelines.
- Train your staff to answer the evaluation questions.
- Assure that TRAINED and CERTIFIED evaluators are using tests and assessments that are reliable, valid, nondiscriminatory, and *current.* If your standardized tests are older revisions, invest in the more recently standardized assessment tools.
- School psychologists are trained to determine the most appropriate assessment tools for each student; however, this autonomy can be detrimental if the psychologist always

uses the same assessments. As administrator, guarantee the appropriateness of the assessments by meeting briefly with psychologist(s) to review evaluation questions and subsequent procedures. If you have several school psychologists and other specialized personnel, meet monthly to discuss this issues associated with appropriate assessment.

- Make sure evaluators use a *variety* of tests including standardized, norm-referenced evaluations as well as Curriculum-Based Measurement (CBM) and Curriculum-Based Assessments (CBA). In addition, *progress monitoring* is an important aspect of a strong evaluation and should be used in the evaluation procedure, especially if the student received prereferral interventions or is being reevaluated. In other words, how is the student responding to intervention based on prereferral or IEP goals and objectives?
- Assure that a complete and appropriate classroom observation is conducted and specifically discussed in the report. The observation should be conducted to match the evaluation questions. For example, if the evaluation question is, *Does the student need direct and explicit instruction in reading?* conduct at least one of the classroom observations in a reading setting. Or if an evaluation question is, *Does the student exhibit aggressive behaviors in unstructured settings?* conduct the observation in an unstructured setting such as lunch, recess, changing classes, etc.

Scope of Evaluation

A second criterion used by hearing officers and judges to determine the "appropriateness of the evaluation" is the *scope* of the evaluation (Etscheidt, 2003). In other words, did the evaluation cover all aspects of the suspected disability? When the evaluation team answers specific evaluation questions, follows up on other suspected areas that may broaden the evaluation, and ensures that all members of the team, including the parents, contribute to the student's evaluation, adequate scope is met.

Tips.
- Ensure that all needs or concerns are addressed. For example, if the student exhibits a language processing problem that was not *originally identified* as an area of concern, the examiner must confirm this added suspicion with standardized assessments and/or a referral to a speech and language clinician. Likewise, any other area of concern needs to be addressed as well. For this example, if a parent suspects that his or her child exhibits behavioral problems, assess this area as well in a variety of school settings.
- Areas most likely to be disputed in the area of scope are functional behavioral assessments, observation of a student in areas of concern, and inadequate review of health records (Etscheidt, 2003). The lesson here is if the team suspects other areas of concern not specified in the original evaluation questions; seek additional evaluations as appropriate to answer the question.

Utility of Evaluation for IEP Development

The third area denoted by Etscheidt (2003) in her review of IEE hearing and court cases focuses on the *utility of the evaluation* for the development of the IEP. Here, the evaluation team must "reasonably calculate" the evaluation so that it provides the IEP team sufficient information to write the IEP document.

Tips.

- Educational strengths and needs with specific recommendations need to be offered by the team in the evaluation so that an appropriate IEP can be authored. What curriculum and instructional techniques could be used to make the evaluation have utility for subsequent writing of the IEP? The evaluation should easily convert to Present Levels of Academic Achievement and Functional Performance (Present Levels).
- Ensure that the evaluation enables the team to understand the *impact of the disability* on educational performance and how it will affect performance in general education settings.
- Recommendations to address the specific needs of the student must be addressed. For example, instead of writing, *The student needs an intensive reading program;* the evaluation should conclude, *The student needs an explicit, multisensory, systematic reading program that focuses on phonemic awareness, phonics, and oral reading fluency.*
- Recommendations for specially designed instruction must be included in the evaluation as well; in other words, what does the staff need to do to provide access to the general education curriculum?
- Attend to aspects of the reevaluation as well. For example, if a parent suspects or requests additional information for reevaluation that the district ignores, an IEE may be warranted and the district may be responsible in the end.

In addition to these three areas, one aspect of an IEE request that is overlooked in the literature and in practice is the LEA's ultimate right to evaluate students who have a suspected disability. We think this is often the first error that an LEA administrator makes when processing IEEs. For example, whatever your prereferral system is, it is important that if you *intend to evaluate* a student, seek informed consent, and consent is ultimately denied by the parent or guardian, the district MUST proceed to DUE PROCESS to gain that permission. Furthermore, if a parent later requests or obtains an IEE and wants reimbursement by the LEA, the district should have a process in place on how it will handle this IEE information.

Although many LEAs want to avoid litigation by any means, simply ignoring a nonconsenting parent or pandering to a parent's request for an IEE may cause an unnecessary delay in a student's right to a free appropriate public education. Trust us on this—seek to perform the evaluation even if it means a due process hearing. You have hired certified, respected professionals to do the job, and no one knows the student as well as the LEA teachers and administrators. The district evaluation will have the breadth and depth needed to write a stronger Evaluation Report and subsequent IEP if conducted well.

Final Tips

- If a Permission to Evaluate consent is not returned within ten school days, take the initiative to phone the parent or guardian to discuss evaluation procedures, especially if the prereferral process was not attended by the parent. Use administrative skills to inquire as to why the consent has not been returned so that you are clear on whether the parent understands the purpose of the evaluation.
- If a parent requests or has alternative concerns of an already identified student and makes that request public, initiate an evaluation as soon as possible to assess the new area of concern.

- *Do your homework!* In the event that a parent requests an IEE after what you consider to be a thorough evaluation, your job is to provide that parent with a list of certified professionals who are available to conduct an IEE.
- Interview three or four private, local certified school psychologists or other specialists to determine if they meet the criteria set forth in IDEA, specifically, are they qualified to conduct an evaluation.
- Write guidelines for the IEE, including a requirement for an observation and consultation with school personnel.
- Meet with evaluation team personnel, including psychologists, teachers, counselors, administrators, and other ancillary staff, to periodically review evaluation procedures. Mini professional development opportunities should be conducted at least annually to review district evaluation procedures.

Pitfalls to Avoid

- Not reading the IEE report thoroughly. In other words, do not be impressed with the IEE length or the qualifications of the examiner. Review the report and determine if the IEE offers additional information not covered in the original LEA report. Devise a plan to address additional concerns.
- Delaying the process. If a parent requests an IEE: (1) determine the strength of the district evaluation or conduct a new one or (2) provide an IEE at public expense.

REFERENCES

Etscheidt, S. (2003). Ascertaining the adequacy, scope, and utility of district evaluations. *Exceptional Children, 69*(2), 227–247.

Freedman, M. K. (1996). IEEs: Who's right, and when? *The Special Educator, 12*(1). Retrieved April 10, 2003, from http://www.lrp.com.

■ ■ ■ ■ ■

CHAPTER FIFTEEN

CONTRACTING WITH OUTSIDE SERVICE PROVIDERS

OVERVIEW

The Individuals with Disabilities Education Improvement Act of 2004 (IDEA 2004) (i.e., PL 108-446) assures parents of students with disabilities the provision of related services if their child requires and can benefit from them. Often, related services are not provided directly by school district personnel, but must be procured outside of the district, or outside of educational resources. In such instances, the local educational agency (LEA) often contracts the needed services with community or agency personnel, venturing into counseling, medical, therapy, or psychological arenas.

In this chapter, we define *related services* and the roles of service providers. Next, we define steps by LEAs in procuring contracted service providers. Then, we provide guidelines and tips that may be helpful in avoiding inadequate contracted services. Finally, we offer resources on related services that might prove useful to the new special education program administrator, who often is in charge of contracting for the related services on behalf of the LEA.

REGULATIONS

§300.24 Related services

(a) General. As used in this part, the term related services means transportation and such developmental, corrective, and other supportive services as are required to assist a child with a disability to benefit from special education, and includes speech-language pathology and audiology services; psychological services; physical and occupational therapy; recreation, including therapeutic recreation; early identification and assessment of disabilities in children; counseling services, including rehabilitation counseling; orientation and mobility services; and medical services for diagnostic or evaluation purposes. The term also includes school health services, social work services in schools, and parent counseling and training.

(Authority: 20 U.S.C. 1401(22))

The federal regulations clearly underscore that students with disabilities must receive related services that enable them to receive meaningful benefit from educational opportunities. In order to provide the opportunity to receive meaningful educational benefit, LEAs sometimes must expand on local resources, relying on the expertise and willingness of community or agency professionals to help support decisions offered to students or families.

Further, the IDEA 2004 added specific services to the definition of "related services" [602(26)], including interpreting services and specific school nursing services. The IDEA 2004 excluded surgically implanted medical devices (such as cochlear implants).

ROLES OF SERVICE PROVIDERS

The roles of service providers providing contracted related services include such tasks as (a) assisting in the identification and evaluation of students' counseling, medical, therapy, or psychological needs that have an impact on educational needs, and (b) directly providing counseling, medical, therapy, or psychological services to students or parents. Below, we explain how federal regulations accentuate the roles of related service providers for each service contracted by the LEA.

Audiology Services

Audiology services include duties performed by trained personnel to address the screening needs and identification of students with hearing loss. Because hearing loss is a low incidence occurrence, and the service provision may not be readily available at a specific locale, many LEAs find it necessary to contract for audiology services when a student is suspected of or evidences a hearing loss.

Accordingly, contracted service providers may make available to LEAs hearing assessment information needed for the student's individualized evaluation report. They may target instructional strategies relevant to the student's specially designed instruction and classroom accommodations. For instance, contracted service providers might focus on the determination of the range, nature, and degree of the student's hearing loss, including referral for medical or other professional attention for the habilitation of hearing. Procured services received by the LEA might include the provision of habilitative activities, such as language habilitation, auditory training, speechreading, hearing evaluation, and/or speech conservation.

Additionally, audiologists often support a student's Individualized Education Program (IEP) team by participating with parents or LEA personnel in the creation and administration of programs for prevention of hearing loss. Contracted services may focus on the provision of counseling and guidance of children, parents, and teachers regarding hearing loss or in the planning and implementation of home-school strategies to determine an individual student's needs for group and individual amplification. Further, contracted services may include an audiologist's help in selecting and fitting the student's appropriate hearing aid, or in working with teachers or parents to evaluate the effectiveness of the student's amplification.

Counseling Services

Counseling services may include contracted duties performed by community-based, qualified social workers, psychologists, guidance counselors, or other agency personnel. For instance, contracted services may entail a local community agency's help to the LEA in creating and maintaining counseling programs held on school grounds. Thus, contracted counselors may aim school-based services at facilitating LEA personnel, parents, and students' acquisition, maintenance, and generalization of active listening skills; provide group guidance strategies on problems facing an at-risk student population, such as tactics to avoid teenage pregnancy or drug dependency; or offer advisement, such as training on coping skills and anger management, parenting skills, problem solving, interpersonal relationships, stress reduction, or self-awareness of emotions, behaviors, and the connection between affect, emotions, and actions.

Early Identification and Assessment

Early identification and assessment of disabilities in children include duties related to the implementation of a formal plan for identifying a disability as early as possible in a young child's life. Contracted services may take the form of early interventionists working directly with family members, LEA professionals, and community agency members who screen and identify infants and young children for needed special education and related services. Contracted roles may also entail the provision of formal assessments needed in the development of an Individualized Family Services Plan (IFSP), appropriate to a young child with identified needs and his or her family.

Medical Services

Medical services are contracted services provided by a licensed physician to determine a student's medically related disability that results in the student's special education and related services. For instance, many LEAs often work with psychiatrists or clinical psychologists in ascertaining data on emotional or behavioral functioning of students with emotional disturbances. Or, contracted services may include consultations with dieticians, nurses, or endocrinologists in determining appropriate meals and drug prescriptions for students with other health impairments, such as those with suspected endocrine or hormonal imbalances. Such contracted services may focus on the identification and assessment of medical issues that hold educational implications to students' service provisions.

Occupational Therapy Services

Occupational therapy services are services provided by qualified occupational therapists. Contracted roles may include working with family members and LEA personnel to develop, improve, or restore a student's motor functions impaired or lost through illness, injury, or deprivation. Such therapists may assess students' needs or provide direct services to students with fine motor issues. Direct services include the provision of interventions, such as improving the student's ability to perform tasks for independent functioning, (e.g., handwriting, typing, computing, cutting, pasting, and other school-related, fine motor skills). Occupational therapists may consult with teachers or family members on preventing initial or further impairment or loss of fine motor function. Many occupational therapists may work in early intervention centers, preschools, or elementary schools, alongside teachers and other therapists, to support a student's early intervention needs.

Orientation and Mobility Therapy Services

Qualified personnel provide orientation and mobility therapy services to students identified as blind or visually impaired. Such services enable those students to attain systematic orientation to and safe movement within their environments in the school, home, and community. Thus, an LEA may contract for the services of an orientation and mobility specialist who works with the parents and student, as appropriate, to teach spatial and environmental concepts and use of information received by the senses (such as sound, temperature, or vibrations). This specialist may help the student to establish, maintain, or regain orientation and line of travel, such as when one uses sound at a traffic light to cross the street. The specialist may work with LEA personnel to support the student's use of a long cane in supplemental, visual travel skills. Or, the specialist's contracted services may focus on teaching specific environmental cues as tools for safely negotiating the home environment to students with no available travel vision or to those with limited residual vision. Such specialists may offer specialized strategies to the students' IEP teams, in order to help students understand and use remaining vision and distance low vision aids. They may offer consultation services to use appropriate visual techniques, and orientation or mobility tools at the home, school, or community location.

Parent Counseling and Training

LEA personnel may contract with family agencies to provide parent counseling and training services that support parents' understanding of the special needs of their child. For example, roles of the contracted family service provider may target the provision of information on child development issues and transition services to parents. Parent counseling and training often focus on parent education and continuing development courses that strengthen parents' skills, allowing them to support the implementation of their child's IEP or IFSP. Specific topics might include advocacy roles parents can play to support school efforts, or transition planning across the life span of students and family members.

Physical Therapy

Physical therapy services are provided by qualified physical therapists. Physical therapists target gross motor areas related to the student's neuromuscular, skeletal development. That is, these professionals may work with teachers or family members to determine a student's proficiency in school-related ambulation, such as running, hopping, jumping, or kicking skills. Difficulties may arise in neuromuscular or skeletal influences affecting the student's coordination and completion of physical tasks or lower body requirements. Also affected may be the student's skills in endurance, posture, memory, and processing.

Contracted services may focus on the specialist's observations, assessments, and instruction centering on the student's coordination and completion of physical tasks, or lower body requirements for standing or sitting in required locations. For instance, the specialist may teach the student balance strategies, based on a physical therapy prescription and according to the directions of the student's personal physician. The therapist may submit reports to the program supervisor or classroom teacher indicating consultative strategies to supplement the physical domain of the student's IEP. Working with family members and LEA personnel, the therapist may develop appropriate physical therapy guidelines and teaching strategies, consulting with the classroom teacher and/or family members.

Many physical therapists conduct individual or small group therapy sessions in accordance with the student's individualized physical therapy prescription. When requested, therapists often participate as a member of the multidisciplinary team in the identification or review and reevaluation of students "thought to be exceptional" or with identified physical needs.

Psychological Services

Many LEAs contract for psychological services that include administering psychological and educational tests, behavioral ratings, and/or other assessment devices. Contracted psychological services also may entail interpreting assessment results; or obtaining, integrating into an evaluation report, and interpreting information about student behavior and conditions relating to student learning.

Many contracted psychologists also consult with other staff members in planning school programs to meet the special needs of students as indicated by psychological tests, interviews, and behavioral evaluations. For instance, key roles for psychologists underscore planning and managing a program of psychological services, including psychological counseling for students and parents and assisting in developing positive behavioral intervention strategies.

Recreation Services

Contracted recreation services may include an assessment of a student's leisure function and his or her needs in therapeutic recreation services. The specialist may conduct a comprehensive leisure assessment of adapted physical education needs, specifying present levels of educational performance in a number of sports and recreation areas in which the student displays interest. Further, the specialist may provide recreation programs in schools and community agencies or offer leisure education, as mandated by a student's IEP. Recreation service providers collaborate with teachers and family members to encourage students' social skills; fine-tune appropriate adult-bound, leisure time goals; ascertain students' interests, pursuits, or preferences; and encourage students' and family members' daily leisure activities.

Rehabilitation Counseling Services

Rehabilitation counseling services provided by qualified personnel in individual or group sessions focus specifically on a special student's career development, employment preparation, independence, and integration in the workplace and community. Services may include vocational rehabilitation services provided by vocational rehabilitation programs funded under the Rehabilitation Act of 1973.

LEAs may contract with community or agency personnel to offer job shadowing opportunities, career options, or meaningful instruction or assistance in preparing the student for life after graduation from high school. Targeted areas may include independent living skills, financial management, citizenship responsibilities, and armed forces or tertiary educational choices, in addition to employment opportunities and career advancements.

School Health Services

Services provided by a qualified school nurse or other qualified health professional comprise school health services. School health services include work by professionals providing diagnostic and evaluation supports in students' health areas. Health-related specialists provide important data related to evaluations of students' nutrition, exercise, sleep, and safety precaution needs. School health services are related to students' educational planning and school involvement needs. Health data help teachers and family members to acquire appropriate diagnostic information, important for students' IEPs. Data help to further ascertain whether students' growth and health are proceeding smoothly and accurately.

Importantly, the new IDEA 2004 added an exception to the definition of "assistive technology device" [602(1)] to exclude surgically implanted or replaced medical devices (e.g., cochlear implants), while including interpreting services.

Social Work Services in Schools

Social work services in schools include preparing a social or developmental history on a student with a disability, or offering group and individual counseling to the student and family. Contracted services often target the social worker's partnership with parents and teachers on those problems faced in a student's living situation (home, school, and community) and that affect the student's school adjustment.

For example, social workers often interact with teachers and other school professionals to support students' growth and development and the development and maintenance of healthy family interactions. Social workers help to determine specific family strengths, analyze family assets and skills, and assess or intervene in unique family experiences. Such actions can provide valuable data to a student's IFSP or IEP team.

Many social workers are responsible for gathering information, making appropriate referrals for psychiatric and/or psychological services, and providing ongoing support to students who are thought to be or have been identified as students with disabilities. Among the contracted services that many social workers provide are direct mental health services to school-age students. Social workers also develop and maintain a liaison with psychiatric services to facilitate referral and/or follow-up on students. Many contracted services also include the provision of casework, group work, and consultative mental health services to give definition and treatment to those students not adjusting to the ongoing educational program at the school site.

Speech-Language Pathology Services

Speech-language pathology services focus on the identification of students with speech or language impairments, the diagnosis and appraisal of specific speech or language needs, and the referral for medical or other professional attention necessary for the habilitation of speech or language impairments. Contracted services often entail the provision of speech and language services for the prevention of communicative impairments and counseling and guidance of parents, children, and teachers.

Among the contracted services that LEA personnel often negotiate with contracted service providers include the scheduling and conduction of therapy classes according to the content of students' IEPs. Further, specialists notify parents, teachers, nurses, administrative personnel, and any others concerned with students' welfare and needs related to articulation, fluency, language, and receptive or expressive communication skills.

Contracted service providers often supply information and counsel in order to achieve the best possible therapy results, and they refer students, through the proper authorities, to the appropriate agencies for supplemental diagnosis and assessment as indicated by specific student needs. Finally, it is imperative that contracted service providers keep adequate records on students receiving speech-language therapy in order to ensure the most effective continuing therapy.

Transportation Services

Transportation services include a student's travel to and from school and between schools, travel in and around school buildings, and the student's need for specialized equipment (such as special or adapted buses, lifts, and ramps), if required on the student's IEP.

LEAs often contract with bus, van, or taxi agencies to offer a variety of transportation options. Contracted transportation services may include the LEA issuance of a paraprofessional or transportation assistant, indicated on the student's IEP. The extra adult present during the provision of a student's transportation services helps to ease transportation concerns and ensure the safe traveling of the student with special needs.

PUTTING PRINCIPLES INTO PRACTICE

So, where does a special education program adminstrator, new to the LEA, begin? In order to define steps in procuring contracted service providers, we offer the following tips.

Tips

- The LEA should keep an updated list and variety of related service contractors available in the service region. It is important to secure the services of two to three companies or service entities that may contract with the LEA in the provision of services that the LEA cannot provide (e.g., two to three companies or service entities per audiology, medical, orientation and mobility, rehabilitation counseling, and transportation services).
- It is important to let the market value work in the LEA's favor. New administrators and supervisors may work with the central office staff to send out periodically an "RFQ" ("Request for Quotations") on services to multiple service entities in their locale. That way, local service contractors will compete against each other to drive down the costs to the LEA.
- As LEA personnel examine the provision of services, it is important to seek out the lowest responsible bidder(s), in order that the contactor can fulfill the contract (i.e., the lowest bidder to provide occupational therapy or physical therapy may not have enough therapists to fulfill the needs for therapy requested by the LEA at that time). It is important to monitor the ongoing costs, in addition to provision of ongoing services in a timely manner.

- New special education program administrators may work with central office personnel in contract language of the service provision. It is important and efficient to have an LEA attorney draw up a "boiler plate" contract to be used with various providers.
- Special education program administrators may work with the central office personnel on managing the actual services and responsibilities of the services. In the contract language, it is important to the LEA to have the authority to manage the contractors' staff so that the LEA has greater control to locate and provide the services where needed. Some service providers may not believe that they have to follow the LEA's timeline for a full day of service, for example, because they don't see the need to attend school until the bell rings. However, if the LEA requires the full day services, it is important to have the jurisdiction to direct the contractor's staff to be on school grounds as needed.
- Special education program administrators may be responsible for overseeing the paperwork provided by contracted service providers. For instance, it is vitally important that contracted service providers providing medical assistance secure reimbursable services by completing the necessary paperwork to enable the LEA to get reimbursement from medical assistance. By overseeing paperwork, the LEA has the jurisdiction to require completed paperwork during mandated timelines.
- Special education program administrators may be responsible for working with contracted service providers to develop and maintain student files on those students requiring related services. LEA policy and procedures should underscore that all information gathered will come under the LEA's authority regarding the confidentiality of student records.

Avoiding Inadequate Contracted Services

Below, we provide guidelines and tips for avoiding inadequate contracted services. This is followed by pitfalls to avoid.

- Special education program administrators may work with the superintendent or executive director to ensure that the contracted service provider has sufficient liability insurance (e.g., an indemnification clause) that contains provisions for the contractor to carry liability insurance at a sufficient rate. (This rate is usually between $500,000 and $1,000,000 per incident that may result from the delivery of the contracted services.) It is important that new administrators are aware that contracted services provided under their jurisdiction may not necessarily be appropriate and sufficient. Accidents may occur and the LEA needs to safeguard its responsibility by contracting service providers that can ensure adequate coverage in case something does go wrong.
- Special education program administrators should be cognizant of contractual language and whether the language is binding and final. That is, LEA personnel should seek to obtain an "out clause" in the language of all service contracts, such that either the LEA or service providers can nullify service contracts within a set period of days.
- It is important to LEAs to seek out contract language so that the service provider provides a long, advanced notice if the service provider does attempt to nullify or void his or her contract. However, on the other hand, it is important that if the provision of the

contracted services were inappropriate or inadequate, administrators would be wise to seek contract language in order to get out of the contract as quickly as possible. A typical contract may entail at least 60 to 90 days initially. Such a condition should be sufficient to provide the LEA and service contractor notice of ending the contract if the services are inappropriate or inadequate and allow the LEA to seek the services of another provider.

Pitfalls to Avoid

The following ideas may help the new administrator or supervisor to avoid common mistakes when contracting for services. Keeping careful and accurate data on contracted services is a wise investment for all new LEA personnel.

- Not having sufficient service providers. Be careful to have more than one service provider for each contracted service. That is, in case the service provider contracted by your LEA goes belly up, the LEA has a backup provider to ensure the continuation of needed services. It is important to have the primary contractors with a majority of the LEA business. However, it is often necessary to have secondary contractors, in case of a break in services.
- Single-year contracts. Avoid single-year contracts so that the LEA does not have to repeat contracts on an annual basis. In order to ensure adequate coverage, LEA personnel may want to seek out multiple-year contracts in lengths of two to three years. Multiple-year contracts help to ensure better pricing for LEAs.

RESOURCES

There are many related service resources available online and in each individual community and state that will be helpful to LEA personnel. The following is a list of national resources that may be helpful to special education program administrators.

Websites

The World Wide Web provides ready access to a variety of resources. Here are some that have been particularly useful to us.

www.cec.sped.org/law_res/doc/law/index.php
Information on the IDEA is provided along with the latest amendments and final regulations. Articles, general information, speeches, training and more are also available.

www.dssc.org
This website is created and maintained by the *Disabilities Studies and Services Center* (DSSC). The DSSC is a division of the *Academy for Educational Development* (AED). The website provides information on the many national projects directed by the DSSC,

such as the *National Information Center for Children and Youth with Disabilities* (NICHY), the *Federal Resource Center* (FRC), and the *Comprehensive School Reform Demonstration* (CSRD).

www.dssc.org/frc/

The *Federal Resource Center* (FRC) for special education is a nationwide, technical assistance network developed through a five-year contract of several partners at the national level. It offers many resources and information concerning special education and related services.

www.wrightlaw.com

This website provides information for special education and related service providers at the federal level. The website information is provided by a special education attorney who represents parents. Included in the website are data on IDEA, Section 504 of the Rehabilitation Act of 1973, and the Americans with Disabilities Act of 1990.

Other Agencies

Other agencies, addresses, telephone numbers, email addresses, and websites that can provide data on the provision of related services are below. Following these are governmental agencies and government-supported organizations.

The Lighthouse National Center for Vision and Child Development
111 East 59th Street
New York, NY 10022
1-800-334-5497 or (212) 821-9200
(212) 821-9713 (TDD)
email: mbeck@lighthouse.org

National Association of Developmental Disabilities Councils
1234 Massachusetts Avenue, NW, Suite 103
Washington, DC 20005
(202) 347-1234
email: naddc@igc.apc.org
URL: www.igc.apc.orc/NADDC

National Easter Seal Society
230 W. Monroe, Suite 1800
Chicago, IL 60606
1-800-221-6827 or (312) 726-6200
(312) 726-4258 (TTY)
URL: www.seals.com

National Federation of the Blind
National Organization of Parents of Blind Children

1800 Johnson Street
Baltimore, MD 21230
(410) 659-9314
URL: www.nfb.org

National Parent Network on Disabilities (NPND)
1727 King Street, Suite 305
Alexandria, VA 22314
(703) 684-6763 (voice/TTY)
email: npnd@cs.com

Spina Bifida Association of America (SBAA)
4590 MacArthur Boulevard, NW, Suite 250
Washington, DC 20007-4226
1-800-621-3141 or (202) 944-3285
email: spinabifida@aol.com
URL: www.sbaa.org

United Cerebral Palsy Associations, Inc.
1660 L Street, NW, Suite 700
Washington, DC 20036-5602
1-800-872-5827
(202) 973-7197 (TDD)
email: ucnatl@ucpa.org

Government Agencies

Administration on Developmental Disabilities
U.S. Department of Health and Human Services
Hubert Humphrey Building, Room 329D
200 Independence Avenue, SW
Washington, DC 20201
(202) 690-6590
(202) 690-6415 (TTY)

Clearinghouse on Disability Information
Office of Special Education and Rehabilitative Services
U.S. Department of Education
Switzer Building, Room 3132
330 C Street, SW
Washington, DC 20202-2524
(202) 205-8241 (voice/TTY)

Indian Health Service
Health Education Programs

5600 Fisher Lane
Room 6A38
Rockville, MD 20857
(301) 443-1870

National Council on Disability
1331 F Street, NW
Suite 1050
Washington, DC 20004-1107
(202) 272-2004
(202) 272-2074 (TTY)

National Institute of Child Health and Human Development
P.O. Box 29111
Washington, DC 20040
(301) 496-5133

National Institute on Disability and Rehabilitation Research
Office of Special Education and Rehabilitative Services
U.S. Department of Education
Switzer Building, Room 3060
600 Independence Avenue, SW
Washington, DC 20202-2572
(202) 205-8134
(202) 205-8198 (TTY)

National Library Service for the Blind and Physically Handicapped
Library of Congress
1291 Taylor Street, NW
Washington, DC 20542
(202) 707-5100
(202) 707-0744 (TTY)

Office of Special Education Programs
U.S. Department of Education MES Building, Room 3086
600 Independence Avenue, SW
Washington, DC 20202-4611
(202) 205-5507

Social Security Administration (Headquarters)
6401 Security Boulevard
Baltimore, MD 21235
1-800-772-1213
1-800-325-0778 (TTY)

Government-Supported Organizations

Abledata: The National Database of Assistive Technology Information
8455 Colesville Road, Suite 935
Silver Spring, MD 20910-3319
1-800-227-0216 or (301) 608-8998
(301) 608-8912 (TTY)

National Clearinghouse on Family Support and Children's Mental Health
Portland State University
P.O. Box 751
Portland, OR 97207-0751
1-800-628-1696
(503) 725-4165 (TTY)

National Information Center on Deafness
Gallaudet University
800 Florida Avenue, NE
Washington, DC 20002-3695
(202) 651-5051
(202) 651-5054 (TTY)
email: judd103w@wonder.em.cdc.gov

National Rehabilitation Information Center (NARIC)
8455 Coles Road, Suite 935
Silver Spring, MD 20910-3319
1-800-346-2742 or (310) 588-9284
(301) 495-5626 (TTY)

CHAPTER SIXTEEN

NAVIGATING THE MENTAL HEALTH SYSTEM

OVERVIEW

Mental health entails one's ability to function (i.e., cope and adjust). According to the *Diagnostic and Statistical Analysis Manual–IV* (DSM-IV, American Psychiatric Association, 1994), there are five axes of functional diagnosis that psychiatrists may use to classify clients. Most important to school settings are *Axis IV: Psychosocial and Environmental Problems* and *Axis V: Global Assessment of Functioning*. Diagnoses are determined over time (DSM-IV, pp. 25–31).

Axis IV: Psychosocial and Environmental Problems can be important to one's mental health over time as "stressors" trigger problems. Coping and adjusting to stressors may impact the diagnosis, treatment, and prognosis of mental disorders. Stressors are grouped into relevant categories as follows:

- *Problems with the primary support group* (e.g., coping with and adjusting to the death of a family member, divorce or separation, removal from the home, sexual or physical abuse, neglect, and so forth).
- *Problems related to the social environment* (e.g., coping with and adjusting to the death or loss of a friend, discrimination, or life cycle transitions, such as marriage, birth of a child, retirement, and so forth).
- *Problems of an educational nature* (e.g., coping with and adjusting to illiteracy, academic disparities, discord with teachers or peers, and so forth).
- *Problems of an occupational nature* (e.g., coping with and adjusting to unemployment, job change, threat of job loss, stressful work schedule or conditions, and so forth).
- *Problems in habitation* (e.g., coping with and adjusting to homelessness, unsafe neighborhoods, inadequate housing, and so forth).
- *Problems related to economics* (e.g., coping with and adjusting to extreme poverty, insufficient welfare support, inadequate finances, and so forth).
- *Problems with access to health care services* (coping with and adjusting to inadequate health insurance, inadequate health care services, lack of transportation, and so forth).
- *Problems related to legal systems or criminal interactions* (e.g., coping with and adjusting to arrest, incarceration, victim of crime, litigation, and so forth).

- *Other psychosocial and environmental problems* (e.g., coping with and adjusting to exposure to disaster or war; discord with nonfamily caregivers, such as physicians, counselors, and so forth).

Based on the Axis V: Global Assessment of Functioning, one's overall level of functioning can range from superior in all areas (in which one is involved in a wide range of activities and has many interests at home, at school, and with peers) to a level of functioning requiring constant supervision due to one's severely aggressive or self-destructive behavior or gross impairment. In essence, an individual's mental health needs can be assessed by how one functions in relationship to coping with and adjusting to life's trials and tribulations.

Why are the above data important to special education program administrators? According to the executive summary and recommendations of the National Advisory Mental Health Council (2002), currently, one in ten children and youth in this country suffers from mental illness severe enough to result in significant functional impairment. Such children and youth with mental health needs are at much greater risk for dropping out of school and suffering long-term consequences, such as poverty, joblessness, or hospitalization. Every year, approximately 9.5 percent of the U.S. population age 18 and older have a depressive disorder. Mental illness often co-occurs, such as depression with anxiety disorders and substance abuse. More than 90 percent of the people who commit suicide have a diagnosable mental illness, commonly a depressive disorder or a substance abuse disorder (Highmark, 2003). No other illnesses damage so many individuals so seriously and pervasively.

Accordingly, there are myriad mental health issues facing students and families evolving from individuals' attempts to cope with and adjust in their lives. Such mental health issues challenge school personnel. For instance, school personnel cannot escape the daily ramifications evolving from the effects of community and domestic violence, conduct problems, depression, eating disorders, homelessness, physical and sexual abuse, high-risk sexual behavior and sexually transmitted diseases, school dropout or refusal, serious mental illness, substance abuse, or suicide.

Such mental health issues affect people of all ages, races, ethnicities, community or neighborhood contexts, cultures, backgrounds, lifestyles, and socioeconomic statuses. Additionally, mental health functioning can be exaggerated by community, home, or school factors; attitudes, behaviors, beliefs, and feelings of family members, professionals, peers, and self; current events; individual reactions and personal skills; and any of the behavioral, cognitive, ecological, or social conditions that may trigger signs in how individuals recognize, respond to, and control their mental well-beings.

School settings cannot escape students' daily mental health functioning; nevertheless, many students and families require support from local educational agency (LEA) and community personnel to create and maintain their healthy, mental well-beings. While not directly responsible for addressing the mental health needs of the local school and family population, special education program administrators can do much to support mental illness prevention as they collaborate with and address the mental health needs of the children, youth, and families they serve.

For example, understanding the reciprocal influences between students and their environments throughout developmental periods is critical. Additionally, by working collaboratively with families, LEA personnel, and frontline agency personnel involved in mental health care service delivery (e.g., behavioral specialists, clinical psychologists, counselors, social workers, and physicians), special education program administrators can support community efforts to confront barriers to effective services. Such barriers include stigma, poverty, and lack of appropriate access to and use of mental health services.

Although the Individuals with Disabilities Education Improvement Act of 2004 (IDEA 2004, i.e., PL 108-446) mandated important changes to the federal special education law, the new law does not directly change special education program administrators' roles and responsibilities in navigating the mental health system. However, in order to navigate the mental health system appropriately, special education program administrators need to have a clear understanding of the LEA's roles in mental health services. Accordingly, in this chapter, we view federal special education regulations, emphasizing the need for coordinated mental health services across agencies and disciplines. We explore students' mental health needs and examine avenues in which special education program administrators can work collaboratively with educational and mental health professionals and families. Then, we provide guidelines and tips that may be helpful to special education program administrators navigating the mental health system. Finally, we offer resources on mental health issues that might prove useful as special education program administrators participate in interagency coordination.

REGULATIONS

§300.244 Coordinated services system

(a) General. An LEA may not use more than 5 percent of the amount the agency receives under Part B of the Act for any fiscal year, in combination with other amounts (which must include amounts other than education funds), to develop and implement a coordinated services system designed to improve results for children and families, including children with disabilities and their families.

(b) Activities. In implementing a coordinated services system under this section, an LEA may carry out activities that include—

(1) Improving the effectiveness and efficiency of service delivery, including developing strategies that promote accountability for results;

(2) Service coordination and case management that facilitate the linkage of IEPs under Part B of the Act and IFSPs under Part C of the Act with individualized service plans under multiple Federal and State programs, such as title I of the Rehabilitation Act of 1973 (vocational rehabilitation), title XIX of the Social Security Act (Medicaid), and title XVI of the Social Security Act (supplemental security income);

(3) Developing and implementing interagency financing strategies for the provision of education, health, mental health, and social services, including transition services and related services under the Act; and

(4) Interagency personnel development for individuals working on coordinated services.

(c) Coordination with certain projects under Elementary and Secondary Education Act of 1965. If an LEA is carrying out a coordinated services project under title XI of the Elementary and Secondary Education Act of 1965 and a coordinated services project under Part B of the Act in the same schools, the agency shall use the amounts under §300.244 in accordance with the requirements of that title.

(Authority: 20 U.S.C. 1413(f))

The federal special education regulations clearly underscore that students at risk for or with identified disabilities may have mental health needs that must be addressed. Such students must receive coordinated mental health services, in addition to mandated educational services.

Mental health services cannot be fragmented and must address the needs of today's students and families. School personnel can and must play a role in the prevention of mental illness and in mental health needs. By mandating a coordinated service delivery system encouraging collaboration and resource sharing, the federal regulations draw attention to the fact that educational entities receiving federal funds must work together with other agencies (e.g., health, social, or welfare agencies) to meet the mental health needs of infants, children, adolescents, and families.

Participation in coordinated services highlights the role of school-based personnel as they work with families and community agency personnel to facilitate students' mental health services. Federal regulations stress the necessity of availability and maintenance of coordinated collaboration activities to foster effective mental health programming and delivery.

STUDENTS' MENTAL HEALTH ISSUES

While not responsible for providing direct, intensive mental health services, it is important that special education program administrators play collaborative roles in interagency mental health efforts. As LEA leaders, they must be aware of student and family issues affecting potential at-risk factors and characteristics of mental illness and mental health needs. They can support research to increase understanding of how children and youth with mental illnesses may benefit from intervention efforts and perhaps develop new or compensatory skills. Further, they can encourage the study of new assessment tools and approaches that combine qualitative and quantitative methods to understand issues associated with students and families from diverse cultures and subcultures, and the cultural contexts.

Special education program administrators can work with interagency personnel to identify how mental health service providers and families manage children's or youths' disorders and why they do or do not engage in the most effective practices. By participating in coordinated, interagency efforts, special education program administrators can support practice efforts that seek to examine why some mental health treatments are not more widely disseminated, what factors underlie complex health behaviors, and the types of decision-making strategies that guide current practice.

We discuss common mental health issues in Table 16.1 by listing signs and signals that affect students' educational involvement and may trigger the need for interagency coordination with school personnel and mental health service providers and families. Avenues in which special education program administrators can work collaboratively with others accompany each.

TABLE 16.1 Mental Health Issues and Possible Responses

COMMON MENTAL HEALTH ISSUE	AVENUES FOR WORKING COLLABORATIVELY WITH LEA PROFESSIONALS, MENTAL HEALTH PROFESSIONALS, AND FAMILIES
Community Violence • Increased community crime • Poverty • Low adult employment in community • Limited community involvement • Limited social agencies	• Examine collaborative strategies within a safe environment (i.e., interagency team format, workshop context, cross-disciplinary professional development offerings) aimed at combating community violence. • Recognize community violence prevention strategies and techniques. Encourage LEA professionals to gain knowledge of and skills in combating violence in order to teach students increased conflict resolution skills. • Support and facilitate innovative community violence reduction practices by offering meeting times and locations on school grounds. • Disseminate knowledge in and practice of relevant mental health area (i.e., prevention of community violence strategies, family services, etc.). • Practice problem-solving scenarios given cross-disciplinary dialogues. • Promote reflective practices and community initiatives to support student and family needs related to community involvement.
Depression • Expressions of sadness, emptiness, or hopelessness • Prolonged sense of guilt • Pervasive feelings of worthlessness • Continuous dissatisfaction with previously satisfying events • Difficulty in decision making • Constant state of anger • Thoughts of death or suicide • Altered sleep or eating patterns	• Encourage teachers to observe differential characteristics of students displaying depression characteristics and make referrals for support services as necessary. • Acquire and practice self and peers' reflective development as collaborative team members on combating depression and mental illness. • Support the use of depression screening and evidence-based preventions for depression in a variety of settings. • Support community goals to reduce or eliminate depression in students and family members: Have LEA personnel examine, discuss, and describe the theories and resulting etiologies, assessments, and interventions related to interventions and long-term strategies. • Communicate/consult across disciplines, agencies, and settings in order to reduce conditions that may trigger depression. • Seek updated and timely knowledge and disseminate to others as warranted on needs of atypical students, needs of their families, and strategies to combat depression and mental illness. • Actively support mentoring programs that document LEAs, family services, and individual mental health goals, values, and concerns in interdisciplinary, coordinated services.

(continued)

TABLE 16.1   Continued

COMMON MENTAL HEALTH ISSUE	AVENUES FOR WORKING COLLABORATIVELY WITH LEA PROFESSIONALS, MENTAL HEALTH PROFESSIONALS, AND FAMILIES
Domestic Violence • Limited parental involvement in school functions • Multiple family disturbances • Police responses to family disturbances • Restraining orders • General unhappiness • Depression, withdrawal, isolation • Family problems, few resources • Social alienation	• Practice collaborative strategies within a safe environment (i.e., interagency team format, workshop context, cross-disciplinary professional development offerings) to combat domestic violence. • Recognize mental health content—concerns of others regarding domestic violence. • Encourage parental involvement in school activities by offering family-friendly services at times and places based on family needs. Offer transportation and babysitting services to encourage family involvement. • Practice problem-solving scenarios to reduce family disturbance. • Support varied service delivery (i.e., workshops) methods to understand and prevent domestic violence. • Support and facilitate innovative educational practices that discourage students' and families' social alienation. • Promote reflective practices: Offer an LEA initiative to support student and family needs on understanding the etiology of domestic violence.
Eating Disorders • Altered eating patterns • Radical changes in weight • Radical changes in appearance • Lack of grooming • Isolated eating habits • Unusual requests for restroom needs • General unhappiness	• Practice collaborative strategies within a safe environment (i.e., interagency team format, workshop context, cross-disciplinary professional development offerings) to combat eating disorders. • Recognize mental health content related to healthy eating practices. Encourage school personnel to teach appropriate curriculum content to students. • Practice problem-solving scenarios with students and family members on effects of eating disorders. • Assume leadership roles relative to area of expertise (e.g., parents as experts on child and family needs; mental health professionals offering behavioral and mental health updates; teachers offering data on realities of eating disorders).
Homelessness • Unknown family address • Lack of stable mailing address or phone contact • Frequency in change of school or district • Habitation in cars, vans, campgrounds, motels, shelters	• Seek to discover data on the accurate number of local homeless students. • Seek out data on students' living conditions and reasons supporting continuation in ineffective home-based sites. Share data with interdisciplinary team members. • Share school resources and educational practices others find useful on supporting family stability. Offer media, library, Internet, technology, and other LEA resources as is feasible.

TABLE 16.1   Continued

COMMON MENTAL HEALTH ISSUE	AVENUES FOR WORKING COLLABORATIVELY WITH LEA PROFESSIONALS, MENTAL HEALTH PROFESSIONALS, AND FAMILIES
Homelessness (continued)	• Seek to foster respectful-beneficial relationships among families, LEA personnel, and community agencies that combat homelessness and family instability. • Recognize the expertise in child mental health. Support mentorship programs to increase the number of racial/ethnic minority professionals who can address the unique needs of minority children.
Physical and Sexual Abuse • Expressed instances of physical and sexual abuse • Chronic fatigue • Poor emotional control • Excessive moodiness • Physical changes in appearance • Excessive or inappropriate clothing • Marked change in sleeping or eating habits • Severe feelings of uselessness • Constant state of anger • Withdrawal from responsibility	• Communicate/consult across disciplines, agencies, and settings in order to gain a deeper understanding of the complexities of physical and sexual abuse as mental illnesses—what causes them, what interventions are effective, and how to get interventions to those who need them. • Acquire and practice self and peers' reflective understanding on signs and signals of students' experiencing physical or sexual abuse. Share as collaborative team members. • Support mental health needs and community goals: Discuss and describe the theories and resulting etiologies, assessments, and interventions related to mental health strengths and needs. Support local practices to combat physical and sexual abuse.
School Dropout or Refusal • Low attendance rate • Chronic tardiness or absences • Low achievement • Low graduation rates • Lack of extracurricular involvement • Limited parental involvement in school functions • Withdrawal from responsibility	• Recognize continued school dropout or refusal as an at-risk indicator of potential mental health concern. • Practice problem-solving scenarios on long-term consequences of low attendance rate, chronic tardiness or absences, low achievement, lack of extracurricular involvement, limited parental involvement in school functions, and withdrawal from responsibility. • Encourage cross-disciplinary efforts and interagency support to facilitate the development of culturally sensitive in-school involvement and commitments that are feasible, cost-effective, and readily disseminated. • Promote reflective practices and LEA initiatives to support student and family needs related to school attendance and graduation rates. • Recognize expertise in child mental health. • Support mentorship programs to increase the number of racial/ethnic minority professionals who can address the unique needs of minority children.

(continued)

TABLE 16.1   Continued

COMMON MENTAL HEALTH ISSUE	AVENUES FOR WORKING COLLABORATIVELY WITH LEA PROFESSIONALS, MENTAL HEALTH PROFESSIONALS, AND FAMILIES
Serious Mental Illness (e.g., Early-Onset Schizophrenia, Bipolar Disorder) • Out-of-proportion anxiety • Carelessness (personal habits, risk-taking, thrill seeking) • Lack of grooming • Sexual promiscuity • Mood swings • Poor emotional control • Withdrawal from responsibility • Isolation	• Support and facilitate innovative mental health practices examining reasons why individuals with bipolar disorder or schizophrenia do or do not follow treatment recommendations. • Support studies on the impact of the long-term use of medications to treat bipolar disorder or schizophrenia, including impact on psychosocial functioning. • Support LEA training seminars, summer institutes, and intensive coursework on adaptability and sustainability of interventions (e.g., different roles of family in the intervention process, strategies for engaging families, and ways of increasing or maintaining treatment fidelity). • Support training seminars, summer institutes, and intensive coursework on the range of service settings where effective mental health services are typically delivered (e.g., schools, primary care, community clinics).
High-Risk Sexual Behavior and Sexually Transmitted Diseases • Sexual promiscuity • Overt sexual advances • Age inappropriate knowledge of sexual behavior • Sexual advances • Provocative dress • Drug or substance abuse • Physical changes in appearance • Excessive medical concerns • Pregnancy	• Assume leadership roles relative to area of expertise (e.g., parents as experts on child and family needs; mental health professionals offering behavioral and mental health updates; teachers offering data on classroom realities). • Support LEA opportunity to share resources and practices others find useful on high-risk sexual behavior and sexually transmitted diseases.
Suicide • Recent marked changes in behavior (weight, change, sleep difficulties, etc.) • Recent change in situation (loss of pet, parent, status, etc.) • Out of proportion anxiety • Carelessness (personal habits, risk-taking, thrill seeking) • Thinly veiled comments ("I'll get even," "I'm a burden")	• Seek the implementation of parenting education in primary care settings on signs and signals and methods to prevent suicide. • Support studies of factors influencing how practitioners and families manage youth disorders and the use of evidence-based treatments to reduce the risk of suicide and increase suicide prevention practices. • Support mentoring for child and adolescent mental health practices in the LEA. Support funding for sabbatical leaves or teaching/mentoring time, provided in the form of supplements to grants to teachers and related service providers.

TABLE 16.1   Continued

COMMON MENTAL HEALTH ISSUE	AVENUES FOR WORKING COLLABORATIVELY WITH LEA PROFESSIONALS, MENTAL HEALTH PROFESSIONALS, AND FAMILIES
Suicide (continued) • Direct comments (talk of suicide to others) • Giving away prized possessions • Collecting drugs, guns • Questions regarding various ways to die • Statements of intent	
Substance Abuse • Physical changes in appearance • Glassy-eyed, disoriented • Excessive fatigue • Chronic moodiness • Poor emotional control • Excessive money • Excessive medical concerns • Carelessness (personal habits, risk-taking, thrill seeking) • Withdrawal from responsibility	• Provide mentoring opportunities that support effective substance abuse interventions and dissemination to the homes, schools, agencies, and other places where children, adolescents, and their parents can easily access them. Support practices and dissemination efforts that are usable. Support partnerships among students, families, LEA personnel, agency providers, and other stakeholders. • Encourage teachers and other school personnel to seek knowledge on specific psychological and behavioral functions that are impaired by prolonged substance abuse, including memory, attention, emotional processing, expression, social cognitive capacities, and child temperament.

GUIDELINES AND TIPS ON NAVIGATING INTERAGENCY COORDINATION

We present guidelines and tips in how special education program administrators can work collaboratively to ensure appropriate and accessible coordinated mental health services (Office of Mental Health and Substance Abuse Services, 2003).

1. Special education program administrators can meet on a regular basis to discuss issues related to interagency collaboration, including mental health needs and required services for students and families. Children and youth with severe mental health needs can gain access to needed services that are planned collaboratively with school personnel, the family, physicians, and mental health agency providers (e.g., agencies representing mental health–mental retardation services, children and youth services, juvenile probation, and so forth).

2. Special education program administrators can become familiar with the roles and positions of mental health care workers that may be involved in school activities. These include staff of *wraparound services,* such as behavior specialist consultants (BSC),

mobile therapists (MT), and therapeutic staff support (TSS). The BSC, usually a licensed doctoral-level psychologist, clinical psychologist, or mental health clinician with documented training in behavioral management and support, is responsible for the interagency team's responsibility to formulate, implement, and monitor a behavioral plan. The BSC helps to record case progress, attends interagency meetings, provides on-call services, attends trainings, and provides guidance to the implementation of a student's or family's individualized medical treatment plan. The MT is a licensed mental health professional that provides therapeutic services to the student and family in the student's natural settings, especially the home. This individual assesses the strengths and therapeutic needs of the student and family and plans and implements therapeutic interventions that are focused on individualized needs. A TSS worker is responsible for direct implementation of the treatment and/or behavior plans with the student and family. This individual observes in the natural settings and uses either behavioral support or crisis intervention techniques, as outlined in the plan, when the student exhibits problem behaviors.

3. In addition to serving as a forum for raising issues of interagency collaboration, special education program administrators can set up meetings to support the LEA and other child-serving agencies to collaborate and oversee training and technical assistance initiatives aimed at improving interagency coordination with the goal of reducing mental illness and increasing appropriate mental health practices in the locale.

4. Special education program administrators can work collaboratively with mental health personnel to support interagency coordination by helping parents, advocates, representatives of other child-serving agencies, and other individuals recognize the importance of identification, screening, and assessment of students who may have mental health needs. LEA personnel often have a crucial role in identifying which students require mental health services. By alerting school personnel to observe and report at-risk students, mental health services can reach those in need more effectively and efficiently. For instance, school personnel may be in the best position to identify those students who require hospitalization because they are dangerous to self or others. School administrators can support teachers' reporting of overt behaviors or threats with acts to further the threats. School personnel may assist families in identifying students' "voluntary" and "involuntary" commitments for examination and receipt of mental health treatment services. School personnel can work with families, mental health care workers, and physicians to obtained signed consent to inpatient treatment services. School personnel also can help to differentiate students requiring hospitalization, partial hospitalization, or outpatient services by presenting to interagency teams behavioral data observed in the school setting.

5. If students require interagency coordination to access appropriate educational placements that offer therapeutic or mental health services, special education program administrators can support active LEA participation on interagency teams. For instance, the new administrator can assign veteran teachers to assess educational implications of the students' needs for behavioral specialists. School counselors and social workers can work with agency personnel on matters to determine barriers preventing students from receiving agreed-upon placements and mental health services. If necessary to resolve

coordination problems, LEA administrators can facilitate the prompt scheduling of meetings of the local interagency team, including the family of the student, school personnel, relevant child-service agencies, and offer immediate and convenient locations.

6. Special education program administrators can support shared data by recognizing the disparity in how educators and medical personnel classify problem behaviors and mental illness (e.g., clinicians rely on the DSM-IV; educators use the classification criteria specified by the IDEA 2004). By having a working knowledge of relevant DSM-IV diagnoses and IDEA 2004 criteria, LEA personnel can communicate more effectively across disciplines.

7. Section 1412(a)(12)(A)(i) of the 1997 amendments to the IDEA requires the state Medicaid agency's financial responsibility to precede the financial responsibility of the LEA. If a student's educational placement is in dispute and not resolved within thirty calendar days (with the exception of the summer months) by the local interagency team, the new administrator or supervisor can report to the state educational agency for appropriate intervention with other state agencies based on the presenting issue(s).

8. The special education program administrator can take a mentoring lead during interagency meetings in advocating the position that the student's diagnosis or treatment services do not replace the parents' decision-making responsibility relative to the resolution of the student's mental health problems. The team is there to support and help to coordinate, but not to replace parental jurisdiction.

9. In collaboration with state educational officials, special education program administrators can seek assistance from interagency councils in order to identify whether there is a need to enhance the capacity of local mental health services in collaboration with school initiatives. When the need to enhance local capacity is identified, the administrator can guide discussions with the student's interagency team, on specific details of capacity-building activities that will be undertaken to remedy the need and monitor individual students' progress in building the identified capacity.

10. In accordance with the 1997 amendments to the IDEA related to interagency coordination, the special education program administrator can hold faculty meetings reiterating how LEA personnel can collaborate to ensure that services should be coordinated among child-serving agencies in order that students with disabilities receive a free appropriate public education in the least restrictive environment.

11. Special education program administrators can allow planning time and workshop or faculty time allotments to educate school staff, board members, parents, students and the community about the roles, responsibilities, and limitations in dealing with mental health issues as these affect students' school performance. Allowing sufficient time for the team members to carry out their responsibilities on the promotion of effective mental health practices is essential.

PUTTING PRINCIPLES INTO PRACTICE

Where does a special education program administrator new to the LEA begin? In order to define steps in navigating the mental health system, we offer the following tips.

Tips

- Special education program administrators can support families and mental health professionals by offering conference rooms and meeting locations at times and places conducive to interagency team members.
- Special education program administrators can support mental illness prevention, wellness promotion, and crisis intervention by encouraging LEA personnel to monitor students' functional outcomes (e.g., academic achievement, improved family functioning, increased school attendance, supportive parent–child relations, and social skills).
- School personnel must be part of interagency teams that receive training in identifying mental health problems and determining whether the presenting problem lies within the responsibility of the school. Special education program administrators can inform the interagency team and family of the problem affecting the student's performance in school, provide information on agency resources and the options to deal with problems, and, where necessary, set up linkages with community agencies or external resources to help resolve problems.
- Special education program administrators can work to encourage local programs that positively influence students, including school, family, peer group, and community services that are individually, developmentally, and culturally appropriate. For example, LEA administrators can work with mental health officials to ensure that teachers, parents, and students have access to early childhood education; before- and afterschool programs; vocational and career education; and local transition services to ease student and family adjustments from elementary education to middle school, high school to adulthood, and between general education and special education.
- Special education program administrators can encourage teachers to view student diversity positively. By working closely with mental health service providers, offering families a greater choice in mental health providers, and having more control over the services provided, LEA personnel can work actively to promote an organized school structure that supports a culture for learning and a climate conducive to appropriate mental health and development.
- In order to advance research on child and adolescent mental illness, prevention, treatment, and services, special education program administrators can facilitate in services and teacher development through schoolwide and classroom programs to reduce school violence, eliminate bullying, create safe schools, and foster resiliency in students, families, and school personnel.
- Special education program administrators can support and operationally activate in their buildings prereferral intervention, tutoring, and reduction in class sizes.
- Special education program administrators can support the active engagement of parenting and adult education on mental health signs and characteristics, community outreach, mentoring, volunteer programs to combat mental illness, and school–community partnerships.
- By supporting prevention and professional development on mental health issues, special education program administrators can promote local in-service topics for educators such as the following: *LEA Personnel in Interagency Partnerships; Mental Health*

Needs of Students and Families; Transition Issues in Interagency Services for Students, Families, and Agency Personnel; and Strategies for Working Effectively with Diverse Students' Families in Mental Health Services.

• Special education program administrators can promote LEA awareness of new initiatives to support students' mental health needs. For example, there is a current federal proposal (H.R. 1170: *Child Medication Act of 2003*) that prohibits schools from making students with behavioral problems take medication in order to attend class (American Academy of Child and Adolescent Psychiatry, 2003). Under this bill, passed by the House in May 2003, states receiving federal education money must make sure school personnel do not coerce parents into medicating their children. Special education program administrators can disseminate information on current initiatives promptly and systemwide.

Guidelines for Avoiding Inadequate Mental Health Services

The following ideas may help the special education program administrator to avoid common mistakes when navigating the mental health system.

• *Do not assume primary mental health roles and responsibilities.* Special education program administrators must be cognizant that mental health issues do impact upon a student's performance in school; however, it is neither the mission of the school nor its responsibility to resolve all problems that impact upon school performance. By collaborating with mental health service agencies, LEA personnel support the mental health needs of its student population—but do not take over the major roles and responsibilities of others.

• *Do not take the place of physicians or parents.* It is important to scrutinize mental illness prevention strategies in school settings, including ineffective psychosocial and psychopharmacological strategies that have been developed. However, school personnel should not be required to take the place of physicians or family members when observing the effects of treatments designed to involve all relevant individuals in a student's life.

• *Don't pass on required responsibilities.* Be careful to observe and monitor mental health personnel's roles on IEP teams. It is not the MT or TSS worker's sole responsibility to devise, implement, and manage a student's behavior plan in the IEP process. Legally, school personnel must be responsible for the behavioral portion to a student's IEP.

• *Don't do it all.* Work with educational and interagency personnel to offer coordinated efforts within and across multiple disciplines. Offer a location and time to support an opportunity for interdisciplinary exchange and integration of knowledge across a range of specialized areas. However, the school site should not be the only site where interagency coordination occurs. Agenda items, meeting priorities, meeting times, and locations should vary to involve active participation of team members.

RESOURCES

Many mental health resources are available online and in each individual community and state that will be helpful to LEA personnel. The following is a list of national resources that may be helpful to special education program administrators.

Websites

The World Wide Web provides ready access to a variety of resources that contain useful mental health service material. Here are some that have been particularly useful to us.

National Institute of Mental Health (NIMH)
Office of Communications
www.nimh.nih.gov
6001 Executive Boulevard, Room 8184, MSC 9663
Bethesda, MD 20892-9663
1-866-615-NIMH (6464), toll-free or (301) 443-4513
(301) 443-8431 (TTY)
(301) 443-4279 or (301) 443-5158 (fax)
email: nimhinfo@nih.gov

U.S. Department of Education
www.ed.gov/pubs/FamInvolve
"Family Involvement in Children's Education: Successful Local Approaches."

National PTA
www.pta.org/programs/pfistand.html
"National Standards for Parent/Family Involvement Programs."

Other Agencies

Federation of Families for Children's Mental Health
1021 Prince Street
Alexandria, VA 22314-2971
(703) 684-7710

Clearinghouse on Disability Information
Office of Special Education and Rehabilitative Services
U.S. Department of Education
Switzer Building, Room 3132
330 C Street, SW
Washington, DC 20202-2524
(202) 205-8241 (voice/TTY)

National Clearinghouse on Family Support and Children's Mental Health
Portland State University
P.O. Box 751

Portland, OR 97207-0751
1-800-628-1696
(503) 725-4165 (TTY)

National Institute of Child Health and Human Development
P.O. Box 29111
Washington, DC 20040
(301) 496-5133

Social Security Administration (Headquarters)
6401 Security Boulevard
Baltimore, MD 21235
1-800-772-1213
1-800-325-0778 (TTY)

Office of Children, Youth and Families
Room 131
Health & Welfare Building
P.O. Box 2675
Harrisburg, PA 17105-2675
(717) 783-4756
(717) 787-0414 (fax)

Office of Mental Health and Substance Abuse Services
Room 502
Health & Welfare Building
P.O. Box 2675
Harrisburg, PA 17105-2675
(717) 787-6443
(717) 787-5394 (fax)
Public Assistance Helpline (TDD) 1-800-451-5886
email: webmaster@dpw.state.pa.us
URL: www.dpw.state.pa.us

REFERENCES

American Academy of Child and Adolescent Psychiatry. (2003). *H.R. 1170.* www.aacap.org/legislation/108/108-4.htm.
American Psychiatric Association. (1994). *Diagnostic and statistical manual of mental disorders* (4th ed.) (DSM-IV). Washington, DC: American Psychiatric Press.
Highmark. (Spring 2003). Quick facts about depression. *Looking Healthward, 5,* 11. Author. www.highmarkbcbs.com.
National Advisory Mental Health Council. (2002). *Blueprint for change: Research on child and adolescent mental health. Report of the National Advisory Mental Health Council's Workgroup on Child and Adolescent Mental Health Intervention Development and Deployment.* Washington, DC: Author.
Office of Mental Health and Substance Abuse Services. (2003). *Memorandum of understanding.* Harrisburg, PA: Author.

CHAPTER SEVENTEEN

RUNNING EFFICIENT AND EFFECTIVE STAFF MEETINGS

GINA SCALA

OVERVIEW

It is important for the special education staff to be able to develop a relationship with their special education program administrator. There is no one who can identify the needs of children in the school better than the special education teacher. These staff members need to be able to come and share their ideas and problem areas with their supervisor. Staff meetings are a critical way of sharing information and training with your staff.

In this chapter, we provide suggestions for running efficient and effective meetings. We also describe methods of incorporating "alternate" ways of getting the staff to remember not only to come to the meeting, but also to participate, control participation, and remember the contents of the meeting.

SUGGESTIONS FOR EFFECTIVE MEETINGS

Many special education program administrators attend more meetings than they would like; additionally, they are frequently asked to chair the meetings. There may also be meetings that are necessary for the well-being of the district and the functioning of the staff. When the special education program administrator announces it is time for a meeting, this can create either a favorable reaction or one of dread. What variables are necessary to implement in order to increase the effectiveness of a meeting? How do you create an environment that facilitates effective meetings? How do you support effective meetings? What practical suggestions are available?

A tremendous amount of time is spent in preparing, conducting, summarizing, and evaluating meetings (Podemski, Marsh, Smith, & Price, 1995). Meetings provide opportunities for staff to get together to create, discuss, confirm, and present ideas, plans, and programs. Although a number of meetings are general in nature, many meetings are legally required for specific educational purposes—for example, multidisciplinary meetings, IEP meetings, manifestation determination meetings, as required by IDEA 2004. Meetings offer a legitimate and predetermined time for groups to get together to pass along information. In addition, meetings offer opportunities for staff to express ideas, clarify procedures, and become actively involved in problem-solving experiences. Many occasions are available daily for informal times for people to get together—natural opportunities and not "official" meetings—that need to be designed to optimize their effectiveness. The caution becomes that an overreliance on informal meetings does not seem to be an appropriate method for long-term problem solving or cohesiveness within an organization. A great deal of material presenting suggestions to increase the effectiveness of meetings has been generated (Akenhead, 1986; Ensman, 1996; Friend & Cook, 1992; Gorton & Burns, 1985; Harris, 1995; Hoch, 2000; Jones, 1995; Legerwood, 1996; Legg, 1991; Manchur, 1991; Manthey, 2001; Rogenski, 1996; Shelton & Bauer, 1994; Wherry, 1986).

With the increased use of technology, a different component has been added to the occurrence of meetings. The need to "meet" in a traditional format (i.e., table, chairs, crowds, and handouts) has been altered to conduct meetings via conference calls, video conferencing, Internet chats, to offer a few. Moreover, costs are reduced significantly since the group does not need to take off work, travel, obtain lodging, and submit expenses. This may suggest one variable that results in effective meetings—the location.

However, prior to conducting a meeting, a legitimate purpose needs to be identified (Fielding, 1995; Legerwood, 1996; Manchur, 1991). Due to the increased professional and personal demands being placed on individuals, a definitive purpose should be established. The purpose seems to produce peripheral outcomes such as interest, anticipation, participation, and commitment.

PUTTING PRINCIPLES INTO PRACTICE

Various suggestions have been offered for conducting a meeting and evaluating its effectiveness. Some of the most documented (cf. Criscuolo, 1984; Gorton & Burns, 1999; Hasley, 1997; Masaokqua, 2002; NEA, 2001; Podemski et al., 1995; Rogenski, 1996) and popular suggestions include:

- Prepare and disseminate a written agenda a few days prior to the meeting.
- Put the game plan in print. Stay on the topic.
- Make presented information connected. Make disconnected information available in print and grouped. In other words, the majority of the meeting should be on *substantive issues.*
- Serve some type of nourishment or refreshment.
- Establish meeting ground rules. Staff should create and confirm the rules. Review the rules prior to the meeting (e.g., set a time limit for speaking).
- Post meeting rules.
- Give opportunities for people to speak and interact.
- Set up action plans for each agenda item with available resources.
- Set definitive beginning and ending times for the meeting. Be punctual.
- Develop opportunities for shared decision making.
- Emphasize comfort—smart boards, chairs, tables, facilities.

- If technology is being used, check availability and participants' comfort and knowledge in using it.
- Consider an appropriate location. Calculate travel time. Consider a permanent or floating location. This may be related to the agenda items. Remember "home turf" sometimes is associated with many advantages (and disadvantages).
- Disseminate written minutes in a timely fashion, generally within one week.
- Make sure the meeting is necessary. If all of the proceedings can be sent in an electronic or written format, participants may debate why their attendance is necessary. Routine information can be disseminated without the need to officially meet. In other words, have a definite reason for the meeting.
- Try to create a theme for the meeting. In addition to presented material, give "how to" information. Participants should leave with practical ideas and action plans. Remember these are professional development opportunities.
- Prioritize problems, then solve them.
- Allow participants the opportunity to accomplish the meeting goal.
- Make sure all participants have the opportunity to offer significant input. Often the meeting is dominated by a few.
- Look for opportunities to celebrate hard work, support, dedication, and successes of staff, faculty, and/or students as meeting themes. This could be extended to support partnerships and community involvement. Moreover, this could be regularly scheduled at each staff meeting—a great way to start a meeting. Consider celebrating birthdays of the month at each staff meeting.
- Take risks; break from the routine, especially when the results are not what were originally anticipated. If the meeting does not seem to be making progress, stop and restart.
- Planning and establishing a functional agenda can identify the specific participants; do not force unnecessary participation.
- Balance the number of electronic and "face-to-face" meetings. Face-to-face meetings build morale and solidarity.

Due to the number of legally mandated meetings, as well as the typically occurring meetings, the entire educational community cannot afford poorly run, unproductive, and disorganized meetings. Meetings must have a definite purpose and reasonable goals. Meetings need to be the vehicle to maintain communication, foster organizational structure, and enhance overall morale (Lindelow, 1989).

Tips

To maximize meeting productivity, the following strategies are offered:

- Start meeting at an odd time, i.e., 3:03 P.M. instead of a traditional 3:00 P.M. It should heighten punctuality of the participants because it is unique and the staff should respond well.
- Allow staff to vent for the first five minutes. After that, stay on task. If the topic strays, give an immediate reminder to get back on track.

- Set a specific start and stop time for the meeting. If you remain on task, you can be done quicker and staff can leave before the designated stop time.
- Pass a brick or token around. If you have it, you speak. If you do not have the brick or token, you wait until it is passed to you. It reduces talking by a few and spreads the talking to others.
- Assign specific time limits for specific agenda items using a timer. When the time is up, the bell rings. Decide if more time is needed on that item, reprioritize the agenda, place it on next month's schedule, and move on.
- Do not sit or stand in front of the group. Facilitate the meeting from within the group.
- Put agendas on colored paper. Use a color that is not generally used for anything else. When the staff receives something on that color paper, it will become an automatic discriminative stimulus for them to read.
- Any meeting resulting in action items should be assigned to a staff member. Solidify each person's responsibility by putting it in writing.
- Take time to laugh. Emphasize humor throughout the meeting. Laughing together will also allow you to cry together. End your meetings on a funny story that had happened within the previous month. Give prizes to the best story. It will set the stage for "can you top that" at the next staff meeting. These opportunities will give the staff something to remember fondly.

Pitfalls to Avoid

- Holding meetings without agenda items. Provide an agenda and stick to it. This allows the staff to know the purpose of the meeting and how to prepare.
- No advance notification. Provide an agenda before the meeting to ensure there is no hidden agenda. Provide information items through email or phone mail.
- Personal gripes aired at the meeting. If a staff member has a serious problem with you or your recommendations, meet with him or her privately. Do not allow anyone to "hijack" the meeting.
- Filling up time. Just because you have ninety minutes for a meeting does not mean all the time needs to be used. Be efficient and end early when possible.
- Rushing through items just to leave early. If a topic needs time, take the necessary time.

Meetings are inevitable. The key is to make them as efficient and productive as possible while maintaining active participation from the staff.

REFERENCES

Akenhead, J. (1986). Use staff chats to build your school's team spirit. *Executive Educator, 8*(10), 23–24.
Criscuolo, N. P. (1984). Staff meetings: Meaningful or meaningless? *NAASP Bulletin, 68*(471), 134–136.
Ensman, R. G. (1996). How to participate in a meeting. *Child Care Information Exchange, 108,* 79–80.
Fielding, M. (1995). Five minutes of fame at ten to nine. *The Times Educational Supplement,* 4115, 20.
Friend, M., & Cook, L. (1992). *Interactions: Collaboration skills for school professionals.* White Plains, New York: Longman.

Gorton, R. A., & Burns, J. (1985). Faculty meetings: What do teachers really think of them? *The Clearing House, 59*(1), 30–32.

Harris, J. (1995). Anybody out there listening? *Child Care Information Exchange, 104,* 82–84.

Hasley, V. (1997). Ten strategies for revolutionizing learning. *Thrust for Educational Leadership, 27*(1), 23.

Hoch, D. A. (2000). The pre-season staff meeting. *Coach and Athletic Director, 70*(2), 12–13.

Jones, R. (1995). Meetings without tedium. *Executive Educator, 17*(9), 18.

Legerwood, P. C. (1996). Not another meeting! *Principal, 76*(2), 42–43.

Legg, J. (1991). Momentum—Successful staff meetings. *Child Care Information Exchange, 77,* 52–55.

Lindelow, J. (1989). *Making meetings more effective.* Sacramento: Association of California School Administrators (ASCA).

Manchur, C. (1991). *How to run productive meetings.* Alexandria, VA: Association for Supervision and Curriculum Development.

Manthey, G. (2001). Tell your stories and make a difference. *Leadership, 30*(3), 17.

Masaokqua, J. (2002). Ten quick ways to improve board meetings. *Board Café.*

NEA. (2001). How do you raise morale among colleagues at work? *NEA Today, 19*(8), 25–28.

Podemski, R. S., Marsh II, G. E., Smith, T. C., & Price, B. J. (1995). *Comprehensive administration of special education* (2nd ed). Englewood Cliffs, NJ: Merrill.

Rogenski, K. (1996). Control your staff meetings. *Thrust for Educational Leadership, 26,* 14–16.

Shelton, M. M., & Bauer, L. K. (1994). *Secrets of highly effective meetings. The practicing administrator's leadership series.* Thousand Oaks, CA: Corwin Press.

Wherry, J. H. (1986). A public relations secret: Enlist entire staff for PR effectiveness. *NASSP Bulletin, 70*(494), 3–13.

CHAPTER EIGHTEEN

BUILDING RELATIONSHIPS WITH SPECIAL EDUCATION STAFF

OVERVIEW

Scores of textbooks and manuals are written on educational leadership. These textbooks provide valuable material on *how to develop* leadership qualities, supervisory skills, and collegial relationships; unfortunately, few focus on the unique role of the special education administrator. Therefore, the following three chapters do not attempt to re-teach educational leadership qualities and skills but rather provide specific ideas and procedures for *Building Relationships with Special Education Staff* (Chapter 18); *Evaluating Special Education Staff* (Chapter 19); and *Working with Other Administrators* (Chapter 20).

Each school entity operates special education programs differently depending on size and population. In a large school district, you may be one of several special education administrators assigned a specific program or building. Conversely, in a small school district, you may be the only special education administrator. Regardless of your circumstances, researchers, spanning decades, identify three primary areas of supervisory characteristics as essential features to success: (1) effective communication, (2) strong interpersonal skills, and (3) effective managerial and technical skills for evaluation of programs and teachers. The goal of this chapter is to review the first two areas of supervisory focus: enhancing "human" relationships with your staff using effective communication strategies and managing special education programs.

REGULATIONS

There are no provisions in IDEA that legislate relationships with your staff; however, to provide students with disabilities a free appropriate public education (FAPE), you need to cultivate strong relationships with your teachers, paraprofessionals, subordinate supervisors, related service providers, and other professionals.

PUTTING PRINCIPLES INTO PRACTICE

The scope of supervisory models range from *conventional,* whereby supervisors attempt to *control* teachers' instructional behaviors, to *collegial,* whereby supervisors *share* leadership with teachers (Glickman, Gordon, & Ross-Gordon, 2003). Regardless of your personal philosophy, training model, or district supervision plan, effective supervisory models focus on supervisor attributes that include interpersonal skills, managerial skills, and technical skills applied to direct assistance of teachers, curriculum, and professional development.

Building Interpersonal Skills

Analysis of diverse individual supervisor dispositions is complex; however, interpersonal skills are your most important resource in developing effective relationships with your staff. It appears clear, through years of research and practice, that when your staff has a sense of purpose, where they work together and are supported by work conditions and management, their professional development and productivity are positively affected (Alfonso, Firth, & Neville, 1981). In addition, interpersonal skills include the ability to motivate, influence, and win cooperation among staff. As a special education administrator, your primary job is to assure FAPE to students with disabilities in your charge—thus, *you must get this part right.*

Know Your Staff. However large the school district, you MUST commit to knowing as many teachers, related service providers, and paraprofessionals as possible. It is a difficult task to assess program strengths and needs, assure FAPE, and evaluate programs when you do not know your staff. Moreover, you need to deal with teachers as individuals. Just like students with disabilities, teachers have unique and varied needs. Be sensitive to differences and respond to each teacher in a manner consistent with his or her professional needs and personality. For example, you will have teachers who are independent, self-motivated, and goal directed and others who are dependent on supervisory input, lack professional motivation, and have difficulty setting goals. Knowing how each teacher approaches instruction will be helpful in responding to their needs. Some general tips include:

- Be *visible* in each building; visit classrooms informally, not just to evaluate the teacher or when there is a problem.
- Find ways to bond with individuals; do not gossip or spread rumors.
- Try to find common interests.
- Schedule at least one meeting a year with each teacher to discuss individually how things are going, set annual goals, and establish instructional priorities.
- Schedule or attend regular building or district staff meetings to show support.
- Attend evaluation and IEP meetings as often as possible or insist that subordinate supervisory staff attend.
- Keep the lines of communication open; you may not want an "open-door" policy, but you should invite teachers to schedule a time to discuss issues.
- Be honest and straightforward in your dealings with all staff. Even if there are personality conflicts, if you stay honest and forthright with teachers, you will eventually earn their trust and respect.
- Plan at least one social event a year for your staff.

Establish Annual Goals and Commitments.   Educational decision making boils down to common values and goals among administrators and staff (Alfonso et al., 1981). This one is easy! As a special education administrator, your supervisory agenda is mandated: You must provide students with disabilities in your district with a FAPE in the least restrictive environment (LRE). It is essential that you keep your focus on this purpose and at the forefront of all supervisory decision making. Your commitment to this simple goal will underscore to the staff your advocacy to students with disabilities, thus strengthening theirs.

One way to achieve common goals in special education is to consistently *keep the child as the focal point* in all decision making. When teachers know that you will stay the course and make programmatic or other educational decisions based on this simple idea, you model advocacy for students with special needs. It is essential that the staff understand that your decisions are based on what is best for the student, not what is best for them, yourself, or other administrators.

Of course, FAPE is a mandated, legislative goal for all special education administrators and special education teachers, but if you are going to translate this goal into action, you must generate commitments from your staff to connect this overriding goal to the classroom environment. One way to achieve this is to set secondary goals each year for specific focus, then commit resources toward achieving those goals. The following are possible secondary goal areas that could be addressed district- or building-wide:

- Writing meaningful goals and objectives for IEPs that include all necessary components.
- Writing positive behavior support plans.
- Outlining safe physical management techniques.
- Providing reading instruction that models current research.
- Providing strategies instruction to allow students to progress.
- Studying and understanding changes in regulations or legislation.
- Providing meaningful transition services for affected students.

Conduct Monthly Meetings.   Because special education changes frequently due to case law, new legislation resulting in new regulations, and local policy changes, it is important to formally meet with staff on a regular basis to keep them abreast of progress toward special education goals and any changes that affect their classrooms. Think about the following suggestions:

- Depending on the size of your district, you can determine if building meetings versus entire staff meetings are more feasible. Either way, set meeting dates for the entire academic year, and distribute a calendar with dates, times, and places of meetings. Try to keep the dates as uniform as possible (e.g., third Monday of each month).
- Begin and end on time; efficiency is always appreciated by staff.
- Provide an agenda and follow it.
- Encourage participation toward the agenda goals
- Stay on specific topics outlined on agenda.
- Mediate any group disputes.
- Verbally summarize meeting.
- Write and distribute minutes as an official record as soon as possible.

- Do not meet if you do not have agenda items; in other words, do not meet for the sake of a meeting. Have a purpose.

Learn to Listen.   Develop good listening skills; this involves listening openly and with acceptance. When teachers come to you with issues or problems regarding students, parents, other administrators, or colleagues, do not:

- Be judgmental.
- Yakity, yak, yak, yak.
- Allow the individual to get off track. Rather, determine quickly what the specific problem is and focus the individual on that specific problem.
- Underreact or dismiss the issue or problem. It is far preferable to help the individual generate solutions—he or she usually knows what to do but wants and needs your support.

Do try to:

- Paraphrase during the conversation to clarify your understanding, then help the individual formulate a plan of action.
- Be a "sounding board." Sometimes there is no solution, but listening with compassion to the individual may make him or her feel better.
- Make time to listen to the "good stuff," too.

Be Visible and Cooperative.   Many teachers perceive "administrators" as far removed from the daily grind of teaching, especially teaching students with disabilities. Teachers should see you in less formal and more spontaneous settings; therefore, find ways to show your skills:

- Teach a lesson once a year in each classroom. This small activity will enhance your own teaching skills. Moreover, you will experience the classroom dynamics and get to know the students.
- Attend as many evaluation or IEP meetings as possible, not just meetings that may be contentious or difficult. This shows teachers that you care about their students and their parents, as well as support their programs.
- Do not ignore your staff. Respond quickly to phone calls or email.
- Show up at meetings when you are scheduled to be there, arrive on time, and call if you will be late.

Be a "Peaceful Warrior."   It is naïve to think that your entire staff will like, respect, or trust you; thus, there will be times you need to interact with teachers on a less cooperative level—the "crucible of human interaction" (Alfonzo et al., 1981, p. 346). In order to maintain a professional demeanor during these trials, you need to develop a thick skin. Try the following:

- Model self-control and professional behavior by hearing the individual out. Do not talk or try to intervene until he or she stops talking.
- Do not take it personally; remember, it probably is not about you.

- Try to resolve the conflict by clarifying, restating, summarizing, and offering compromises, if feasible.
- Make sure you are in a private place during any contentious discussions.
- Do not feign that you care or promise a course of action you are unwilling to execute just to appease a person. This may escalate anger and subsequently diminish trust and respect.
- Allow your staff to vent their anger and frustration in a respectful manner; once an upset person calms down, you can successfully work toward conflict resolution.
- When engaged in a confrontation, stand your ground by being direct and forthright. Never raise your voice or use abusive language.
- Do not allow a subordinate to be abusive; it is unproductive, unprofessional, and should not be tolerated.

Sometimes your staff will have conflicts with each other. When this is the case, use the same guidelines as above but work toward mediation and allowing the teachers to resolve the conflict with you.

Always Model Professional Demeanor.
- Dress professionally.
- Speak professionally.
- Do not gossip.
- Arrive and end on time.
- Be in control.
- Be consistent; your staff often depends on your professional demeanor to help them navigate meetings.

Managing Special Education

The management of special education programs is complex. Many supervisors complain that they are drowning in a sea of paperwork, phone calls, referrals, IDEA updates, and other urgent emerging issues, including budgetary planning and assessment of program needs. To manage programs effectively, you must learn to allocate your resources—specifically time and money.

Get Organized.   The special education administrator must attempt to remove barriers so that teachers can teach and students can learn. To that end, you need to develop a systematic process for conducting the daily business of special education. Begin by using a daily planner to organize your schedule (see Figure 18.1).

- Keep a detailed appointment book, computerized or otherwise, with you and make a copy for your assistant.
- Add notations during the day, especially reminders for long-term projects.
- Try to reserve specific days for visiting specific buildings. During those days, schedule meetings, observations, and other building business.
- Reserve a specific time to return phone calls and review mail and email each day.

MONDAY

8:00-9:00	Office: Return phone calls; prepare for day	X
9:00-10:00	Visit Elementary School 1. ~IEP Meeting for Student A	
10:00-11:00	Observe Mrs. K. Focus evaluation on behavior management	
11:00-11:30	Check into office; return phone calls	
11:20-12:00	Working lunch with guidance counselor	
12:00-1:00	~Multidisciplinary evaluation meeting for Student B	
1:00-2:00	Observe Student X in regular class for evaluation report	
2:00-3:00	~IEP meeting for Student C	
3:00-4:00	Return to office to close day; prepare for Tuesday	

FIGURE 18.1   Example of Daily Planner Activities

- Reserve one day a week for "office only." You need time to clear your desk and focus on administrative paperwork.

Invest in a Computerized Student Case Management System.   One major feature of supervising special education programs is case management. Depending on your district's size and circumstances, you may have subordinate supervisors who can split duties between elementary and secondary programs or other differentiated case management arrangements. However, whatever your district's organization, *you* must come up with a systematic plan to track students, and ALL teachers must follow the same plan for consistency.

To that end, all special education teachers must have the tools and training necessary to "case manage" students, including the assessment of students for writing evaluation reports and Individualized Education Programs (IEPs) and conducting evaluation and IEP conferences.

Many commercial companies have developed specialized software for case management of evaluations, IEP development, and other necessary paperwork. These software programs are designed to streamline the writing of IEPs and provide various perks toward case managing based on each district's needs. The Council for Exceptional Children (CEC) recommends the following two programs; however, you should investigate your own state's resources for the most viable program to meet your financial and programming needs.

- *IDEAPro™: Chalkware Education Solutions.* This software is a powerful IEP-writing tool that includes a number of IDEA supportive documents, modifiable menus, fast search capabilities, user-customizable library of goals, and benchmark data.
- *Excent®: Horizon Software Systems, Inc.* With Excent®, IEP software is integrated into its district information management system. This program can be customized to conform to all district and state forms and procedures. It includes a Medicaid encounter and

tracking component, data verification, and electronic state reporting capabilities. It also has integrated student management software and districtwide reporting systems. More information on both programs can be reviewed on the Council for Exceptional Children website: www.cec.sped.org.

Regardless of which case management system best fits your district's unique needs, ensure that teachers are trained to use the system effectively and have the proper equipment to use it (i.e., computer hardware).

Develop a Special Education Staff Handbook.   When trying to manage a varied staff, it is critical that you develop a procedures manual for both new and experienced staff members. In the long run, a special education manual will save you time and provide staff members with various forms and procedures in special education. As suggested by Miros (2001), in addition to manual forms and documents, you should include: (1) their purpose, (2) advice on how to complete forms, (3) to whom and when to submit specific forms or requests, (4) where to obtain copies, (5) how to access forms electronically, and (6) how and when to suggest revisions. A review of the manual should also be an agenda item for your first staff meeting to underscore additions, changes, or revisions. The following is a list of possible items[*] to include in a manual:

- A copy of IDEA regulations and standards; including any state differences for practice.
- Referral procedures for the district, including prereferral responsibilities.
- A flow chart of multidisciplinary procedures with teacher responsibilities highlighted.
- Hard copies of all pertinent forms, including consent for evaluation and reevaluation, Notice of Procedural Safeguards, invitation to IEP team meeting, Notice of Recommended Educational Placement, and district IEP forms.
- Special education report card supplements.
- Forms for teachers, parents, and other staff to complete for assessment purposes.
- Purchase order forms.
- A list of possible curricular accommodations for students.
- Behavior plan forms.
- Discipline procedures.
- A list with contact information of all other special education staff including central office administrators, secretarial staff, instructional assistants, and related service personnel.
- A list of other service providers or consultants.

[*]You should also include any other pertinent district information that you deem necessary.

Allocating District Resources.   School finance experts define an educational budget as translating educational needs into a sound financial plan (Brimley & Garfield, 2002); however, as a special education administrator you probably have limited formal training in accounting principles. Nevertheless, with your job comes the stewardship of a large program budget appropriated by federal and state funds as well as local district sources. Understanding your funding sources is essential for budgetary decision making, and as a special education administrator, you are responsible for thousands, and in some cases millions of dollars (Brimley & Garfield, 2002).

In order to identify program needs, you need to have the pulse of your special education program. In other words, if you have followed the advice proffered in this book, you will be a visible leader who knows your district, building, staff, and student needs. More specifically:

- Familiarize yourself with all special education funding resources available to the district, including federal and state contributions, incentives, and grant monies.
- Ask your district business manager or superintendent for an approximate budget figure.
- Always begin by analyzing total district staffing needs since these expenses are the most costly. You will be able to anticipate most staffing costs by reviewing current staffing loads coupled with student IEP needs; remember to consider students who are moving in, changing educational programs, and graduating.
- A needs assessment is a valuable process, because teachers gain "ownership" of ideas by contributing to the change process (Alfonzo, et al., 1981). In addition to helping you prioritize instructional needs and evaluation focus, a needs assessment can help you to establish budget priorities.
- Then, ask teachers to provide you with a "wish list" of texts, materials, supply needs, and professional development opportunities. Have them categorize those needs into three categories: (1) resources that would make my program *ideal* for providing FAPE, (2) resources that would make my program adequate for providing FAPE, and (3) resources that I need to provide the most basic FAPE. In this last section, ask them to tell you what students *will not* receive because of lack of resources, training, and materials.
- Collate the information and share the results of the needs assessment with your staff.
- Have the staff brainstorm ideas on how to plan for meeting the needs (can be done at a specific staff meeting).
- Involve teachers in the process of planning speakers and presenters; have curriculum reviews.
- Conduct a cost analysis of professional development needs, materials, and trainings.
- To save money, if possible, have several teachers trained as trainers to help lower professional development costs.
- Textbooks, software, and other "big ticket" items must be researched for evidence that they work with students with disabilities and paired with instructional priorities.
- Require teachers to rank order their budget requests using the same "wish list" format.
- Once "big" programmatic needs are planned within the special education budget, predetermined monies should be delineated evenly for each teacher to purchase general supplies.
- DO NOT allocate more monies to one teacher over the other if the monies do not match instructional priorities.
- Remember the special education budget is dynamic in that students and staff needs are constantly changing to meet FAPE; therefore, plan for unexpected costs and additional resources.

Finally, the more visible, proactive, and organized you are as a special education administrator, the more secure your special education staff will be in providing students with disabilities a free appropriate public education—the ultimate goal.

REFERENCES

Alfonzo, R. J., Firth, G. R., & Neville, R. F. (1981). *Instructional supervision: A behavior system* (2nd ed.). Boston: Allyn and Bacon.

Brimley, V., & Garfield, R. R. (2002). *Financing education in a climate of change* (8th ed.). Boston: Allyn and Bacon.

Glickman, C. D., Gordon, S. P., & Ross-Gordon, J. (2003). *Supervision and instructional leadership: A developmental approach* (5th ed.). Boston: Allyn and Bacon.

Miros, R. (2001). How to select and evaluate special education staff. In D. F. Bateman & C. F. Bateman, (Eds.), *A principal's guide to special education.* Arlington, VA: Council for Exceptional Children.

■ ■ ■ ■ ■

CHAPTER NINETEEN

EVALUATING SPECIAL EDUCATION STAFF

OVERVIEW

Each school district develops an evaluation framework that is often based on national or state teaching and certification standards coupled with district needs. Moreover, the school district may not require that you formally evaluate your staff; rather, the building administrator is responsible for all formal staff evaluations. Regardless of your district's method, an effective special education administrator will actively seek ways to provide formal and informal *feedback* to special education teachers. Past research has shown that teachers who receive the most feedback on instructional technique, classroom management, and program effectiveness are also the teachers who are most satisfied with their teaching abilities (Glickman, Gordon, & Ross-Gordon, 2003). In addition, many researchers point out that teachers often change instructional behaviors independently after their instructional behavior has been described by an observer (Brophy & Good, 1974). This chapter will provide guidelines on how to observe and evaluate special education teachers using a clinical supervision structure, including providing direct feedback and assistance to teachers, and how to develop or adapt an existing teacher evaluation framework.

REGULATIONS

There are no provisions in IDEA 2004 that legislate how to effectively evaluate your staff; however, to provide students with disabilities a free appropriate public education (FAPE), you need to develop a strong system of formal and informal feedback to your staff to improve overall instruction.

PUTTING PRINCIPLES INTO PRACTICE

Traditionally, teachers are observed once or twice a year by a building administrator who is trained as a "generalist" and may not possess the training to conduct a robust evaluation for the special education teacher. Because teaching students with disabilities is complex, it is highly recommended that you use a *formative evaluation* framework to observe and evaluate your staff. In other words, observe your staff throughout the year and provide ongoing feedback to improve instruction with the purpose that effective teachers provide FAPE.

Observing and Evaluating Teachers

Establishing Instructional Priorities.   In Chapter 18, you were advised to establish annual goals and commitments from teachers based on overall IEP goals and objectives toward providing FAPE. Once you and your teachers establish instructional needs, you can work toward establishing instructional priorities for teacher improvement. The special education administrator must be skilled at analyzing special education instructional priorities with overall district, building, and individual teacher needs. This unique vision will help you to guide special education teachers toward refining their needs into positive practice.

- Begin by meeting with each teacher in the first month of school to pinpoint instructional goals, then make commitments. For veteran teachers, encourage instructional growth and refinement; for novice or struggling teachers, begin with general elements of effective instruction.
- Together analyze each teacher's class IEP goals and objectives to help determine overall classroom needs.
- Commit to observing the teacher in the classroom environment at least twice during the year.
- Commit to observing the teacher in an IEP planning meeting at least once a year.

Clinical Supervision.   The most common structure for conducting an effective evaluation is *clinical supervision* (Cogan, 1973; Goldhammer, 1969). The clinical supervision structure is straightforward and does not require extensive training; in fact, it requires five simple sequential steps:

1. *Meet with the teacher prior to an observation(s).* In this step your role is to determine the reason and purpose for the observation with the teacher (Glickman et al., 2003). Most researchers advocate for the administrator and teacher to collaborate on the purpose of the evaluation; however, since you should conduct at least two observations, two different types of preobservation meetings or a combination are recommended based on the experience and tenure of the teacher.

Observation 1. As mentioned in Chapter 18, if you have already established annual instructional goals and commitments with each teacher at the beginning of the year, your evaluation focus will be easier to pinpoint at observation time and will keep the goals consistent. As an example, if the teacher's annual instructional goal is to decrease use of verbal and nonverbal reprimands, your observation could focus on that specific behavior and anecdotal data. However, it is important to note that you may identify several areas of instructional focus annually. This type of observation is useful for veteran teachers who have mastered elements of effective instruction and are seeking ways to improve specific skills.

Observation 2. General frameworks for observation and evaluation are often based on elements of effective instruction and their effect on student learning; therefore, it is important to observe and evaluate special education teachers on general effective practices. To that end, reserve *at least* one visit to observe general practices or combine the annual focus goals with general instructional goals. This is a matter of observation style and preference; design a system that works best for you and the teacher. The domains for general instructional practices are discussed in the next section.

Observation 3. Special education teachers and related service staff have additional administrative responsibilities that directly affect FAPE—that is, to conduct reliable and valid assessments for IEP development, conduct IEP planning meetings, keep track of timelines, and monitor progress. It is wise to observe each teacher in an IEP planning meeting and include skills within an observation and evaluation framework. Ideas for systematically incorporating these skills into a framework will be discussed in the next section.

Finally in this step, decide on the *time of the observation* and the *time for the post conference* or follow-up to the observation. Remember to always keep your appointments.

2. *Observe.* Observation is a matter of individual style, and there are many ways to observe classrooms. In fact, a considerable collection of textbooks on the market offer in-depth observation techniques. However, the choice of observation tool depends on the *purpose* and *focus* of the observation, which you established in step 1 of the clinical supervision structure. In this step, simply follow through with the focus of the preconference for all observations. In our example in Observation 1, the teacher goal identified as decreasing the use of verbal and nonverbal reprimands in the class, you may want to use a frequency chart to observe behaviors (Figure 19.1). Quantitative and qualitative instruments can be used and may include visual diagramming, verbatim scripting, open-ended narratives, focused questionnaire coupled with district observation form, a framework checklist, behavior matrix, coded combinations, and performance indicators (Glickman et al., 2001). Develop an observation tool that meets your observation needs. Technically, observation is the act of noting (Glickman et al., 2001); therefore, it is important in this step to just *take data,* not analyze it.

Time	Reprimands	Type of Reprimand	Notes
9:00-9:05	III		
9:10-9:15	I		
9:20-9:25	III		
9:30-9:35	I		
9:40-9:45	II		
9:50-9:55	I		
Total	**11**		

FIGURE 19.1   Teacher Reprimands

3. *Analyze and interpret.* It is important to reflect on the observation, lay out your data, and study the information. Glickman and colleagues (2003) suggest using an analysis work-sheet as a guide that can include: (a) writing the major findings of your observation and (b) interpreting what you believe is desirable or not desirable about the major findings. This will help guide you to administrator judgment. *You can structure your observation form to provide both visual data and interpretive data.* Here are some additional tips:

- Make it a practice to review and interpret data as soon as possible after the observation; if you wait too long, you may forget salient information.
- Make it a practice to write your data prior to the post-conference meeting. Make a space for teacher comments and final post-conference recommendations (see framework below).
- Be as objective as possible when interpreting the data. If you are unable to be objective, ask another administrator to observe as a reliability check or review the data.

4. *Post conference.* Once you have completed your analysis, it is time to meet with the teacher for a post conference; this is conducted to discuss your analysis with the teacher and finalize a plan for instructional improvement. It is important to begin this discussion by point-ing out something positive about the instruction, then move to exactly what you observed. Many researchers have established effective techniques for discussing this information; this will be up to you. However, if you follow the suggestions in Chapter 18 for developing inter-personal relationships, you should be prepared to discuss results with your staff.

Regardless of the status of the teacher, veteran versus novice, you cannot help him or her improve instruction if direct assistance is not provided. By arranging observations, pro-viding feedback, and establishing a plan for improvement, you are sending a message that teachers and their jobs are important. Discuss a plan for improvement that is specific for the next observation and offer direct assistance, in whatever forms are appropriate, as needed (Glickman et al., 2003). Some direct assistance options:

- Offer to demonstrate a lesson or a specific teaching technique.
- Arrange for the teacher to visit another classroom to observe a specific instructional method.
- Co-teach by modeling how to plan, execute, and evaluate a lesson.
- Provide necessary training, resources, and/or materials.
- Assist with student assessment.
- Problem solve together.

The outcome is that you and the teacher need to select which approach would work best for that teacher. You may not need to provide any direct assistance at all; however, that is something to determine at the post conference.

5. *Critique the previous four steps.* Just as a teacher uses clinical teaching to adjust in-struction, you need to review whether the format and procedures you used were satisfactory and whether you need to make revisions for the next observation (Glickman et al., 2003).

For a more in-depth review of clinical supervision and observation formats, refer to the refer-ences and suggested readings at the end of the chapter.

Developing or Adapting an Evaluation Framework

One specific evaluation framework does not exist that meets the needs of all school districts or administrators; however, extensive research reveals four common domains that encompass effective teaching: (1) planning and preparation, (2) classroom environment, (3) instruction, and (4) professional responsibilities (Danielson, 1996). Many school district evaluation tools include all or some of the elements of these four domains and accompanying component skills. An abbreviated review of each domain is examined below with component skills and suggested additional areas (underlined) specific to special education teachers:

Planning and Preparation. According to Danielson (1996), planning and preparation define how a teacher organizes and designs instruction. This is particularly important for special education teachers as they endeavor to provide FAPE. Instruction must be systematically planned using effective teaching methods. Component skills may include:

- Demonstrates knowledge of content and pedagogy

  - Uses research-based content (e.g., systematic phonics approach to teach reading).
  - Uses appropriate scope and sequence.
  - Adapts and/or modifies general education curriculum to meet the unique needs of students.

- Demonstrates knowledge of students

  - Understands individual strengths and needs; adjusts content or instruction to meet unique needs.
  - Can interpret assessment results to plan and adapt instruction.
  - Individualizes instruction.
  - Uses varied approaches to teaching content (e.g., uses manipulatives).
  - Uses clinical teaching (test, teach, test model).
  - Uses errorless teaching techniques.

- Selects instructional goals

  - Uses assessment data to pair IEP goals and objectives with instructional goals.

- Demonstrates knowledge of resources

  - Knows the general education curriculum and resources available; adapts materials to meet the needs of students.

- Designs coherent instruction

  - Uses a direct instruction model for teaching students with disabilities.

- Assesses student learning

  - Uses progress monitoring techniques.
  - Uses reliable and valid standardized assessments.

- Uses formative assessment.
- Uses curriculum-based measurement.
- Uses curriculum-based assessment.
- Uses varied data collection methods.
- Effectively synthesizes assessment data for writing evaluation reports, periodic reports to parents, and present levels of performance on the IEP.

Classroom Environment.   Most researchers agree that teachers must master at least the fundamentals of classroom management before skilled instruction can occur (Danielson, 1996). For special education teachers, mastering the classroom environment is paramount to their success. Specifically, attention to establishing classroom routines and rules, attending to the physical environment, and setting expectations for student behaviors are prerequisites to effective instruction (Brophy & Good, 1986; Danielson, 1996; Porter & Brophy, 1987). In addition, these factors correlate positively with maximizing academic learning and engaged time (Brophy & Good, 1986). Consider that when students with special needs are highly engaged in learning, FAPE is easier to attain. Component skills may include:

- Creates an environment of respect and rapport

- Establishes a culture for learning

- Manages classroom procedures
  - Organizational routines are in place and followed.
  - Time on task is maximized with teacher organization.

- Manages student behaviors
  - Evidence of positive and effective behavior management system.
  - Rules are visible with obligatory consequences.

- Organizes physical space
  - Classroom arrangement maximizes small group and individualized instruction.

Instruction.   The primary focus of FAPE is to improve student learning. Through volumes of research we know that effective special education teachers communicate the goal and relevancy of the lesson, offer a strong model and guided prompts, provide frequent review, use appropriate materials, and utilize a lesson structure that maximizes student understanding by relating to past learning (Brophy & Good, 1986; Zigmond, Sansone, Miller, Donahoe, & Kohnke, 1986). Moreover, teachers who provide direct, frequent, and timely feedback enhance learning (Rosenshine & Furst, 1971). Component parts may include:

- Communicates clearly and accurately
- Uses effective questioning and discussion techniques

- Engages students in learning
- Provides feedback to students
- Demonstrates flexibility and responsiveness

Note: Under each component in this section, add information that is specific for your special education teachers.

Professional Responsibilities. Special education teachers in particular have many roles outside of and in addition to those in the classroom: preparing IEPs with assessment data, writing IEP goals and objectives, conducting IEP planning meetings, participating in collaborative teaching, and attending to legislative timelines, to name a few. Teachers who excel in these activities are highly regarded by colleagues, parents, and administrators (Danielson, 1996). In fact, according to Porter and Brophy (1987), effective teachers accept personal responsibility for student learning and behavior; therefore, the link between teacher collaboration and students is well established in the literature. For special education teachers, this relationship is even more important because providing FAPE requires vigilance to legislative mandates including procedural safeguards. Component parts may include:

- Reflects on teaching

  - Uses a clinical teaching structure requiring teachers to continuously assess, teach, and reassess.
  - Uses progress monitoring.

- Maintains accurate records

  - In this section, customize your observation to include areas of record maintenance that *you* require your teachers to sustain. For example, if your teachers are responsible for keeping timelines for reevaluation and IEP development, task analyze those skills to include in this section.

- Communicates with families

  - In this section, you can create many areas of focus for the special education teacher, including how he or she sustains contact with families, how he or she conducts IEP planning meetings, how he or she interacts with family members.

- Contributes to school and school district

- Shows interest in growing and developing professionally

- Displays professionalism

  - Presents information to colleagues and families in a professional manner.
  - Maintains professional demeanor when confronted by a colleague or family member.
  - Is prepared for all meetings.

- IEP development

  - Organizes all paperwork for IEP development, including assessment reports, invitations to meetings, and whatever other responsibilities you require of your teachers.
  - Prepares Present Levels of Academic Achievement and Functional Performance using standardized, formative, and curriculum-based measurement data.
  - Reports data using measurable, precise language from which goals and objectives can be constructed.
  - Relates data to instructional goals and objectives.
  - Provides work samples.
  - Goals and objectives include a specific behavior related to present levels, a condition under which the behavior will be performed, and the criteria for success.
  - Includes behavior plan, if needed.
  - Includes transition plan, if needed.
  - All elements of IEP are completed.

- IEP planning meeting

  - Parents are properly invited to the IEP meeting, given opportunity to participate in the meeting, and are given full notice of their procedural rights.
  - The IEP team is properly constituted.
  - The present levels are explained using understandable language without jargon.
  - Teacher handles any disputes or disagreements in a professional manner.

All domains can be easily adapted to meet the needs of your school district and special education staff. The point is to customize your evaluation process to include areas exclusive to special education teachers and their responsibilities.

Note: Readers desiring an in-depth study of Danielson's work can find references at the end of this chapter.

REFERENCES

Brophy, J. E., & Good, T. L. (1974). *Teacher-student relationships: Causes and consequences.* New York: Holt, Rinehart and Winston.

Brophy, J. E., & Good, T. L. (1986). Teacher behavior and student achievement. In M. C. Wittrock (Ed.), *Handbook of research on teaching* (3rd ed.). New York: Macmillan.

Cogan, M. (1973). *Clinical supervision.* Boston: Houghton-Mifflin.

Danielson, C. (1996). *Enhancing professional practice: A framework for teaching.* Alexandria, VA: Association for Supervision and Curriculum Development.

Glickman, C. D., Gordon, S. P., & Ross-Gordon, J. (2003). *Supervision and instructional leadership: A developmental approach* (5th ed.). Boston: Allyn and Bacon.

Goldhammer, R. (1969). *Clinical supervision: Special methods for the supervision of teachers.* New York: Holt, Rinehart and Winston.

Porter, A. C., & Brophy, J. E. (1987). Synthesis of research on good teaching: Insights from the work of the Institute for Research on Teaching. *Educational Leadership, 45*(8), 74–85.

Rosenshine, B., & Furst, N. (1971). Research on teacher performance criteria. In B.O. Smith (Ed.), *Research in teacher education.* Englewood Cliffs, NJ: Prentice-Hall.

Zigmond, N., Sansone, J., Miller, S., Donahoe, K., & Kohnke, R. (1986). Teaching learning disabled students at the secondary school level: What research says to teachers. *Learning Disabilities Focus, 1*(2), 108–115.

SUGGESTED READINGS

Acheson, A. A., & Gall, M. P. (1992). *Techniques in the clinical supervision of teachers* (3rd ed.). New York: Longman.

Pajak, E. (1993). *Approaches to clinical supervision.* Norwood, MA: Christopher Gordon.

■ ■ ■ ■ ■

CHAPTER TWENTY

WORKING WITH
OTHER ADMINISTRATORS

OVERVIEW

The role of the special education administrator is unique and complex among administrative positions. Your job is to advocate for students with disabilities, their teachers, and parents. This role is not always a popular one; therefore, your interaction with administrative colleagues is critical as you develop trust and respect as an administrative team member. This chapter will first outline ideas for working with the *superintendent, school board,* and *building principal.* Next, *general tips* for balancing student advocacy with the mission and goals of the organization are discussed.

REGULATIONS

There are no provisions in IDEA 2004 that legislate your relationship with administrative colleagues; however, to provide students with disabilities a free appropriate public education, you will need to foster strong relationships with your administrative peers.

PUTTING PRINCIPLES INTO PRACTICE

The Superintendent

The superintendent is the educational leader and CEO of the school district. He or she sets the tone of the administrative team, and his or her vision guides the mission and goals of the school. Therefore, your relationship with the superintendent is critical for your stakeholders—students with disabilities, their parents, and teachers.

Whether you are new to a school district or are being considered for promotion, prior to accepting a position as a special education administrator you should investigate the *superintendent's support* of special education. *Without superintendent support,* your job will be more complicated. Your *operating budget, technology needs,* and *personnel issues* are highly dependent on the superintendent's understanding and acceptance of special education. Moreover, the superintendent's attitude toward special education is a model for the administrative team; unfortunately, if he or she does not support special education, it will affect your relationship, interactions, and effectiveness with other administrators.

Your role as an advocate for students with disabilities is undermined when you are unable to perform your job under IDEA guidelines. When a superintendent is "closed off" or uninterested in special education, it can compromise your position with parents and personnel. As an example, consider that you are preparing your budget for the new school year and you have determined that you need an additional speech and language pathologist. You have based this budgetary request on data that you collected showing your current speech pathologist is unable to provide appropriate services to students at the high school. Weekly speech pathologist contact charts reveal that nine high school students received 50 percent less speech and language therapy than was outlined in their IEPs. You also determine that this is a chronic problem not a situational one. Armed with this information, you determine that a part-time speech pathologist is appropriate, and you have worked out a budgetary plan for new personnel. When presented to the superintendent, it is immediately vetoed as unnecessary because a "parent has not complained." In fact, the superintendent suggests that high school students should be dismissed from speech services since they are too old to benefit from them. See the problem with an unsupportive superintendent?

Let's ask the next logical question: What do you do when a superintendent is *unsure, unwilling,* or *uneducated* about special education? The following tips will help you to establish procedures for dealing with this type of superintendent. Furthermore, the following tips are also good practice to use with superintendents who are supportive and knowledgeable about special education.

- Schedule a weekly meeting with the superintendent to discuss impending issues that may have budgetary, legal, or programmatic implications and consequences. Most superintendents do not like surprises, especially budgetary ones, so keep the superintendent informed. In addition to being good administrative practice, weekly meetings demonstrate conscientiousness on your part and help to build rapport and trust.
- Do your homework! One of the most effective ways to persuade superintendents of special education needs is to collect data to support your cause. Be prepared with relevant legislation, regulations, and information on current district operations and how new programs may impact the budget, personnel, or other areas important to the operation of the district. In addition, a cost analysis of any program change is essential.
- Show probable programming effects and list the consequences of not following legislative mandates.
- Be prepared to answer difficult questions by anticipating the types of information the superintendent will want to know. Using the same example of the part-time speech pathologist, think through all of the possible questions he or she could ask regarding a new position, including the utilization of room space, how the new speech pathologist can be used in other areas, and how many exceptional students will benefit from the service.

The School Board

The members of the school board are not "administrators"; however, all district decisions are ultimately approved by this board of directors. Because the school board is comprised of citizens who may not fully understand the complexity of the special education maze, it is a good policy to inform them about what they need to know when they need to know it, rather than providing a "crash course" in special education legislation at the beginning of every school year.

One exception to that rule is in the area of discipline. It is your job to advocate for the student and provide guidance to the school board on federal and state laws governing discipline and students with disabilities. This is *the* area where you should spend time educating the school board at least annually. In addition:

- Create a Special Education Discipline Handbook specifically for the school board that outlines IDEA and state legislation regarding discipline *without* educational jargon.
- The handbook should include a flow chart of district disciplinary procedures and timelines that visually depicts the course of action taken by teachers and building principals or their assistants.
- Try to attend any disciplinary hearings that are scheduled for students with disabilities in order to advocate for any student's free appropriate public education. In addition to behavioral data, provide an educational history and documentation of IEP goals and objectives. This background will be useful to the school board in understanding any student's disability.

When requesting programs or services that will have budgetary impact, provide the school board with a rationale embedded in IDEA legislation, when applicable.

- Do your homework! As in the case with the superintendent, an effective way to convince the school board that you need a service, program, or other budgetary consideration is to be prepared with data to support your cause.
- Because you are working with lay people, try not to condescend to the board; but do try to provide them what they need to know using straightforward language absent of educational jargon.
- Handouts can be helpful—specifically graphic organizers that help the board understand your request. Providing a cost analysis is always beneficial.

The Building Principal and Assistant Principal

Your relationships with the building principal and assistant principal are critical as they influence their administration of special education programs and services. If you take a cursory look at most graduate school programs in educational leadership, you will discover courses that focus on finance, general supervision, technology, curriculum, school and community relationships, and school law; rarely are principals trained in issues of special education. Therefore, it is important to help principals understand their important role in the administration of special education programs and services in their buildings.

Depending on the size of the school district, you may need to work with a handful or a roomful of building administrators. In some school districts, usually smaller ones, you may be assigned the role of district LEA with subordinate instructional assistants who help serve that role in your absence. However, in other school districts, the role of LEA is performed by the building principal or assistant; consequently, it is essential to nurture a working relationship with all building administrators so that students with disabilities can access a free appropriate public education. Here are some tips:

- If possible, participate in interviews for new principal personnel so that you can ask specific questions related to special education and gauge how open the individual is to special education in general.
- Build into your budget funds to purchase *A Principal's Guide to Special Education* (Bateman & Bateman, 2001). This excellent resource will guide building administrators through the complicated maze of IEP development, discipline issues, inclusion, due process, and other related special education issues.
- Using the book as a guide, annually provide professional development opportunities for building principals on any changes in legislation, regulations, or policy, emphasizing their role.
- All new building administrators should be trained in established district special education procedures and responsibilities so they understand their role in the special education process—especially if they are serving as the LEA.
- Model leading an evaluation team meeting and IEP meeting for new principals and assistant principals, then observe several meetings they lead to assure they understand your procedural expectations.

Because principals or their assistants are responsible for enforcing discipline at the building level and are on the front line in terms of student safety, they are often conflicted about how to proceed when a student with a disability needs to be disciplined. Moreover, many principals need to be reminded that they are not the sole arbiter of discipline decisions for students with disabilities—thus, spend a great deal of time teaching all building principals and their assistants about these issues related to exceptional students.

- Encourage building administrators to develop or enhance building-wide discipline plans to comply with the provisions of IDEA.
- Create a discipline handbook to help establish a consistent, step-by-step district discipline procedure for students with disabilities. The manual should include ideas for providing positive behavioral supports, dealing with suspensions and exclusions from school, and providing a safe learning environment for all students. When developing a procedural manual, invite several principals and assistant principals to participate in its development.
- Provide training in positive behavioral support for all principals. Take advantage of any training or professional development offered in your area that may help principals execute positive building-wide discipline plans.
- Insist that principals collect detailed anecdotal behavioral data. In addition, each discipline incident needs to be reported to the teacher and documented consistently. This data will be essential if the district needs to proceed to a hearing.

Another area of special education that principals need to know and understand is the concept of "inclusion" and what an inclusive philosophy should reflect. The principal is the educational leader of the building, and as such, his or her attitude and philosophy regarding students with special needs sets the tone for the building and is critical for determining how students with disabilities access the general education curriculum.

- Bateman and Bateman (2001) discuss the history of inclusion and provide a detailed review of the regulations in terms of a continuum of services; however, many inexperienced principals may have difficulty interpreting what this means. Your job is to ensure that all principals understand that inclusion, like all of special education, is individualized based on each student's needs on a continuum.
- Help principals budget for and provide coverage for general education teachers to be active, not passive, participants in the evaluation and IEP process. In other words, require the general education teachers' full participation so that they understand the process.
- Enlist their help when budgeting for more support teachers and paraprofessional support so the students in their buildings are provided with appropriate programs. Moreover, teachers will perceive they are receiving the support they need from all administrative levels.
- In conjunction with the principal, provide training and professional development to the building staff in accommodating students with disabilities in general education classrooms.
- Remind building administrators they are the principal for all students. It is their responsibility to assure FAPE on a daily basis.
- It is important that you know how each building operates, how the teachers interact, and how the building is organized to make informed and instructive decisions *with* the principal in matters of inclusive education.
- Finally, the principal needs to be visible in special education classrooms. Many special education teachers complain that the principal is intimidated or uninterested in what happens in their classrooms; for that reason, encourage principals to be involved, to get to know the students and their parents, and to be a voice supporting special education in their own buildings.

General Tips for the Administration Team

Know IDEA Legislation. The administrative team will look to you for guidance on all issues related to special education. For the administrative team to trust you, we think that the following ideas will help facilitate your understanding of IDEA and related special education legislation.

- Keep a copy of IDEA regulations and your specific state guidelines in your plan or date book for easy access. CDs explaining IDEA legislation will be available through the Council for Exceptional Children (website listed below) and *IDEA Partnership Projects; Western Regional Resource Center at the University of Oregon; National Information Center for Children and Youth with Disabilities;* and *Educational Development Center, Inc.*
- Keep your contact or compliance person at the state department of education on "speed dial." In other words, seek help when you need it.

- Network formally or informally with other district supervisors in your area to discuss relevant and similar issues and problems.
- Attend workshops and law institutes that review new guidelines, new legislation, and court rulings, at least annually.
- Attend special education leadership training when offered.
- Train the administrative team annually on changes in IDEA, Section 504, and ADA that are pertinent to keep them abreast of current policy and planned practice.
- Keep important websites on legislative policy bookmarked on your computer to access up-to-date information on IDEA legislation and other relevant matters of special education. Several comprehensive sites are listed below; however, the department of education in your home state may have good website resources to explore as well.

  - *Council for Exceptional Children* (CEC): Public Policy Legislative Action Center: www.cec.sped.org
  - *Federation of Children with Special Needs* (FCSN): IDEA news: www.fcsn.org
  - *The Special Education Advocate:* Online newsletter about special education law, advocacy, research, and other related topics: www.wrightslaw.com
  - *Office for Civil Rights Fact Sheet: Your Rights Under Section 504:* In schools that receive federal funding, students with disabilities are entitled to reasonable accommodations under Section 504, regardless of whether they receive special education services and programs: www.os.dhhs.gov
  - *A Parent and Educator's Guide to Section 504:* www.pathfinder.minot.com
  - *U.S. Department of Justice AHD Home Page:* This website helps you understand the basic provisions of ADA—specifically, how to explain them to parents or teachers: www.usdoj.gov
  - *Office of Special Education and Rehabilitative Services:* The U.S. Department of Education's Office of Special Education and Rehabilitative Services (OSERS) supports special education programs and research: www.ed.gov/offices/OSERS

Keep the Student as the Focal Point.   All administrators have personal agendas for their district, building, curriculum, or finances. Your agenda is mandated; you must ultimately provide students with disabilities a free appropriate public education in the least restrictive environment. In order to stay this course, you must keep the student as the focal point as you make programmatic or other educational decisions. Although your advocacy for students with disabilities may not always be popular, it is important that the administrative team know your decisions are based on *what is best* for the student.

- Do not cater to one administrative team member over another when making decisions about a student with a disability. For example, it is human nature that you may like one principal better than another principal; therefore, you may cater to that "favored" principal when scheduling meetings, IEP meetings, or assigning new staff. Work hard at resisting that urge and use a systematic plan and schedule based on specific timelines and legislative mandates.
- Listen to all administrative team members for ideas; but always keep your decisions based on the student's needs and the most effective way of meeting those needs.

Budgetary, staffing, and other administrative reasons can be considered; but should never drive your decisions.
- Ignore the "squeaky wheel." Many administrative colleagues mistakenly think their building needs supersede all others. You are in the position to view all district needs, thus it is important to continue with your organized schedule based on district needs. Do not reinforce inappropriate administrative behavior.

Help Administrators Deal with Parents of Exceptional Students. Many administrators at all levels, maybe even you, panic when dealing with angry or unhappy parents of students with disabilities. Superintendents, principals, and special education administrators worry about litigation, due process, or mediation hearings because they are often costly to the district and psychologically difficult for staff. Thus, a mistake that many administrators make at the first sign of trouble is to immediately pander to a parent's request in an effort to solve the problem.

- Teach the administrative team and remind yourself *not* to pander to parents. The school has a right to reflect on demands and requests of parents and guide decision making in an educationally sound manner. As an example, let us look at a first-grade student with a learning disability. Evaluation results reveal that the student is only able to write three words per minute. Classroom data shows that the "average" first-grade student is able to write eight to ten words per minute. The proposed IEP goal: *The student will write at least five words per minute using capitalization and punctuation.* The parents disagree and want a clause in the IEP stating that the child should not be required to write at all unless the occupational therapist is in the room. Teach the LEA to stay the course by keeping the child as the focal point and making educationally sound decisions based on what the student needs, rather than weighing the cost of implementing the request versus a due process hearing.
- On the other hand, it is also important not to be too rigid with parents. Remind your administrators that parents are an integral part of the team and an effort must be made to collaborate.
- Underscore in all your professional development with the administrative team that if they are prepared, their staff is prepared, and they make sound educational decisions based on the student's strengths and needs, they should be in good standing with parents. This steadfast and consistent focus will help guide district decisions in a positive way.

Be an Active and Visible Educational Leader. Special education is all about relationships, so nurture your administrative ones. Even when colleagues disagree on issues, if you have a good rapport, stay the course, and make sound educational decisions based on the needs of the student, the administrative team will learn to respect your choices. To augment this process:

- Be visible in buildings. It shows you are interested in building and district cohesiveness when you interact with staff. Depending on the size of the district, plan to spend several hours a week in each building observing special education classes, attending multidisciplinary and IEP meetings, and meeting with parents. If you do not make the time to visit individual buildings, staff may view your decisions as arbitrary. Therefore, schedule time to visit district buildings.

- Diversify your interests. In other words, participate in other district committees and activities. This way, you get a global view of district mission and goals.
- Take an active role in district curriculum development to represent special education and promote programs and interventions that are scientifically based on validated research practices.
- Be proactive in your interactions with administrative team colleagues. Find the courage to ask questions, disagree with issues, and be forthright in your needs. If you stay honest, you will gain the respect you need to fulfill your mission.
- If you are going to be a strong administrator, you need to develop a thick skin. If you take every slight personally, you will burn out quickly in this already difficult job. Remember, if you consistently keep the student as the focus of your decisions, everybody wins.
- Keep your sense of humor; most people will appreciate that quality.
- Provide all administrators with the Special Education Manual you developed for your staff as a reference to practice.

REFERENCES

Bateman, D., & Bateman, C. F. (2001). *A principal's guide to special education.* Arlington, VA: Council for Exceptional Children.

INDEX

504 accommodation plans, 27
504 definitions, 21, 22
504 need, 23
504 regulations, 24

Accounting codes, 167
Accounting principles, 167
Americans with Disabilities Act, 14, 15
Annual report, 88, 89
Appeals, 13, 54
Appropriate education, 9, 25

Budget
    calculating, 172
    contracting services, 177
    cycle, 165–166
    direct cost, 174–175
    e-Rate, 178
    functions and objects, 167, 168–171
    indirect costs, 176
    Medicaid loophole, 178, 211
    per-pupil tuition rate, 173
    purchasing consortia, 177
    rehabilitation act, 191
    request for proposals (RFP), 177
    request for quotations (RFQ), 193
    resources, 179–180
    revenue codes, 167
    salary and fringe benefits, 174–176, 177–178
    staffing, 174

Child find, 26, 59
Community agencies, 73
Computer monitoring, 93
Contiuum of alternative placements, 104, 112
Cumulative school file, 69

Discipline, 12, 51, 56
    district handbook, 245
Disproportionality, 90

Due process, 7, 39
    expedited, 40, 47
    hearing, 56

Eligibility, 80
Evaluation, 6, 25, 26, 67
Evaluation process, 75

Family agencies, 73
Family Educational Rights and Privacy Act
    (FERPA), 15, 16
Federal funding
    commingling, 153
    distribution, 160
    equitable participation, 157–158
    excess costs, 153, 154, 172–173
    extended school year, 162
    IDEA 2004, 151
    management, 155
    maintenance of effort (MOE), 155–156
    resources, 163
    risk pools, 153
    section 611 of IDEA, 156
    supplemental, 154
Free appropriate public education (FAPE), 23, 24,
    90, 109

General education curriculum, 121

Hearing officers, 13, 110
HR 1350, 76, 79, 81

IDEA, 2, 23, 28, 51
IDEA 2004, 10, 59, 67, 76, 77, 78, 87, 91
IEE (Independent Educational Evaluation), 46, 47
    appropriateness, 183–184
    due process, 185
    evaluation questions, 184
    scope, 184

utility, 184–185
IEP, 6, 7, 44, 45, 97, 98, 99, 102, 115
    administrative management, 228–229
    amending, 102
    team, 100, 101
IFSP, 5
Impartial facilitator, 45
Inclusion, 3
Initial evaluation, 75

Learning disabilities, 80
Least restrictive environment, (LRE), 3, 24, 70, 103
Local education agency, 73, 88, 97, 101
Local resources, 229–230

Mainstreaming, 3
Manifestation Determination Review, 53
Mediation, 42, 46
Medical device, 99
Mental health, 120
    behavior specialist, 209–210
    bipolar disorder, 208
    Child Medication Act 2003, 213
    community violence, 205
    coordinated services, 204
    depressive disorder, 202, 205
    Diagnostic and Statistical Manual IV, 201
    domestic violence, 206
    dropout and school refusal, 207
    eating disorders, 206
    high risk behaviors, 20
    homelessness, 206
    interagency collaboration, 209–210, 212
    mental health issues and responses, 204–205
    physical and sexual abuse, 207
    resources, 214–215
    schizophrenia, 208
    substance abuse, 209
    suicide, 208
    wraparound services, 209–210
Monitoring, 87
Multi action plan, 119
Multi-year IEP, 102, 103

No Child Left Behind (NCLB), 12, 87
    fiscal implications, 166
Nonacademic settings, 107
Notice, 79

Office of Civil Rights, 22, 27, 29
OSERS, 29

PL 94–142, 1
Parent groups, 129
    advisory groups, 129
    collaboration, 129
    establishing, 129–130
    maintaining, 129
    participation, 129
    resources, 131–135
Parental consent, 76
Parental involvement, 4
Peer-reviewed research, 99
Placement, 25, 26
Preplacement evaluation, 25
Prereferral, 67, 69
Principal collaboration, 245
Private school placements, 107, 108, 109
Procedural safeguards, 4, 27, 40
Pupil personnel meeting (PPM), 72

Reevaluation, 26, 78
Referral, 67
Referral process, 68
Rehabilitation Act of 1973, 14, 21, 22, 51
Reimbursement, 109
Related services, 5
    audiology, 188
    contracts, 193–194
    counseling, 188–189
    early identification and assessment, 189
    liability, 194
    meaningful educational benefit, 187–188
    medical services, 189
    occupational therapy, 189
    orientation and mobility training, 190
    parent training, 190
    physical therapy, 190–191
    recreation, 191
    rehabilitative counseling, 191
    resources, 195–199
    roles of service providers, 188
    school health, 192
    social work, 192
    speech and language, 192–193

transportation, 193
Resolution meeting, 40
Response to treatment, 81, 83
Revenue codes, 167
Rowley, 9

Schaffer v. Weast, 40
School boards, 244–245
School calendar, 74
School newsletter, 74
School website, 74
Screening, 67, 68
SEA, 62, 88
Seriously bodily injury, 13
Short term objectives, 99
Special education staff evaluation, 233–240
    clinical supervision, 234–236
    framework, 237–240
    observation, 23
    post-observation, 236
    pre-observation, 234–235
Special education staff meetings, 217–219
    alternatives, 218–219
    effectiveness, 218
    monthly meetings, 225

rules, 218
Special education staff relationships, 223–230
    case management systems, 228–229
    demeanor, 227
    interpersonal skills, 224–227
    listening, 226
    managing staff, 227–229
    organization, 227–228
    resource allocation, 229–230
    special education handbook, 229
    visibility, 226
Student handbook, 120
Suggestion box, 72
Superintendents, 248–250
Suspension, 26

Team, 75
Three-pronged process, 110
Transfer, 101
Transition, 8, 100, 115
    middle school, 139, 144–145
    within and between schools, 137–147
Tuition reimbursement, 109, 110

Unilateral withdrawal, 111

Ward of state, 77